ALLIANCES, OUTSOURCING, AND THE LEAN ORGANIZATION

ALLIANCES, OUTSOURCING, AND THE LEAN ORGANIZATION

Michael Milgate

Q

QUORUM BOOKS
Westport, Connecticut • London

Library of Congress Cataloging-in-Publication Data

Milgate, Michael, 1966–
    Alliances, outsourcing, and the lean organization / Michael Milgate.
      p. cm.
    Includes bibliographical references and index.
    ISBN 1–56720–365–5 (alk. paper)
    1. Organizational effectiveness. 2. Strategic alliances (Business). 3. Contracting out. I.
Title.
HD58.9.M55   2001
658.1′6—dc21   00–042558

British Library Cataloguing in Publication Data is available.

Library of Congress Catalog Card Number: 00–042558
ISBN: 1–56720–365–5

First published in 2001

Quorum Books, 88 Post Road West, Westport, CT 06881
An imprint of Greenwood Publishing Group, Inc.
www.quorumbooks.com

Printed in the United States of America

For M.S.R

CONTENTS

PREFACE

This book combines a number of themes that ought to be on the management agenda of both international organizations as well as small and medium-sized enterprises including how an organization can leverage more competitive advantage from its core competencies through alliances, partnerships, and outsourcing. The smart money is on alliances and partnership activity intensifying during the early decades of the century. There is a growing body of literature and debate over outsourcing being yet another management fad that the expression of the failure of managers to manage their resources. As a result many clients of outsourced services are dissatisfied with the level of service and quality provided now that it has changed from being an in-house function. In addition, while many alliances deliver rich business benefits, too many fail because organizations entered alliances for the wrong reasons. This book, therefore, raises some timely issues and, hopefully, provides some pointers as to how to be successful when entering into these ventures.

Throughout the book, all references to monetary values are in the currency where the transaction took place. The daily exchange rate fluctuations make it difficult to calculate an exact figure, and the value may be more meaningful in a historical setting. There is also the added complexity of the author being an Australian and trying to convert from, for example, £ to A$ to U.S.$. The exchanges that would be used in the United States are not used here as they would still have to be converted to A$, which would add to the inaccuracy of the values.

1

THE LEAN ORGANIZATION

BUSINESS DRIVERS BEHIND THE "LEAN" ORGANIZATION

Ours is a world of paradoxes. For an organization to grow, it must think and act lean. In order to compete, it must cooperate. In order to become global, the organization must act local. Staff should be empowered, but the organization should not lose control. The organization must change but should retain traditional values. It seems that business policy-makers must address trends and issues that are like riddles wrapped in mysteries enshrouded in enigmas (to paraphrase Winston Churchill's description of the former USSR).

This book sets out to remove at least some of the levels of obfuscation. The central thesis of this book is that the big business winners in the new millennium will be those organizations that focus most successfully on their core competencies and leverage them through a range of strategic alliances[1] and outsourcing to create a *best of everything* network.

So, what is driving it all? It is not hard to identify the business drivers that increasingly make the lean organization approach attractive to business managers across our world.

- It offers the opportunity to reap economies of scale and scope. When corporate giants such as Fujitsu, General Motors, IBM, and

ICI are actively seeking and exploiting alliances, it is clear that the world's economy is just too big for even the mightiest organizations to exploit all the opportunity alone.

- It provides an entry mechanism into increasingly global markets. From aerospace to pharmaceutical, automobile manufacturing to publishing, engineering to fast food, markets are now global. From Albuquerque to Adelaide, from Zurich to Zetland, people drive the same cars, watch the same television sets, and eat the same hamburgers or sushi.

- It delivers a weapon to burst through the barriers created by economic regionalism. The world is dividing into powerful economic regions: Europe, Japan, North America, and Southeast Asia. Each provides enticing market opportunities but erects multiple barriers to entry. These barriers may be cultural, economic, or legislative. The lean organization uses alliances to find ways through or around these barriers.

- It provides a counter-balance to market uncertainty. There has never been a time when business had access to more information and sophisticated analysis; or a time when it was more uncertain what will happen next. Market uncertainty makes the lean organization want to share risks with others.

- It pools expertise to cope with the quickening pace of technological change. This has a twin impact—first on what products are made and second on the way products are made. Few organizations have the resources to monitor all the technologies or the capital to take advantage of all those that offer the chance of winning a new competitive edge. The lean organization uses partnerships to pool resources to exploit technologies.

- It provides strength to cope with economic uncertainty. The wired-up world is a more volatile place than ever before. An earthquake can set a stock market tumbling and a change of government can send a currency into free-fall. Growth and slump cycles steadily roll round the world's economies.

- It accommodates the pressures of time. Business is conducted at a faster pace than ever before, with shorter product development periods and shorter product life cycles. Being first to market with a major innovative drug, car, or aircraft wins matchless business benefits for a few months, or possibly a few years. However, being first is tougher than ever before. The lean organization uses partnerships to help achieve this leading position.

None of these issues stands alone. Technological change has become increasingly rapid and global in nature, resulting in smaller differences between markets in different parts of the world. The globalization[2] of markets is giving opportunities for organizations to realize economies of scale and scope. These factors have lowered unit costs enough for large organizations to take advantage of them.

However, a side effect of technological change and globalization has been shortening of product life cycles. This has led to increasing investment demand both to install new technologies and to develop new products.

Competitive advantage has, therefore, gone to the organization able to adopt the new technologies, achieve economies of scale and scope, serve global markets, and change its product range regularly. Since few companies have resources and competencies to meet these stringent requirements, there has been widespread resort to alliances to meet the needs of this new economic order.

Yet, how do you become a lean organization? There is no blueprint, no packaged solution to creating a lean organization. There are six building blocks that help in becoming a lean organization:

- core competencies (Chapter 2);
- strategic partnerships (Chapter 3);
- effective strategic outsourcing (Chapter 4);
- new management disciplines (Chapter 5);
- partnership culture (Chapter 6); and
- technological enablers (Chapter 7).

These are described in the next section and then in detail in Chapters 2 to 7. Chapters 8 to 11 look at various issues, such as probity when dealing with a publicly funded organization (culture and cultural mismatches).

Why a Lean Organization?

The term *lean organization*, is borrowed and adapted from "the lean enterprise," which was first used by Womack and Jones.[3] They defined the lean enterprise as "a group of individuals, functions, and legally separate but operationally synchronized companies."[4] This thinking grew out of their ideas about "lean production" most effectively deployed in their book *The Machine That Changed the World*."[5] Womack and Jones see the lean enterprise as being defined by a "value stream."[6] The mission of all the members "is collectively to analyze and focus a value stream so that it does everything involved in supplying a good or service (from development and production to sales and maintenance) in a way that provides maximum value to the consumer."[7]

Womack and Jones suggest that there are many examples of organizations improving specific activities in a single organization:

> But these experiences have also made us realize that applying lean techniques to discrete activities is not the end of the road. If individual breakthroughs can be linked up and down the value chain to form a continuous *value stream* that creates, sells, and services a family of products, the performances of the whole can be raised to a dramatically higher level.[8]

They believe value-creating activities can be joined, "but this effort will require a new organizational model: *the lean enterprise*."[9]

Womack and Jones point out that lean enterprises must adopt new principles for regulating their behavior. First, they must learn how to cooperate with other organizations as well as to compete; and sometimes do both at the same time. They must learn how to accept decisions of organizations from different industries and cultures, how to coordinate their activities, and how to resolve disputes. Above all, they must learn how to share equitably the profits and other gains from their alliances.

Womack and Jones suggest that a "lean enterprise" differs from the "virtual corporation" and from Japanese *keiretsu* and Korean *chaebol*. On the one hand, virtual organizations "in which 'plug-compatible' members of the value stream come and go, fail to grasp the massive costs of casual interactions."[10] On the other hand, members of the lean organization are not cemented into long-term relationships through cross-shareholdings, like *keiretsu*. "Participants in the lean enterprise must be free to leave if collaborators fail to improve their performance or refuse to reveal their situation."[11]

The Lean Organization's Building Blocks

There are six building blocks required to give an organization the opportunity to become a lean organization: core competencies, strategic alliances, effective strategic outsourcing, new management disciplines, a partnership culture, and technology enablers.

Core Competencies

The first building block for the lean organization is core competencies. These are "the collective learning in the organization, especially how to co-ordinate diverse production skills and integrate multiple technologies."[12] For example, Honda and Seagate Technology and the engineering organization GKN were able to develop three benefits over competitors from the core competencies. First, these competencies deliver potential access to an increased variety of markets. Honda's competencies in small engines have been leveraged into outboard marine engines, lawn mowers, motorcycles, and family cars. Second, the competencies make a significant contribution to perceived customer benefits. Seagate Technology, which was able to deliver more disk storage space at a better price than its competitors, was highly prized among leading personal computer (PC) manufacturers, who comprise its main customer base. Finally, competence provides a unique edge. It is something that is difficult for customers to imitate. GKN surrounded its automotive products with such a web of special design and support relationships for its customers that it has a clear edge in competing for business with its core products in the highly competitive automotive component market.

Strategic Alliances

The second building block is strategic alliances. These come dressed in a variety of structures, such as joint ventures, collaborations, consortia, and business networks (such as the Japanese *keiretsu* or the Korean *chaebol*). Three common reasons that organizations use alliances are:

- to provide extra leverage for an organization's core competencies in order to win long-term sustainable competitive advantage;
- to move an organization into long-term and developing commitments to new markets, territories, or technologies that were previously closed to it; and
- to provide a platform for kinds of organizational learning that are central to future business success, but would otherwise be unobtainable.

The corporate observer will rightly note that there is nothing new in this. Organizations such as Corning, for example, have used them as a cornerstone of business since the 1940s. As Dicken has noted: "What is new is their current scale, proliferation and the fact that they have become *central* to the global strategies of many firms rather than peripheral to them. Most strikingly, the overwhelming majority of strategic alliances are between competitors."[13]

Dicken is overstating his case when he says the "overwhelming majority" of alliances are between competitors. Certainly a significant number are, but as will be discussed later in this book, two intensely competitive organizations rarely make happy partners. Dicken is correct, however, in stating that the scale and proliferation of alliances are what distinguish are current activity from the past.

Consider, for example, the scale and proliferation of global strategies of IBM and Fujitsu, both competing for a leading position in the world's multibillion dollar information technology market. Both have entered a range of alliances in an attempt to encircle the other's business. Aware of the growing power of the Pacific Rim in information technology (IT), IBM has had or has alliances, for example, with Matsushita (in low-end PCs), Rioch (for hand-held PCs), Toshiba (for display technology), Mitsubishi (for mainframes), Canon (for printers), and Hitachi (for larger printers). IBM works with manufacturing companies, such as Nissan Motor and Nippon Steel, on applications of its systems for factory environments, a strategy that builds on leading-edge manufacturing techniques as well as providing a secure foothold in the market for Japanese IT products. IBM tackled the growing Japanese telecommunications market through alliances with NTT for value-added networks.

Fujitsu has an equal approach to alliances. Its aim is to encircle IBM. The stated business strategy is to build a federal global business organization. Fujitsu plans to become a network of organizations in borderless alliances. In pursuit of this aim, Fujitsu has formed a range of global alliances to challenge IBM's dominance of IT markets.

The alliance game is being played with mounting enthusiasm by other major industries such as aerospace, automotive, pharmaceuticals, financial services and consumer goods. Sometimes this game spawns unlikely bedfellows. For example, what brings together Mercedes Benz and Swatch, the low-cost Swiss watchmaker? Answer: the desire to develop a microcompact city car. What shared dream links Binney and Smith, the maker of children's crayons, and MicroGrafix, a software developer? Answer: the development and marketing of creative paint-and-draw software for children. In each of these cases, the participants pool very different core competencies in order to invent products for entirely new markets.

Effective Strategic Outsourcing

The third building block is effective outsourcing. When outsourcing first became fashionable (if it ever did) for noncore activities such as accounting, office services, and IT, the main aim of managers was tactical: to save money, rather than strategic to develop business from a defendable position.

Strategic outsourcers—such as Marks and Spencer for clothes and grocery items, Ford for automotive components, and Nike for sports shoes—recognize that outsourcing is the way to access best-of-breed R&D product development and manufacturing skills in a host of often unrelated product areas. By turning their suppliers into strategic partners, these organizations and others have added value to their business relationships by learning from the competencies of their partners and winning new benefits from previously unrealized synergies.

Other organizations see outsourcing as a route to developing new competencies of their own, and ultimately leveraging themselves into new business areas. For example, New Holland, the Fiat subsidiary that manufacturers agricultural machinery, has outsourced its European spare parts logistics to a new joint venture organization formed with Andersen Consulting. New Holland is learning from Andersen's skills in change management and information systems how to build a world-class logistics operation. Within months of this alliance, the managers were receiving calls from other organizations that wanted to outsource their own logistics operations to the new joint venture.

In the long term, New Holland will build a growing European logistics business that will partly offset the effects of the long-term decline in the agricultural machinery and spare parts market. For its part, Andersen Consulting is learning how a sophisticated Europe-wide logistics operation works. It is also gaining organizational knowledge that can be used to leverage it into other outsourcing or consultancy opportunities.

Even organizations outsourcing business support activities (the old heartland of outsourcing) now recognize that they, too, have a significant strategic dimension. For example, a roadside windscreen replacement organization outsourced its IT because it saw that what had been a support activity in the past had become a strategic issue. Its IT supplier will use the knowledge of leading edge IT to develop the client's IT so that it offers improved customer service, in a market place where there are few competitive differentiators.

New Management Disciplines

If managers are to reconcile the paradoxes that are at the heart of the lean enterprise, they need to master a raft of new management disciplines. It turns out that many of the skills that worked so well in the old-style hierarchal organization ruled by command-and-control culture are now re-dundant or, at best, marginal in this new business environment.

In many organizations, whole groups of managers have been removed as part of radical downsizing operations. Those who remain usually need new attitudes, behaviors, and skills to survive and thrive in a business environment where alliances and outsourcing now figure as significant factors. As Womack put it, a career in the lean organization "consists of solving increasingly difficult problems in a multiskilled group."[14]

There are three new management disciplines that are critical for managers within a lean organization to master if they wish to survive. First, they must be able to manage multiple relationships. Increasingly, managers could find they have to work through a mixture of internal teams and external alliances, in addition to outsourcing partners in order to achieve the business results for which they are responsible.

Second, managers must be able to wear lightly a testing management schizophrenia: the ability to cooperate and compete at the same time with the same organization. Rover, the British car manufacturer owned by BMW, for example, cooperated for a time with the Japanese motorcycle and automotive organization, Honda, on manufacturing and automotive technologies. Rover also competes with cars that are the result of this cooperation in some of the same markets. This means that both Rover and Honda managers have had to manage this source of tension within their alliance, within their respective organizations, and within themselves.

Finally, managers need to be able to learn from alliances. This is where Japanese managers, more used to cooperating through *keiretsu*, are more skilled than those from Europe, North America, or Australia. However, the most skillful Western exploiters of alliances have learned fast.

Faced with a multitude of opportunities, how does a business make choices about the partnerships and alliances it enters? A large telecommunications provider[15] operates in a business in which several industries are converging. It finds several industries converging on its traditional core telecommunications business. It sees new industries being created out of this convergence. However, this in turn puts pressure on the organization to build its business in potentially different ways. Consequently, the organization has identified five drivers for more alliances:

1. The need to create sustainable competitive differentiation;
2. The desire to build more comprehensive product portfolios;
3. The race to bring products to market more quickly;
4. The drive for greater cost efficiencies; and

5. The pressure for higher standards of customer service.

In deciding on alliance priorities, the organization decides how to spread its investment between different emerging technologies. For example, the organization could focus on value-adding telecommunication services, but this is already a crowded market. Or the organization could invest in basic telecommunications infrastructures, but this requires huge capital and there is a long payback. The organization could target telecommunications equipment manufacturing, but there are already well-established players in this market. Or the organization could either develop applications or produce content for transmission over telecommunications lines, for example, feature films.

Figure 1.1
How Industries Converge

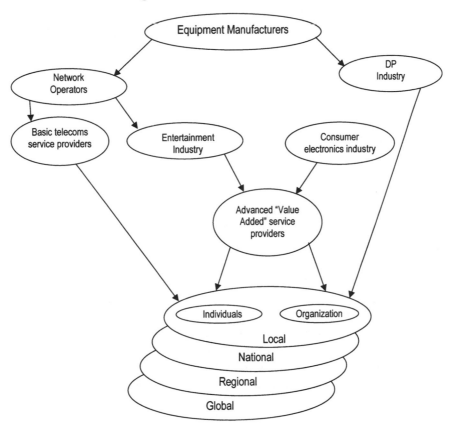

Next, the organization chooses which partners to work with in order to exploit the chosen technologies. In fact, the organization is choosing to work with a range of alliance partners including other telecommunication operators as well as entertainment providers, computing companies, equipment manufacturers, systems integrators, sector specialists, and management consultancies.

The organization harvests five main benefits from working with alliance partners:

1. It discovers new commercial opportunities and sources of revenues;
2. It participates in the creation of standards and common procurement specifications, for example, for broadband signaling;
3. It acquires knowledge and new competencies;
4. It leverages business advantage from the benefits of scale; and
5. It creates visibility and credibility, especially as the organization wants to be perceived as a global provider of telecommunications services.

Partnership Culture

At Asea Brown Boveri (ABB), the Swedish and Swiss engineering and electrical group, the staff works in 1,300 small companies—few have more than seventy employees. The companies are linked together in a culture of teamworking and cooperation that underpins a matrix organization.

Many of the paradoxes at the heart of the lean organization are resolved through adopting the appropriate approach to culture and organization. In particular, there are three important issues. First, an organization must adopt a structure that promotes partnership. There is no one paradigm, however, nor any fixed formula for implementing a particular paradigm. An organization may choose to model itself as a federal organization, cluster organization, or a starburst organization. The organization must then use that template to construct an organization that promotes a culture that best enables its staff to perform their roles and responsibilities effectively.

Second, those organizations most adept at operating as lean organizations develop high-performance business teams throughout their organizations. Moreover, these teams frequently cross functional boundaries within their organization. Organizations with experience of cross-functional teams have a head start in partnering and alliances. They understand the issues involved in building teams and the dynamics of making them work to achieve business objectives. It is not surprising that organizations that enter multiple alliances and partnerships, such as Fujitsu, General Motors, and IBM, are skilled in the art of leveraging business value through the operation of teams.[16]

Finally, managers need to develop a new range of skills for working in a networked organization—whether it is federal, cluster, starburst, or any other model. Managers need two types of skills. The first includes the skills managers need in order to develop and leverage their networks. For example, communication both within and between networks is essential. ABB CEO, Percy Barnevik, adopted the principle of overcommunicating to ensure that staff at all levels of the organization have all the information and, more important, all the understanding they need in order to perform their roles and responsibilities. However, the leaders in network organizations must also teach their staff to manage the stress inherent in this kind of organization and how to develop their networks to deliver more business benefits.

East versus West—Can the West Learn from Keiretsus*? Keiretsu*—literally, societies of business—are those formidable Japanese industrial combinations that lie at the heart of the country's economic strength. There are two predominant types of *keiretsu*. The first are those that are bank-centered (containing twenty to forty-five companies centered on a bank). They enable organizations to share risk and provide a mechanism for allocating investment to strategic industries. The second is the supply *keiretsu*. These are groups of companies integrated along a supplier chain dominated by a major manufacturer. Supply chain *keiretsu* are headed by organizations such as Toyota, Sony, and NEC.

What Can Western Businesses Learn from Keiretsu? The first lesson is that patient capital earns its just rewards. The banks at the center of the *keiretsu* are reliable sources of long-term finance for their other members. However, the Japanese still take a tough view. They will not underwrite a business that is not viable in the long run. In addition, there are strong cross-shareholdings between *keiretsu* members. Typically, anything between 15 and 30 percent is never traded at all. To a significant extent, the success of members of a *keiretsu* is bound up among one another. As Harrison notes: "Such cross-holding frees corporate managers to a significant extent from concerns about the availability of investment capital and encourages them to adopt a longer-term planning horizon than that which characterizes especially British and American corporations."[17]

The second lesson is that long-term, multilayered relationships deliver benefits above those gained from short- or medium-term contracting relationships. *Keiretsu* members trade extensively among themselves. Van Kooij suggests that this outsourcing of production to other *keiretsu* members may account for up to three-quarters of the value production in *keiretsu* such as NEC, Panasonic, and Sony.[18] This creates what has been described as relational contracting, which is highly effective at diffusing innovation throughout a network of companies and sharing risk. However, relational contracting is not a recipe for poor quality and second-rate design. An organization that fails to meet standards will be expelled from the *keiretsu*.

It is doubtful whether an organization with a "Western" managerial style could engage in so much cross-ownership without exciting the attention of monopolies and regulatory authorities. Nevertheless, some organizations are trying to win some of the other benefits of *keiretsu*, such as stable capital and long-term relational contracting. Some Japanese think that Richard Branson's Virgin group looks and acts like a Western *keiretsu*.

Technology Enablers

Some of the best exploiters of the lean enterprise use information technology in creative ways to leverage more value from their core competencies and to facilitate the smooth workings of their alliances and partnerships. Yet, there are few fixed patterns for the use of technology enablers; still less any simple how-to guide to apply IT to a partnership or alliance.

Some organizations have developed the use of technology enablers in an advanced way. For example, e-mail and electronic data interchange are used extensively in many organizations today. These developments have allowed important business partners to share information and knowledge in collaborative projects. They also encourage distributors to tap directly into product databases to acquire information about latest prices, availability, and order placing. It is impossible to generalize about the ways that technology would be used to facilitate partnerships. It is evident that there is a large role for the "obvious" technologies such as e-mail, electronic data interface (EDI), and videoconferencing. However, others can also play a useful role.

Beyond its role in partnerships and alliances, IT also has a role to play in helping companies leverage more value from their core competencies. For example, computer systems now allow managers to log a potential problem onto the IT system in the evening and have some possible answers and information from the IT provider's staff elsewhere in the world on their PC when they return to their office in the morning.

The "Best of Everything" Organization—Myth or Reality?

Can organizations that follow these principles create a "best-of-everything" organization in which each participant contributes its own core competencies? Also, what is the relationship between a "best-of-everything" organization and a lean organization? There are two answers. First, some major organizations are making a conscious effort to slim their organizations and focus on best-of-everything principles Second they focus on their core competencies, core businesses, and core products. They sell off noncore businesses, discontinue noncore products, and adopt a vigorous outsourcing strategy for noncore activities of what is left—the core business.

The global role model for this kind of activity has to be Jack Welch at General Electric. In 1981, when Welch became CEO, the sprawling organization included businesses as diverse as aerospace high technologies, medical equipment, home videos, and carpets. Welch based a new business strategy for General Electric on the simple principle that every business in the new portfolio had to be either first or second in its market. Otherwise, he added ominously, he would "fix, close or sell it." Since then, Welch has sold businesses worth over U$11 billion. He has slimmed the organization's headcount from over 400,000 to approximately 293,000, while boosting revenues from U$27 billion to over U$100 billion over the same period of time.

Interestingly, Welch has encouraged General Electric businesses to enter many partnerships and alliances and he has reformed the culture of the organization. The old bureaucratic structure, he bluntly stated, meant that staff adopted the posture of "face to the CEO, ass to the customer." (However, there are not too many CEOs who would be happy with the implications of a complete 180–degree turn.) Welch based this business revolution on six principles:

- Control your destiny, or someone else will;
- Face reality as it is, not as you wish it to be;
- Be candid with everyone;
- Do not manage—lead;
- Change before you have to; and
- Only compete when you have the advantage.

Welch has been remarkably successful; yet, other companies that are not moving down the slimmer-organization, best-of-everything route have had more difficulty. IBM, for example, cut tens of thousands of jobs, focused its business in smaller operating units, and entered thousands of partnerships. Yet, it is still to be completely successful in its new global role. Welch's success was in changing the General Electric culture, a shift IBM is finding difficult.

But the other side of the coin is equally fascinating. Looking beyond the corporate giants, there are a small number of fast-growing new companies that are basing their operations on lean organization and best-of-everything principles. One example of this is Virgin Cola. This joint venture was formed between Richard Branson's Virgin Group and the Cott Corporation of Canada. It initially launched a rival to Pepsi and Coke in the United Kingdom. Virgin Cola purchases the cola syrup from the Cott Corporation, outsources UK production to a factory in Pontefract, Yorkshire, and leverages sales through special arrangements with selected national retail chains. In its first three months, Virgin Cola shifted £50 million of product with only four employees.

In the United States, Topsy Tail, an organization that makes a range of hair-styling products, topped U$80 million in sales only three years after starting business, and they accomplished this with just three employees. Product manufacturing was outsourced to a tool manufacturer, two injection molders, a package designer, a logo designer, freelance photographers, and a printer. Packaging and distribution was outsourced to three fulfillment houses, television commercials to a video production organization, customer mailings to a direct marketing organization, and publicity to a public relations agency. Control of new product development and marketing strategy, the core competencies of the organization, is the only area done inhouse.

One of the management academics behind this approach to business is James Brian Quinn. He explains the strategic imperative behind the best-of-everything organization:

> By developing a few strategically selected core service activities in greater depth than any competitor, carefully surrounding these with strong barriers to entry, and constructing an effective strategic "block" between suppliers of outsourced services (or products) and the downstream market-place, a company can create a genuinely focused strategy and the most effective possible maintainable competitive edge.[19]

All this activity is changing the shape of global business. The world's economy is still dominated by large organizations. Rather than dwindling away as all this downsizing activity might suggest, large organizations are diffusing their operations both through network organizations and through an increasing range of alliances.

What seems to be happening is that new alliances of organizations are growing. Often they have a major organization at the heart and are surrounded by a series of concentric rings of other suppliers—medium-sized organizations on the first ring, then smaller organizations, and finally individual contractors. But the major organization sets the pace for the alliance and decides key policy issues. This "concentration without centralisation," as Harrison[20] calls it, is, effectively, another way of describing the phenomenon of the lean organization. Harrison suggests that there are four foundations to this new organizational model: "First, managers are vigorously paring down the mix of activities (and the number of employees) they deem central to the firm's existence, while relegating the rest to positions at a greater "distance" from corporate headquarters."[21] This creates core-ring and other network forms of organization. "Second, more and more companies are finding new ways to use computerised manufacturing and management information systems to coordinate these far-flung activities and increase the flexibility with which they enter and exit different markets, alter production designs, and monitor their employees' performance."[22] This is the burgeoning array of technological enablers that facilitate the new organizational forms and methods of working.

"Third, the most successful of the big firms have been busily constructing so-called strategic alliances among one another, both within and, especially, across national borders."[23] Finally, Harrison argues that "within more and more of the big firms and their principal sub-contractors, we are witnessing systematic attempts by managers to elicit the more active collaboration of their most expensive-to-replace workers in the 'mission' of the corporation.[24] This is often referred to as "empowerment" and is facilitated by a range of new organizational forms, often based on teams, and underpinned with collaborative partnership cultures designed to facilitate the free exchange of information.[25]

It is in thinking like this that some of the paradoxes mentioned here begin to be reconciled. For example, a lean organization is not shrinking but, like Welch's General Electric, is creating the circumstances in which it can grow—nearly trebling revenues in a decade.

The lean organization competes vigorously, but uses cooperation as one of the weapons in its competitive strategy. Rover, for example, jumped to the top of the European quality league among carmakers by learning from Honda, while competing in the same market.

The lean organization achieves global reach, yet builds a local face for its business in each of its markets. None of this is easy, as regular management convulsions in large organizations regularly testify. What becomes clear is that there is no blueprint for creating the lean organization. Each alliance is, literally, unique, and in creating and operating it managers must address a unique agenda of issues. Nevertheless, that does not mean there are no best practice guidelines to steer by.

The remainder of this book examines, with increasing focus and detail, the six building blocks of the lean organization and some of the more important issues associated with alliances and outsourcing. Finally, there is a summary of the questions that managers must ask, and answer, as they transform their organization into a lean organization.

The following discussion of the Virgin Group illustrates a number of themes: how to run a lean organization by focusing on core competencies and leveraging value from alliances, and outsourcing.[26]

The Power of Values

The rapid growth of the Virgin group possibly illustrates better than any other organization the overarching theme of this book; that is, the ability to leverage core competencies through alliances and outsourcing to create a lean organization.

In more conservative or traditional Western business environments, the Virgin approach has been seen as somewhat eccentric. There is no denying the success of the organization. Over the past twenty or so years Virgin has progressed from a music and entertainment organization with revenues of £50 million to a diversified global organization with revenues of more than £3 billion in 1999. Too often, the view of the Virgin credo by outside managers is: "It might work for them but it would not work for anyone else." Virgin's circumstances are unique. It is, for example, one of the largest private companies in Great Britain. To translate its management philosophy and practices into other businesses is near impossible, argue some outsiders.

This book supports the view that organizations like Virgin are at the forefront of a new business order in which the kind of management strategies Virgin has followed will be important ingredients for corporate success. Virgin is now a diverse group of companies with a substantial global presence. According to Kochan, Virgin ranked in the 100 greatest brands in the world.[27] Virgin is also growing fast. Virgin is also profitable. It is entering and claiming significant shares in new markets. However, this has come about without most of the traditional trappings of the multinational. There is no head office, little sense of management hierarchy, and a minimum of corporate bureaucracy. Virgin may well be the ultimate lean organization.

Even to speak of the Virgin group of companies is somewhat misleading. There is no "group" as such because the financial results are not aggregated into a central holding company. Each business runs its own affairs. The "group," if it has to have a name, is bound together by a degree of shared ownership, shared leadership, and shared values. The "group" consists of an ever more variegated array of wholly owned businesses, alliances, and outsourcing arrangements.

Virgin is an organization with a lean management that is both agile and nimble. When Virgin wants to move into a new business area, it assembles a team that can move fast and seize a business opportunity. Virgin has no cumbersome committee system that delays decision making. Instead, strategic decisions about new business ventures are led by the chairman, Richard Branson, with a group of senior managers who are summoned on an ad hoc basis for their counsel.

For example, when Virgin decided to move into the cola market taking on Coke and Pepsi, a small team of managers made the decision after a series of informal meetings with its Canadian partner, Cott Corporation, at Richard Branson's home. With the decision made, Virgin was able to call upon a range of management talent in the "group" to get the venture off the ground. After three months, Virgin Cola had shifted £50 million of the product with only four employees.

The cola experience has been replicated many times in Virgin. Richard Branson recognized that he did not need to construct a large central management structure in order to grow the business. Consequently, when a new venture comes along, an ad hoc team is formed in order to evaluate the idea and, if relevant, bring it to market. A central company, Virgin Management, houses a team of management talent that can be seconded to other parts of the "group" when the need arises. This is a style of management that some other organizations have craved, but few have yet emulated in such a successful way.

Why does Virgin succeed where others fail? The answer is partly in the history of Virgin and partly in its culture. When Richard Branson built his music business in the 1970s, signing artists such as Phil Collins and Boy George, Branson concentrated on managing the artists and copyrights and the marketing of intellectual property rather than building record/CD manufacturing, distribution, and marketing operations. Virgin as a result frequently outmaneuvered larger, but structurally "flat-footed" competitors. Managing the music business, in which the rights to "properties" are often shared through complex arrangements, creates the management mind-set that regards alliances as a natural way of doing business. For Virgin, if it worked for music, there was no reason why it would not work in airlines, drinks (alcoholic and nonalcoholic), financial services, hotels, and retailing.

The diversity of the Virgin group raises another question. With so many different businesses, can Virgin have any group-wide core competencies?

The separate businesses within the "group" can develop core competencies on their own. At the "group" level, it dodges the central question: Does a group such as Virgin need core competencies in order to manage its diversity of businesses?

Virgin's core competency is the ability to identify relevant business opportunities and manage the organic growth of new businesses. On the face of it, Virgin looks like any other diversified multinational: skilled at mergers, acquisitions, and leveraging improved financial returns from an asset base. The Virgin approach, however, is different from this and important in explaining its success. The Virgin core competency focuses on building businesses that can generate their own growth potential. Virgin has had its acquisitions and divestments, for example the sale of its record/CD label to Thorn EMI. Virgin is a story of organic growth; £50 million to £3 billion in twenty years could not occur without considerable recourse to alliances and outsourcing. There is considerable management competency demonstrated by Virgin in managing business ventures that harness these kinds of arrangements.

Virgin considers several hundred potential new business opportunities every year but only a small number of these ever reach the starting post. Virgin has four core values that should be present in varying degrees in every Virgin business. These values are quality, competitiveness, innovation, and fun. With the later value, Virgin seeks to create a sense of enjoyment in using its products and services, not necessarily available from rivals. Richard Branson has explained:

> If we launch a new product people assume that we will come up with something a bit different. . . . But it's also synonymous with fun and with entertainment in the broadest sense. The value of the name is enormous. We get asked to put the Virgin name to many things but we say no to most of them."[28]

Branson's point is that people associate the name Virgin with certain attributes and characteristics. It is essential to ensure that whatever venture the "group" undertakes, it is faithful to these attributes and characteristics.

Some financial and management commentators have suggested that the "group" that Branson has built is a Western version of a Japanese *keiretsu* or Korean *chaebol*. In many respects, the Virgin "group" does look like a *keiretsu*. For example, members of the company in the "group" manage their its affairs autonomously but regard themselves as part of the wider Virgin community, from which they derive their core values and attributes. The nature of the "group" is such that there is not the extensive interweaving cross-ownership among the Virgin "group" that is in a *keiretsu* or *chaebol*, but there is certainly a wide pattern of ownership as a result of alliances.

The Virgin Network of Alliances

There were twenty-four groups within Virgin by 1998. Each has its own alliance and outsourcing networks. Some of these groups are:

1. Virgin Travel Group runs Virgin Atlantic Airways (the airline), Virgin Holidays (a travel and holiday company), and Virgin Aviation Services (a freight company).
2. Virgin Entertainment Group runs cinema chains, Megastores in the United States, Japan, and Europe.
3. Virgin Retail Group operates Virgin Retail (Our Price and UK Megastores), Caroline International, and Sound and Media.
4. Virgin Trading Company sells Virgin cola, vodka, and other beverages, Virgin Limobikes, snack foods, lifestyle products, and clothing.
5. Virgin Entertainment Group operates Virgin Digital Studios (525, Rushes, West One TV, Virgin publishing, John Brown Enterprises, and Rapido TV.
6. Ginger Media Group operates Virgin Radio.
7. Virgin Hotels Group operates the Virgin Clubs in the United Kingdom, Spain, the Caribbean, and naturally, the Virgin Islands.
8. Virgin Direct Limited operates Virgin Direct Personal Financial Service Limited.
9. Victory Corporation with Virgin Vie and Virgin Clothing.
10. Virgin Retail Group with West Coast Trains and CrossCountry Trains.
11. Virgin Helicopters.
12. V2 Records.
13. Storm Model Management.

Japanese *keiretsu* are often organized around a large financial organization (for example a bank). The financial organization builds a long-term relationship with the companies in the *keiretsu*. Consequently, the financial organization usually takes a longer-term view of the prospects of its *keiretsu* members than most Western banks do of their customers. This means that the financial organizations invest in their *keiretsu* members for the long rather than the short term. Virgin does not have a bank at its heart (though it has formed an alliance with a large insurance company), yet it has acquired the *keiretsu* approach to investment.

The fact that Branson's family trust still owns a significant portion of the company and that the "group" is largely free from debt allows Virgin to take the long-term view, free from investors fixated by short-term returns (another feature that makes it appear more like a *keiretsu* or *chaebol* than a Western organization).

To some extent, like *keiretsu* or *chaebol*, some of the products of Virgin Publishing turn up in Virgin stores, and the Virgin airline stocks Virgin Cola. However, this feature of vertical integration is less marked than in Japan or Korea. Also less marked are the interlocking directorships that feature in *keiretsu*. The running of each Virgin company is as an autonomous entity, although executives from Virgin Management or elsewhere in the "group" might parachute in from time to time to lead specific projects.

The *keiretsu* approach, even in a European modified form, infuses several key aspects of the management style of the Virgin "group." For example, Branson favors small businesses. He believes that fifty to seventy staff members ought to be about the maximum size for a business unit. Of course, as the group grows, it becomes harder to hold individual businesses down to the seventy maximum. Virgin Travel, for example, has no more than a thousand staff. Even here, the company is looking at how to retain the small-unit principle. For example, it is experimenting with ways to divide up cabin-crew members into self-contained teams.

The philosophy behind this small unit approach is empowerment. The Virgin view is that this is more a way of living than a corporate strategy. Branson will sometimes disagree with those running the various companies, but let them go ahead because they have been hired for their capability to perform and run the various businesses. This approach is essential in such a widespread, diverse, and fast-growing group, for it decentralizes decision making and creates nodes of real responsibility right through the enterprise.

Another feature of the Virgin managerial style is the ability to create true cross-functional management. An example of this approach is Virgin Travel. Where other airlines have group functional directors or general managers at the top of the business with several layers of managers beneath them, Virgin manages with a pool of six directors, commonly referred to as "the six pack." The benefits of this approach are that it reduces functional boundaries within the organization and creates clear centers of responsibility for end-to-end services. It also serves the desire to maintain small business units by making each director the center of a dedicated team of head office staff.

To draw the *keiretsu* parallel too far is dangerous. The strength of the *keiretsu* model is that it predisposes the management of each company to want to cooperate with others in all manners of alliances and outsourcing arrangements. In order to do this it adopts the kind of flexible management style that facilitates external cooperation. Virgin has approached both of these issues in a way similar to most *keiretsu*.

A question for other Western organizations is: how far does the *keiretsu* provide a realistic model for a network of lean cooperating businesses? Virgin's experience suggests that the *keiretsu* model can be made to deliver benefits in Western organizational culture. A *keiretsu* is more than an organizational model. It also implies a system of beliefs and behaviors about how loosely confederated groups of different businesses might work together for mutual advantage. It is because these beliefs and behaviors are embedded deep in the Virgin culture that this approach works so well for it.

Beyond Virgin's corporate organization and management style, there are a number of other lessons that other organization can learn from the Virgin "group."

Cutting the Deals: Why the Virgin Is Not a Rookie

Virgin, on occasion, actively seeks out new business ventures; for example, Virgin Radio in Great Britain. On other occasions, the approach comes from outside the organization. However, in every deal, two factors are uppermost in the minds of Virgin's senior managers. First, the Virgin name must be protected. This means that Virgin nearly always requires management involvement in every business venture it joins. Only rarely has it licensed the Virgin logo for use by others. Second, the venture must measure up, at least somewhat, to the four attributes previously mentioned that identify a Virgin business. So how does this work in practice? The examples of vodka, cola, and insurance throw illumination on these points and underscore other elements of Virgin's approach to alliances.

Virgin Vodka is the result of an alliance between Virgin and William Grant, the distillers whose most famous brand is Glenfiddich whiskey. William Grant approached Virgin in 1992. The whiskey distiller wanted to launch a vodka product and had researched possible brand names, including the usual array of Popovs, Romanovs, and other aristocratic sounding Russian names. The market researcher being used had just been in a Virgin store and came to the conclusion of "why not a Virgin Vodka?" The researcher included the name "Virgin Vodka" in the questionnaires and it came out as the most popular name. Then the managers from William Grant wanted to see if Virgin would be interested in using the name of the new drink. This was one occasion when Virgin did licenseits name—to William Grant to test market the product. The market testing showed significant potential and the two companies formed an alliance to sell the product in Great Britain.

There is a story behind Virgin Cola, potentially a major Virgin business. Virgin had been asked several times to brand a cola. When Cott Corporation approached Virgin, two factors were different. First, the experience with the vodka had demonstrated potential in the fast-moving consumer goods (FMCG) market, a useful counter-cycle business to some of Virgin's other activities. Second, Cott Corporation had more than an idea; it had an actual cola recipe. If Virgin was going to put its name on a cola it would have to be good. The problem with many of Coca-Cola and Pepsi's rivals is that they are perceived by many consumers to have an inferior taste. The Virgin team considering the proposal thought that Cott's formula was one of the best that they had tasted outside the formulas of Coca-Cola's and Pepsi.

Virgin was not completely convinced, although the cola is aimed at a younger market and has synergy with other Virgin businesses. Branson's research among senior Virgin managers was negative. However, after more thought the idea started to grow. The British retailer, Sainsbury, had successfully launched a cola product under its own brand. There seemed to be no reason why Virgin should not also launch a product, trade on its brand name attributes, and offer a product below the cost of the big two.

The launch of Virgin Cola showed how Virgin leverages business benefits through alliances and outsourcing. The Virgin Cola company is an alliance with Cott Corporation. Cott supplies the syrup from North America. The production of the cola, using this syrup, is outsourced to a factory in Pontefract in Yorkshire. Distribution of the product is outsourced. Initially, sales have been leveraged through a series of special agreements with key British retail chains (including Tesco, Thresher, and Martin's news agents). After the initial period, sales are being expanded through other outlets. This approach allowed Virgin to sell £50 million in the first three months with only four full-time employees.

The alliance with Norwich Union to create Virgin Direct moved the "group" into financial services for the first time. As with Virgin's entry into the airlines business, Virgin is seeking to change the ground rules of competition. Virgin Direct will sell a range of purpose-designed financial products. There is no commission for sales people and disclosure of expenses and charges is completely open. Virgin Direct is aiming its products at the mass market and is trading strongly on the attributes identified in the Virgin brand name.

Some common themes run through these and other Virgin alliances. First is that each is set up with extreme care. When the development of an alliance is undertaken, all details have to be very clear. Partners must work together to establish priorities and make clear the time and resources each is prepared to commit to make the alliance work.

Virgin spends considerable time in setting up each alliance. Much of the time is spent defining what will happen in any one of a large number of different contingent situations. Because of experience, Virgin can spend a shorter length of time defining for the prospective partner(s) the way that Virgin wants to work. If the prospective partner(s) does not want to work that way there is no point in forming the alliance and it saves time for both parties.

The second success factor in the Virgin alliances is the culture and skills that managers bring to the formation and management process. Working with alliances and outsourcing are a way of life within the Virgin group. This is deeply embedded in the organization's culture and imbues the style with which managers and staff work. To support this culture there is a vast amount of practical experience of managing alliances, experience that is codified in a manual—the "Virgin System." The manual is effectively a blueprint for running alliances. It shows how to analyze the upside and downside of alliances and provides guidance and methodologies for management. For example, it provides a method for assessing the skills needed in the enterprise and for judging the opportunity costs of using those skills in that alliance or elsewhere in the group.

A third factor is the way each alliance is structured. Every alliance is structured so that there are cut-off points at which fundamental decisions about its future direction can be taken. These cut-off points often relate what the alliance partner(s) is faced with in making major decisions about committing new capital or embarking on some form of expansion.

Another factor is the way in which the alliance is managed. Generally, Virgin sets up an alliance management team with its partner(s). The aim is to make the venture as independent as possible. This gives responsibility to the alliance management team for its own decisions, but it also acts as a catalyst to meld together the managers from both sides of the venture into one unified team. They are free from the close day-to-day surveillance by their respective parents that might encourage them to keep too much of an eye on what the parent is thinking—to the detriment of the venture's own interests.

An important feature of most Virgin alliances is that the chairmanship rotates between the partners. This underlies the equality of the contribution that each brings to the alliance irrespective of the ownership position.

How far can Virgin grow and remain a lean organization, leveraging its competencies through alliances and ventures? Virgin is sixty times its size of 1983, yet it retains the same culture and approach to business. The cola venture shows what can be achieved with a small staff through a network of alliances and outsourcing.

Virgin's active approach to retaining small business units and a hands-off management approach units has created a group with considerable entrepreneurial energy and skills. These are all critical ingredients in Virgin's success. Other businesses have adopted some of these approaches, but the secret seems to be bringing them all together at the same time.

NOTES

1. Throughout this book, the term *alliance* is used for all cooperative ventures; that is, joint ventures, collaborations, and consortia.

2. For useful discussions on globalization, see R. Boyer and D. Drache (1996), *States against Markets* (London: Routledge); P. Hirst and G. Thompson (1996), *Globalization in Question* (Cambridge: Polity Press); A. Hoogvelt (1997), *Globalisation and the Postcolonial World* (Basingstoke: Macmillan); and A. Scott, ed. (1997), *The Limits of Globalization* (London: Routledge).

3. J. P. Womack and D. T. Jones (1994), "From Lean Production to the Lean Enterprise," *Harvard Business Review* 72 (2):93–103.

4. Ibid., p. 93.

5. J. P. Womack, D. T. Jones, and D. Roos (1990), *The Machine That Changed the World* (New York: Simon and Schuster).

6. Womack and Jones (1994), "From Lean Production to the Lean Enterprise," p. 93.

7. Ibid,, p. 94.

8. Ibid., p. 93.

9. Ibid.

10. Ibid., p. 103.

11. Ibid.

12. C. K. Prahalad and G. Hamel (1990), "The Core Competence of the Corporation," *Harvard Business Review* 68 (3):82.

13. P. Dicken (1998), *Global Shift* (New York: The Guilford Press). The level of proliferation in alliance formation is supported by K. W. Glaister and P. J. Buckley (1994), "UK International Joint Ventures," *British Journal of Management* 5:33–51; and K. W. Glaister, R. Husan, and P. J. Buckley (1998), "UK International Joint Ventures with the Triad," *British Journal of Management* 9 (3):169–180.

14. J. P. Womack (1992), "The Lean Difference," *Prism* (First Quarter): 105.

15. This organization has requested that it remain anonymous.

16. For a detailed discussion on the importance, benefits, and difficulties of teams, see J. Lipnack and J. Stamps (1995), *The Teamnet Factor* (Essex Junction, VT: Oliver Wight); J. Lipnack and J. Stamps (1994), *The Age of the Network* (New York: John Wiley and Sons); J. R. Katzenbach and D. K. Smith (1993), *The Wisdom of Teams* (Boston: Harvard Business School Press); J.R. Katzenbach (1998), *Teams at the Top* (Boston: Harvard Business School Press).

17. B. Harrison (1997), *Lean and Mean* (New York: Guilford Press), p. 159.

18. E. van Kooij (1990), "Industrial Networks in Japan," *Entrepreneurship and Regional Development* 2.

19. J. B. Quinn (1992), *Intelligent Enterprise* (New York: The Free Press), p. 97.

20. Harrison (1997), *Lean and Mean* p. 23.

21. Ibid., p. 9.

22. Ibid., p. 10.

23. Ibid.

24. Ibid.

25. For a detailed discussion on empowerment, see R. Johnson and D. Redmond (1998), *The Art of Empowerment* (London: Financial Times/Pitman Publishing London). Empowerment is a concept that has often been misunderstood by practicing managers. For managers who like to have control over their employees' every action (a theory Y approach), it is a great threat. For those managers who like to give their employees the room to use their skills and ability to the limit (a theory X approach), this is the chance that they have sought. The managing director of the Australian subsidiary of an American multinational corporation once told me that every employee in the organization was empowered to work within the limits of his job description and that empowerment had worked well in this organization. This person did not accept their definition of empowerment as something that allowed people just to do their normal duties; instead, the managing director believed that empowerment was supposed to allow them to go outside their normal boundaries to achieve results.

26. Throughout this book, the material used to base the case studies on has been sourced from the business press (such as *Forbes, Fortune, Wall Street Journal, The Financial Times*, and *Business Week*) as well as from academic case notes and supplementary material from the Harvard Business School and European Case Clearing House (at Cranfield University in Great Britain), public domain documents such as annual reports and media releases, and from personal correspondence with people within these organizations.

27. N. Kochan, ed. (1996), *The World's Greatest Brands* (Basingstoke: Macmillan).

28. S. Farish (1994), "The Branson Factor", *PR Week* (9 September), p. 6.

2

CORE COMPETENCIES: THE HEART OF A STRATEGY

CORE COMPETENCIES: DISCOVERING THEIR ROLE

The concept of core competencies is at the heart of an effective business strategy for a lean organization. Yet, two factors, both in their own ways disturbing, were identified during the research for this book.

First, it is surprising how few managers, including some senior people making an important contribution to an organization's strategy, were clear about the concept of core competencies and their role in a business strategy.[1] When asked about their own competencies, managers often replied by naming their main product or service, or referring to a vague concept such as "market leadership" or "customer service."

Second is the number of organizations that were embarking on alliances and outsourcing without first defining the core competencies that should be nurtured in-house to retain long-term competitiveness. These were organizations setting out on an alliance in a reactive rather than proactive way. Too often, an alliance is seen as a way of "plugging a gap" or "covering a weakness" rather than exploiting a strength. In these cases, alliances are more likely to undermine rather than boost the long-term competitiveness of the organization. This occurs because the alliance partners fail to focus on developing core competencies and leveraging business opportunities from them. The result was a "hollow" organization in which key competencies had been eaten away through overreliance on outside partners; rather than a "lean" organization, where the core competencies are enhanced because alliances are designed to strengthen the competencies while outsourcing is used to provide noncore services. Or, to borrow from George Orwell: lean good, hollow bad.

The combination of these two deficiencies provides a recipe for strategic confusion and long-term decline. Indeed, it is hardly surprising that so many alliances should fail when they are not completing flourishing in-house competencies. In fact, the findings of other researchers are reinforced: that ill-advised alliances can undermine an organization's core competencies to the extent that it becomes so "hollowed out" that it is unable to grow into the future.

There are some examples of this in British and American television manufacturing industries. Excessive outsourcing of R&D and manufacturing of key components to Japanese suppliers detached the homegrown industries from the key technological developments needed to be competitive in the next generation of products.

The picture is not all black. Some organizations have grasped the subtleties in the concept of core competencies and have exploited their own competencies in effective ways. GKN, for example, built a more robust business based on the strength of two group-wide competencies: the ability to manage asset-intensive businesses and the skills involved in forging complex design and production relationships with customers. The Virgin Group has developed a competence in managing rapid organic growth through alliances in businesses that display four core values: quality, competitiveness, innovation, and fun. Note that in neither of these successful examples does the heart of the competence lie in a single product. Rather, it resides in a more complex set of technologies, skills, and business processes that enable the organization to deliver a capability that cannot readily be replicated by a competitor.

Quinn suggests that each division, and possibly the entire organization, should select and define the dimensions for the skills and activities required to give the organization the dominating depth needed for competitive advantage in serving its customers in both the short and long term. Quinn also suggests that because customers' needs change over time, these selected bases of competency should not only have enough depth to prevent others from preemption, but be broad and flexible enough to respond quickly to an unknown future.[2] It is, as the old business saying wrongly suggests, no longer enough to make a better mousetrap and the world will beat a path to your door. Instead, you need the core competence to make better and better mousetraps to catch ever more guileful mice.

In unraveling the complexities of core competencies the discussion will proceed to:

- The origin of the concept;
- The links between core competencies and core products; and
- The issues involved in developing a business strategy based on core competencies.

THE ORIGIN OF COMPETENCIES: A DEFINITION AND EXPLANATION

The ideas behind the notion of core competencies were originally developed by Prahalad and Hamel.[3] They argue that the real sources of competitive advantage lie not in products or organizational forms, but in "management's ability to consolidate corporatewide technologies and production skills into competencies that empower individual businesses to adapt to changing opportunities." To explain this they use the analogy of a large tree: "The trunk and major limbs are core products, the smaller branches are business units, and the leaves, flowers, and fruit are the end products. The root system that provides nourishment, sustenance, and stability is the core competence."[4]

Interestingly, in this analogy the core competence is out of sight, under ground. This accurately reflects the fact that a core competence is not a feature that is necessarily noticed by a casual observer. The customers of an organization experience the core competence when they buy a product or service, but they do not necessarily notice it.

As Prahalad and Hamel point out: "Competencies are the glue that binds existing businesses together."[5] They represent "the collective learning of the organization, especially how to coordinate diverse production skills and integrate multiple streams of technologies." If all this seems somewhat vague, Prahalad and Hamel[6] provide three tests that can be applied to core competencies:

- "A core competence provides potential access to a wide variety of markets." They give the example of electronic display systems that enable an organization to participate in businesses such as calculators, miniature television sets, monitors for laptop computers, and automotive dashboards. Canon's competencies in lens systems, laser engines, and miniature motors leverage it into businesses such as copiers, laser printers, fax machines, and camcorders.

- The core competence makes a "significant contribution to the perceived customer benefits of the end product." For example, Seagate Technology's competencies enable it to deliver ever higher performance disk drives to PC manufacturers at a fixed price. In a more unusual way, Virgin's ability to imbue its businesses and products with the core value of "fun" provides it with a means of differentiating itself in the airline business where plane seats from one destination to another are largely a commodity product.

- The core competence "should be difficult for competitors to imitate." Prahalad and Hamel point out that it will be difficult to imitate if "it is a complex harmonisation of individual technologies and production skills. A rival might acquire some of the technologies that comprise a core competence, but it will find it more difficult to duplicate the more or less comprehensive pattern of internal coordination and learning." Seagate, for example, has built market dominance in disk drives by ensuring it "owns" the key technologies that underpin its core products. This ensures the organization controls the development of the technology, which competitors must follow, and determines how and when new technologies are brought to market.

A Checklist for Core Competencies

Core competencies often have the following characteristics:

- Architectural support;
- Continuously reviewed and enhanced;
- Difficult to copy;
- Emobodied, exploited in multiple products or services;
- Enduring and understood;
- Envied by competitors and benchmark organizations;
- Monitored through performance measures;
- Recognized internally;
- Reinforced through training and development;
- True competitive asset; and
- Truly distinctive.

Where an organization defines its core competencies successfully, then leverages off those competencies to develop market strength, it excels the performance of its competitors. Two examples of successful exploiters and one unsuccessful example illuminate this argument:

- During the 1980s, Canon developed core competencies in three key technologies: precision mechanics, fine optics, and microelectronics. These enabled Canon not only to develop well in its original camera marketplace, but to move into copiers, a market that it had never previously tackled. In less than a decade, it had built a leading market share. Within Canon, managers are encouraged to share competencies and to take a broad and creative view of the ways in which they can be used. For example, when the organization developed its first microprocessor-controlled copiers, it drew on assistance from its photo products group, which had already developed a microprocessor-controlled camera.

  Like other organizations that successfully exploit their core competencies, Canon makes a distinction between its market share in end products (for example, copiers), and its manufacturing share—or the share of the total market—by providing own-label products to others as well as its share of the core products sold to others (for example, laser engines). Canon's success comes from its dominating success in core products.

- Sony has developed considerable competence in miniaturization. This competence transcends a whole range of products and gives it a compelling competitive advantage in many different areas. In order to develop this competence, Sony has built skills in technologies as diverse as microprocessors, miniature power sources, power management, packaging, and manufacturing. Sony harnesses these different skills into a stream of knowledge—what Stalk, Evans, and Shulman call "capabilities"—that creates competence and, at the same time, makes it very difficult for any competitor to emulate.[7]

- Atari is an example of an organization that lost sight of its core competence and paid the ultimate price. In the early 1980s, Atari developed a major position in the fast-growing market for video games. The competencies in this market center on the entertainment industry more than electronics. For example, successful organizations that produce video games have competencies such as understanding fashion trends and marketing to young people.

Atari decided it wanted to become a more broadly based consumer electronics product company and in the process lost the primary focus on its main video games competencies. Within years, it had lost the market to Nintendo and Sega. Atari failed to understand that its key competencies were in electronic entertainment systems, rather than consumer electronics generally.

The first two of these examples illustrate how core competencies may create a strategic level for building sustainable competitive advantage. The final example demonstrates the market-destroying impact of losing sight of core competencies in a quest for ill-considered expansion.

However, just what are the business forces that make core competencies such a potent factor? Why are some organizations able to leverage more value from their investment spending than rivals are? Consider this fact: NEC, the Japanese computers and communications organization, invested considerably less in its annual R&D budget from 1980 to 1990 than either IBM or AT&T. Yet, NEC generated 23 percent annual growth during that decade, considerably ahead of both its U.S.-owned rivals. The main reason is that NEC was more effective in leveraging its core competencies during the decade, chiefly through alliances.

In fact, understanding why NEC beat IBM and AT&T during this decade goes a long way to explaining the machinery that translates core competencies into competitive advantage. NEC not only identified its strategic objective—to exploit the convergence of computing and communications (what it calls C&C)—but also created a "strategic architecture" or governance process to focus management energies on achieving the objective. NEC's managers focused on building technology and management competencies in three areas: distributed processing; very large scale integration (VLSI) microprocessors; and digital telecommunications systems, such as ISDN. Senior managers also communicated their strategic intent widely to other parts of the organization and entered into many alliances with the aim of learning the technologies and skills it needed to realize its ambition. Unlike IBM and AT&T, NEC focused its investment more effectively and leveraged huge extra value from its alliances.

The theory behind this approach has been most effectively developed by Prahalad who suggests:

The key to understanding competence is that although it incorporates a technology component, it also involves the *governance process* inside the organization (the quality of relationships across functions, across business units), and *collective learning* across levels and functions inside the company.[8]

Prahalad argues that understanding this more complex web of interrelationships that forms core competencies explains, for example, why an organization like Hitachi grew from U$12 billion to U$68.6 billion in revenues in a decade, while a rival, Westinghouse, with a similar portfolio of businesses, managed to grow from U$8 billion to U$12 billion.

Prahalad advises managers to think of the factors that leverage the working of core competence in terms of an equation:

Competence = Technology x Governance Process x Collective Learning

The key to understanding the power process behind this equation is to know that the three factors that form a competence are "multiplied" by one another, not "added" to one another. So, for example, if an organization with 1,000 technology units has only 20 units of governance process and 5 units of collective learning, its competence equals 100,000 units. However, an organization with a fifth of the technology (200 units) leveraged by 100 units of governance and 500 units of collective learning builds a competence of 10,000,000 units.

The math behind the Prahalad equation is open to debate: multiplying three different management variables, which are difficult to measure with mathematical accuracy anyway, is rather like multiplying gallons by acres by ounces. However, the principle behind Prahalad's equation valuably underscores a central truth about competencies: The development of a competence is the cumulation of several critical features, not one.

This is an important insight for decision takers and makers. Those organizations that are most effective in placing their core competencies at the heart of their business strategies and of leveraging value from them, such as NEC, balance their activities on all the factors that make the competence powerful. GKN, for example, has competencies in particular technologies, such as driveline systems, but it leverages those with a governance process that provides competency in managing the complex design and production relationships that are the key to selling automotive products such as this. Moreover, it underpins the whole with in-depth collective learning based in the competencies needed to manage asset-intensive businesses, of which the manufacture of automotive parts in just one.

Yet, while this analysis portrays the potential business power of core competencies, it leaves two questions unanswered: How does an organization discover its core competencies? and Should core competencies be underpinned with core products?

HOW HONDA UTILIZED CORE COMPETENCIES

A famous advertising campaign for Honda in the United States was the slogan "Six Hondas in a Two-Car-Garage." It illustrates several issues about core competencies. The slogan would not work in Britain where households at the time considered themselves lucky to have a one-car garage, but the lessons are the same.

First, how does an organization discover its core competencies? In Honda's case, it was a combination of meeting a clear customer need while differentiating from competitors. During the 1950s to 1970s, Honda developed its skill in building small motorcycles, an essential form of transport in Tokyo and other parts of crowded Japanese cities. This enabled it to develop considerable competencies in small engine design (the first core competence).

Nevertheless, Honda also had to outflank competitors, such as Toyota, which had more capital than Honda had. So Honda focused on developing a highly effective assembly operation (the second core competence) and outsourced most of the nonengine fabrication. Capital-starved Honda developed low-cost ways of manufacturing its own engine components (the third core competence). Honda also built up skills in managing supplier networks in order to counter the more extensive market reach of its better-funded competitors (the fourth competence). These four competencies provided the platform for expansion in the 1970s, 1980s, and 1990s (see Figure 2.1).

Figure 2.1
How Core Competencies Generate Products

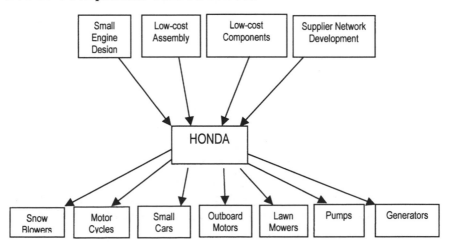

So how does an organization leverage extra value from its core competencies? In Honda's case, it used them to move into adjacent markets. For example, it has diversified its product range, leveraging off its small-engine and low-cost assembly competencies. Those other Hondas in the two-car garage could now include an outboard motor, a lawn mower, a power tiller, and a snow blower. Honda has won market share for all these products through its skills in managing supplier networks.

However, does diversification run the risk of diluting the power of core competencies? Honda has tackled this danger by developing an organization that encourages unit managers to share skills; the organization's small engine competence, and others, are developed in a way that does not compromise a range of products. For example, while an engine in a power tiller could be comparatively noisy (the noise does not matter when the tiller is in the middle of a field), the engine in a lawn mower needs to be quiet (because the neighbors do not like the noise). Honda ensures that business unit managers define their own needs (for their own products), but makes sure that all keep a view on the overall needs of the organization. In this way, the competencies are developed in a strategic fashion for the benefit of all.

COMPETENCIES AND PRODUCTS: THE LINKS

The first step in developing and nurturing competencies is to develop a clear understanding among senior managers of the three elements (technology, governance process, and organizational learning) that make up a competence. One way to consider this is to think of the elements as the atoms and the competence as the molecule. All the atoms must be present in the molecule if the competence is to be stable and effective as a tool of business leverage (see Figure 2.2), but there may be more atoms of one element than others. How the atoms are combined is a matter for legitimate debate in the organization.

A second point to consider is that core competencies should stand the test of being core. In other words, the competence must be central to business success. Snyder and Ebeling suggest three tests for this:

- Does the core competence contribute significantly to the ultimate value of the end product?

- Does it represent a unique capability that provides enduring competitive advantage?

- Does it have the potential to support multiple end products or services?[9]

Figure 2.2
Core Competencies: The Molecular View of the Atoms in a Core
Competence

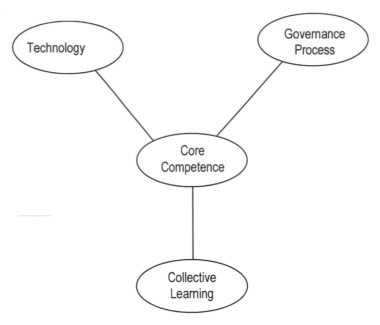

Snyder and Ebeling warn against adopting a "laundry list" approach to defining core competencies. Instead, they recommend using three techniques
to uncover an organization's competencies and to build management consensus about how they should be defined.

Activity-Based Benchmarking

Activity-based benchmarking helps managers focus on where the organization currently wins its competitive advantage. Jennings and Westfall
recommend that "strategic benchmarking" should take place against three
criteria: customers; competencies; and competitors.[10] They point out that
one of the problems in benchmarking competencies is defining the criteria
of excellence for the competencies themselves. They suggest one possible
set of criteria are those used in the Malcolm Baldrige awards. In fact, these
criteria do match off quite conveniently against the three competence elements defined by Prahalad.[11]

Employee and Asset Distribution

Snyder and Ebeling suggest that a compelling argument about core competencies can be derived from studying the organization's internal configuration.[12] By this, they mean examining where the current weight of effort and activity seems to be concentrated.

On the other hand, sometimes a simple insight is as effective as a sophisticated analysis. When Charles Lazarus noted that the only product area where the then U.S.-based Interstate Department Stores made a profit was toys, he decided to focus on that line only, and changed the name to Toys Я Us. Within fifteen years, the organization had built a set of impressive competencies around toy retailing, had won more than 20 percent of the retail toy business in the United States, and had expanded vigorously overseas.

CRITERIA FOR BENCHMARKING CORE COMPETENCIES

The criteria for excellence in the Malcolm Baldrige Awards are the best available standards for measuring core competencies. The Baldrige criteria provide a formal framework that helps an organization focus on those issues it needs to address when it sets out to identify where its strengths lie. Moreover, the range and structure of the Baldrige criteria underline the fact that competencies generally grow from an interrelated set of strengths.

The Baldrige criteria are:

1. Leadership
   - Senior executive leadership
   - Quality values
   - Management for quality
   - Public responsibility
2. Information and analysis
   - Scope of management
   - Competitive comparisons and benchmarks
   - Analysis of quality data and information
3. Strategic quality planning
   - Strategic quality planning process
   - Quality goals and plans

4. Human resources utilization
   - Human resource management
   - Employee involvement
   - Quality education and training
   - Employee recognition and performance measurement
   - Employee well-being and morale
5. Quality assurance of products and services
   - Design and introduction of quality products and services
   - Process quality control
   - Continuous improvement of processes
   - Quality assessment
   - Documentation
   - Business process and support service quality
   - Supplier quality
6. Quality results
   - Product and service quality results
   - Business process, operational and support quality results
   - Supplier quality results
7. Customer satisfaction
   - Determining customer requirements and expectations
   - Customer relationship management
   - Customer service standards
   - Commitment to customers
   - Complaint resolution for quality improvement
   - Determining customer satisfaction
   - Customer satisfaction results
   - Customer satisfaction comparison

WHAT-IF? SCENARIO DEVELOPMENT

Snyder and Ebeling suggest that a "senior management deadlock can often be broken by working out the implications of selecting a single core competency as a guide for future action."[13] For example, managers could ask themselves the question: What would our organization look like in five years if we organize around competence X? Although this approach can be useful in focusing on the implications of organizing around a specific competence, it needs to be used in conjunction with other techniques. For example, focusing on only one "atom" of the competence can produce dangerously misleading results.

This is particularly the case when it leads to a decision to outsource a technology that has long-term core implications. Chrysler, for example, created long-term problems for itself by outsourcing a growing proportion of its engine manufacture to Japanese organizations. Unlike Honda, which recognized the key competence of retaining engine technologies in-house, it became more dependent on external suppliers for a substantial proportion of a critical element in its product.

Once a core competence has been abandoned, it is difficult to retrieve. As Prahalad and Hamel put it: "When it comes to core competencies, it is difficult to get off the train, walk to the next station and reboard."[14]

This raises a further question: Should core competencies be underpinned with core products? Core products are the components or subassemblies that actually contribute to the value of the end products. A point to grasp here is that it is possible to build a commanding position in a "core product," yet still possess only a small share of the global market for the "end-product." Prahalad and Hamel quote the examples of Canon (mentioned earlier), which has a dominating position in the global market for desktop laser printer engines, and Matsushita, which has a large market for key VCR components.

There is an important iterative relationship between core competencies and core products. Core competence gives an organization a lead in the three atoms—technology, governance process, and collective learning—that provide a sustainable long-term competitive advantage. As Prahalad and Hamel explain: "The manufacture of core products for a wide variety of external (and internal) customers yields the revenue and market feedback that, at least partly, determines the pace at which core competencies can be enhanced and extended."[15]

The heart of this argument is that success with core products do not necessarily involve dominating end-user product markets (although that may also be the case). Indeed, the development of a core competence sometimes provides a platform to leverage sales into several different end-user markets. For example, Eastman Kodak's core competencies in imaging systems provide an entry to end-user markets such as cameras and copiers. "A dominant position in core products allows a company to shape the evolution of applications and end markets," say Prahalad and Hamel.[16] As an organization multiplies the number of application areas for its core products, it can consistently reduce the cost, time, and risk in new product development. In short, well-targeted core products can lead to economies of scale and scope.

BUILDING AND BUYING: DEVELOPING A COMPETENCE STRATEGY

Once an organization has defined its competencies, how can it build them into an enduring source of competitive advantage? In addition, if it judges its underlying competencies too weak to sustain its business vision, can it acquire competencies more quickly through mergers, acquisitions, or alliances?

Those organizations that leverage their core competencies most effectively consciously organize around them. In other words, the competencies become the strategic focus for management activity. At Virgin, for example, a central management team constantly explores new ways to leverage new businesses from its competence in managing organic growth through alliances. There is a top management vision of the competencies, and that vision is communicated right through the organization.

Moreover then, in their different ways, organization structures are not allowed to impede the development of the competence. In the case of Virgin, the organization actively plucks management talent from different divisions when it is launching a new venture. In the case of Seagate, the technology competence is actively developed in a cross-divisionalized way. For example, the organization diversified through acquisitions and alliances into other products capable of handling data-intensive computer applications. In both these cases, appropriate skills are shared across both Seagate's functions and its strategic business units (SBUs). This is significant because it has been argued that the SBU approach, still the organizational paradigm in many organizations, is the enemy of core competence development. Top management can see that overemphasis on SBUs results in only one part of the global battle for competitiveness—to put competitive products in the marketplace today.

The reason for this is that SBUs tend to be judged by short-term rather than long-term results. Moreover, where the business is fragmented into semi-autonomous SBUs, no one SBU has a responsibility for developing competencies for the organization as a whole. Yet, those organizations with the most successful competencies—for example, Honda's small engines and Sony's miniaturization—develop competencies that they exploit in different ways through all or most of their SBUs. Excessive focus on SBUs to the exclusion of the interests of the organization as a whole damages competencies development.

SBUs can constrain competence development in two other ways. First, in the absence of competencies that are widely accepted by all SBUs, an individual business unit tends to exploit only those skills that seem immediately relevant to it. Consequently, the opportunity to develop a competence that can fertilize many different businesses and products is lost.

Second, what Prahalad and Hamel call "The Tyranny of the SBU" leads to "imprisoned resources."[17] Managers of an SBU regard the competencies they develop as their sole property. This leads to selfish behavior in which a competence can be jealousy guarded or even hidden from the rest of the organization. As Prahalad and Hamel note, "This may be compared to residents of an underdeveloped country hiding most of their cash under their mattresses."[18] This is not a problem at Virgin, where the organization's SBUs are positively raided for talent when needed to launch a new venture.

Overall, an organization that is too targeted on the individual performance of its SBUs, as many still are, has erected a significant barrier to the development of organization-wide core competencies. Given that mangers recognize the need to develop and enhance competencies, the following actions should be implemented.

Communicate Competencies around the Organization

It is important for staff at all levels to understand the basis of the organization's competencies, for this will impact their own attitudes and behaviors toward their work. Where competencies are widely communicated, there is more of a common sense of purpose in sustaining and building those competencies for long-term advantage.

Organize around Competencies

Those organizations that most effectively exploit their competencies more effectively organize around them. They develop an organizational structure that both enables the competencies to be leveraged for present-day business benefit and to develop them for future business benefit. These organizations very often have flatter organizational structures with strong horizontal- or process-based information flows. In this way the necessary skills to leverage the competencies are harnessed from all parts of the organization.

Target Investment on the Competencies

The effective competence exploiters target investment on all aspects of the competence. That means that not only the technology but also the governance processes and organizational learning needed to leverage business benefit from the competence. Those organizations that target investment only on the technologies are less effective in leveraging business benefit. By targeting investment on all aspects of the competence, an organization is better placed to perform what Prahalad calls "creative bundling,"[19] which allows the competence to be exploited in many different ways. For example, Sony's miniaturization skill produces a dazzling array of different products.

Understand and Develop the Competence

This is one of the most critical and most important features of competence management. A competence atrophies if it is not developed over time. Managers need to think profoundly about the true nature of the competence. For example, during 1994 Eastman Kodak started to look at its own core competence. Previously, it identified this as an ability to produce film for cameras. It then started to position itself as an "imaging" organization, which is leading it into technologies such as electronic imaging. Eastman Kodak is developing its competence in a creative way in order to ensure that it can leverage into growing business opportunities in the future. Significantly, Eastman Kodak said that it plans to seek alliances as a way of developing this competence.

Many organizations are increasingly looking to enrich existing competencies or learn new competencies through a range of alliances, mergers, or acquisitions. Is this a viable strategy? And what ground rules apply when approaching competence development in this way?

The use of alliances is potentially one of the most effective ways to develop and exploit competencies. However, many organizations fail to exploit the opportunities in alliances because they lack the learning skills needed to acquire competencies from alliance partners.[20] There are also important issues in assessing the viability of a partner or acquisition target as a source of core competence. Kozin and Young suggest three important elements needed for an acquisition whose primary purpose is to obtain core competencies.[21]

ELEMENTS TO OBTAIN CORE COMPETENCIES

Planning and Screening

It is important to distinguish between a target organization's key success factors and its existing or potential core competencies. Whereas the success factors drive the target's performance in current markets, the core competencies determine its future possibilities. The potential acquiring organization should draw up a list of the core competencies required for future business success in the light of the target's vision and its business environment. The next step is to consider competencies as an additional factor in the acquisition process.

Due Diligence

An organization must dig deep to uncover the source of the competencies in the target it wishes to acquire. Questioning of the target's customers and competitors to find out where the target odds a differentiated value to the market is encouraged. Competencies are embedded in people and those key people are often not the senior managers. It is more often the case that a collection of line or staff managers has joined unconsciously to develop and maintain a core competence. It is important to structure the acquisition in such a way as to ensure that these people are retained in the organization. It is possible to value the core competencies in a target by focusing on the extra cash flows that might be generated from the synergistic use of the core competencies once they are merged with the acquirer's activities. This is, of course, an added value after accounting for the cash flow from the target's products and services and an additional cash flow that might be generated from revenue and cost synergies created from normal change of ownership or business combination.

STEPS IN IDENTIFYING AND EXPLOITING CORE COMPETENCIES

There is no fixed formula for finding and using core competencies. Those organizations that are most successful use all or most of the following steps:

Step 1—Search out existing strengths. Effective and sustainable competencies usually derive from existing strengths. However, the secret is to find ways to composite isolated strengths into competencies that can deliver value.

Step 2—Win management agreement about competencies. In those organizations that exploit their competencies most effectively, senior managers agree on what the competencies are. This helps to set a priority agenda for future management action and the use of investment and people resources.

Step 3—Build on the competencies. A competence is a living organism. It requires constant care and attention to remain fresh, relevant, and able to contribute value. Competencies that do not receive adequate resources soon wither on the vine.

Step 4—Exploit competencies creatively. The true test of an effective core competence is the ability of the organization to use it in many ways. For example, Sony's miniaturization competence spawns a host of products and businesses. It takes creative thinking to squeeze the juice out of a core competence.

Step 5—Develop competencies into the future. A core competence can become dated or limiting. It needs to be developed so that it is still of value in the developing markets.

POST-ACQUISITION INTEGRATION

After a deal has been completed, it is essential to secure a target's core competencies so that they can be integrated into the acquirer's business. This is partly a function of persuading key individuals from the target organization to remain. It is also partly a question of communicating in order to create a sense of "comfort." The key is to successfully achieve integration in the dissemination of expertise and knowledge across the organization's functions.

Only a few organizations give much thought to how an acquisition's core competencies will be assimilated. As such, they may be failing to harvest as much value as possible from the merger or acquisition. However, many more organizations seek to leverage more value from their own competencies and learn about the competencies of others through strategic alliances and partnerships. This is the topic of the next chapter.

NOTES

1. This may be a result of divergence in the interpretation of management (including functional areas such as marketing R&D, HRM, etc.) theories and concepts by practitioners rather than academics. This author is engaged in a multicountry study looking at how practitioners interpret the numerous concepts and models that are to be found in the strategy literature.

2. J. B. Quinn (1992), *Intelligent Enterprise* (New York: Free Press).

3. C. K. Prahalad and G. Hamel (1990), "The Core Competence of the Corporation," *Harvard Business Review* 68 (3):81.

4. Ibid., 82.

5. Ibid.

6. Ibid., pp. 83–84.

7. G. Stalk, P. Evans, and L. E. Shulman (1992), "Competing on Capabilities," *Harvard Business Review* 70 (2):57–69.

8. C. K. Prahalad (1993), "The Role of Core Competencies in the Corporation," *Research Technology Management* 36 (6):46.

9. A. M. Snyder and H. W. Ebeling (1992), "Targeting a Company's Real Core Competencies," *Journal of Business Strategy* 26: 26–32.

10. K. Jennings and F. Westfall (1992), "Benchmarking for Strategic Action," *Journal of Business Strategy* 13 (3): 22–25.

11. Prahalad (1993), "The Role of Core Competencies."

12. Snyder and Ebeling (1992), "Targeting a Company's Real Core Competencies."

13. Ibid., p. 30.

14. Prahalad and Hamel (1990), "The Core Competence," p. 85.

15. Ibid.

16. Ibid, p. 86.

17. Ibid., pp. 86, 87.

18. Ibid., p. 87.

19. Prahalad (1993), "The Role of Core Competencies."

20. See C. Argyris (1990), *Overcoming Organizational Defenses: Facilitating Organizational Learning* (Upper Saddle River, NJ: Prentice Hall); C. Argyris (1992), *On Organizational Learning*, 2nd ed. (Oxford: Blackwell Business); A. De Geus (1997), *The Living Company: Growth, Learning and Longevity in Business* (London: Nicholas Brealey).

21. M. D. Kozin and K. C. Young (1994), "Using Acquisitions to Buy and Hone Core Competencies," *Mergers and Acquisitions* 29 (2).

3

STRATEGIC ALLIANCES: MATCHING, NEGOTIATING, IMPLEMENTING

THREE DIMENSIONS OF STRATEGIC ALLIANCES

The business world is awash with alliances that the partners call strategic. However, what exactly is a strategic alliance? Moreover, in what forms can it manifest itself? This chapter answers these questions before moving on to examine how an organization might match itself against potential partners, negotiate, and then implement an alliance.

In the extensive literature on alliances, various authors attempt to produce a succinct definition of a strategic alliance. For example, Mattsson suggests that it is "a particular mode of interorganizational relations in which the partners make substantial investments in developing a long-term collaborative effort and common orientation toward their individual and mutual goals."[1] Apart from being verbally indigestible, definitions such as this fail to capture the important features that make an alliance "strategic" as opposed to, say, tactical. A true strategic alliance attempts to achieve the following three objectives:

1. To provide extra leverage for the organization's core competencies in order to deliver long-term sustainable competitive advantage;
2. To move the organization into long-term and developing commitment to new markets, territories, or technologies that were previously closed to it; and

3. To provide a platform for the kinds of organizational learning that are central to its future business success, but would otherwise be unobtainable.

Implicit in this package of objectives is the notion of strategic reshaping and development of the business objectives of the organization. Strategic reshaping means dramatically enhancing an existing platform or constructing a new platform for sustainable business success. Everything else is tactical. However, an alliance may take several forms.

The first type is the joint venture. A joint venture would normally operate in territories where the partners are not individually strong. For example, the alliance between Volvo and Renault helped two motor vehicle manufacturers compete more effectively in global markets. In the case of joint venture, the partners "nurture" their offspring and attempt to build it into a successful business in its own right that contributes to the financial success of the partners.

The second type is the collaboration. It is not a joint venture with a corporate status in its own right. Consequently, it sometimes has fuzzy or gray boundaries. Managed in the right way, that is a strength because it provides a flexible relationship that may be developed or reduced without major problems. It is most appropriate where there is uncertainty about the nature of the task or where the alliance is not limited to a distinct or separable business with specific assets. Examples of collaborations include those groupings of computer companies that cooperate over developing industry-wide standards.

The third type is the consortium. While the majority of alliances are limited to two partners, there are many alliances that have more. The most successful of these endeavor to build on the complementary strengths of each partner, yet often there is some overlap. On the other hand, the consortium clearly involves a number of partners. For example, a consortium led by Digital Equipment, Ford, Texas Instruments, U.S. West, Carnegie Group, and Alcorp developed a new software tool. Consortia are often set up to carry out a specific function, sometimes precompetitive R&D, which is too expensive for one organization. There are also manufacturing consortia, for example, Airbus Industrie. By achieving critical mass, a consortium achieves scale, scope, and learning economies not otherwise available. Relationships with partners are, typically, somewhat at arms length.

ALLIANCE FORMATION: MATCHING AGAINST POTENTIAL PARTNERS

Why do organizations want to enter alliances? There is a wide range of possible reasons, but some common themes appear more often than others.

We discussed the external factors that lead organizations to form more alliances in Chapter 1. However, there is also a range of internal motivators that drive organizations toward alliances. In many cases, there are several motivating factors and, indeed, a combination of motivators creates an even stronger impetus for alliance formation. The most common are:

To access new geographical markets: This is a common factor in many alliances in consumer goods industries. It is especially true of alliances that link organizations in different parts of the globe. For example, the alliance between Rover and Honda in the United Kingdom was partly motivated by the desire of each to penetrate, respectively, the Japanese and European car markets.

To enter new product areas: This is a reason for organizations wanting to extend their business into adjacent market areas or move into completely new market areas. For example, Eastman Kodak's alliance with Canon enabled it to move into the market for low- to medium-volume copiers, adjacent to its existing high-volume market. Virgin's alliance with Norwich Union enabled it to move into the market for financial services, which is completely new to Virgin.

To access and learn about new technologies: This is especially a motivating factor in industries such as cars, aerospace, computers, and communications. For example, Thomson Consumer Electronics in France formed an alliance with the Japanese organization, JVC, in order to improve the manufacturing and assembly skills it needed to build high quality videocassette recorders.

To bring products to market more quickly: This is frequently an important factor in alliances in the high-technology industries where time to market is a critical factor to win business advantage from new technologies. For example, Compaq Computer and Microsoft Corporation created an alliance to develop "plug and play" computer systems, a system that a buyer can use immediately without the need to load software programs.

To access key management skills: This has proven to be an important factor in manufacturing industries. A driving force in many alliances between European or U.S. organizations and Japanese organizations has been a desire to learn about Japanese manufacturing practices, especially those relating to quality improvement

To develop new distribution channels: This is sometimes, but not always, related to a desire to move into new geographical markets. For example, Virgin entered an alliance with Blockbuster Entertainment to develop and own megastores in the United States and jointly own megastores in Europe and Australia.

To lower costs: There can be a desire to lower costs in one or more different ways, for example, manufacturing, distribution, or research and development. This motivator, however, is especially strong in the latter case in computer and aerospace industries, where the entry cost for new technologies is increasingly straining the budgets of even the largest organizations. For example, one can point to an alliance between Sun Microsystems, Fujitsu, Texas Instruments, Philips, and others in developing the reduced instruction set computer (RISC) technology. The Airbus Industrie consortium, involving organizations from several European countries, spreads the huge investment costs and risks involved in bringing new civil aircraft to market.

To access an effective brand name: This is important where an organization plans to enter a consumer market but faces powerful opposition from already entrenched brands. For example, despite low product development and manufacturing costs, few organizations could contemplate launching a new cola brand against the entrenched duopoly of Pepsi and Coca-Cola. However, Cott Corporation's alliance with Virgin is designed to win a small but valuable part of the huge world cola market. The attributes that consumers attach to the Virgin name make it ideal for a product aimed at an essentially young market.

THE IMPORTANCE OF STRATEGIC AND CULTURAL FIT

Strategic fit is essential in order to found an alliance, but both it and cultural fit are essential if an alliance is to develop and deliver benefits to all parties. The best-case scenario for an alliance exists when both parties have a high strategic fit and cultural fit. Organizations need to understand where they fall into this matrix before they enter an alliance. The implications of cultural mismatch will be discussed in detail in Chapter 10.

However, what comes through in many research projects on alliances is that it is not just strategic fit, but also strategic intent, that is the critical factor for long-term alliance success. Strategic intent defines what each of the partners expects to gain from the alliance. For example, does the partner expect to gain access to new technologies, markets, or distribution channels? What does the partner expect to learn from the alliance? Lei says: "Accurate assessment of the benefits and costs of entering a strategic alliance demands a comprehensive understanding of not only how changing technologies and new skills contribute to building competitive advantage, but also how the partner's rate of earning and strategic intent influence the evolution of the alliance."[2]

Learning from partners is paramount. Successful organizations view each other as a window of opportunity on their partner's broad capabilities. Organizations use the alliance to build skills in areas outside the formal agreement and systematically diffuse new knowledge throughout their organization. Strategic intent is an essential ingredient in the commitment to learning.

A vision of both the organization's own and its partner's strategic intent is a clear prerequisite not only for developing an alliance over time but also for harvesting real value from the alliance as it develops from year to year. There are two critical issues here: what the partners regard as the strategic intent of the alliance; and what strategic intent each partner has purposed for the alliance. Partners need to share the same ambition for their alliance, to provide a platform for developing for their mutual gain. There is, therefore, a shared strategic intent for the alliance. Similarly, each partner has a shared strategic intent as its reason for working within the alliance.

It is clear that when partners' strategic intent for an alliance diverges or when the individual strategic intents for entering the alliance are mismatched, the alliance is unlikely to develop strongly or deliver value. Ultimately, it may fail. For example, the alliance formed between General Motors and Daewoo, the Korean industrial group, to build the Pontiac LeMans finally failed because each partner had different strategic intents. General Motors wanted to keep costs down—it had originally been attracted to South Korea by the low labor costs—whereas Daewoo wanted to upgrade the car to sell in its domestic market.

How can organizations ensure they achieve a successful strategic match and that strategic intents are satisfactorily aligned? Following is a series of questions every potential alliance partner should ask itself about strategic match:

What are the broad, readily apparent objectives of this strategic alliance for each partner?

How can the two parties complement each other to create common strengths from which both can benefit?

How important is the strategic alliance within each partner's corporate portfolio?

Are there any problems with the alliance due to its relative closeness to the core business of the partners?

Are the partners "leaders" or "followers" within the particular business segment?

Do they combine to create strength, or is this a case of the "sick joining the sick?"

Are the partners sufficiently similar in culture?

THE SEARCH FOR ALLIANCE PARTNERS

Most organizations that form successful alliances develop a clear understanding of the kind of partner they want before they even start to search for an organization. For example, the Royal Bank of Scotland knew it wanted a banking organization in a major European country that was of similar size and had compatible ambitions within European banking. There were about six banks on the possible short list, but the search was short-circuited when managers made contact with Banco Santander, which was also searching for a partner.

This mixture of formal and informal contacts characterizes the search process for alliance partners. One of the key factors in the ease with which an organization might find an alliance partner, or conversely, attract suitable alliance partners, is its status and standing within its own industry and the business world in general.

Some organizations are repeatedly cited as attractive alliance partners, for example, Fujitsu and Toyota among Japanese organizations; Texas Instruments and IBM in the United States; and the Virgin group among United Kingdom organizations. It is not surprising that organizations such as these should be attractive alliance partners to smaller organizations. What is more interesting, however, is that they are often attractive alliance partners to one another. This reflects the fact that even large organizations are becoming more concerned about focusing on their core competencies and leveraging them by using alliances and partnerships.

Moreover, often alliance partners collaborate in one market while competing in another. This raises two important questions for organizations starting a search for an alliance partner. First, how can they collaborate with a potential partner without putting their own core marketplace at risk? When Rover and Honda had their alliance in the United Kingdom, for example, they both marketed cars that were the same vehicles except for their badging in the same markets. Yet, they concentrated on fighting back to back against common competitors rather than face to face against each other.[3]

Second, will collaboration strengthen the combined power of both in the markets? There is a difficult balancing act here. On the one hand, an alliance between two large competitors to attack the same market is likely to attract unwelcome attention from monopoly and anti-competition law regulators in most of the world's developed markets. On the other hand, a venture between two weak partners is likely to produce only an enfeebled alliance that is ineffective in attacking the market. In an alliance weak plus weak does not equal strong.

Ideally, the partners will be of comparable size (so one does not dominate the other, but it has to be said that there are many successful alliances that break this rule); have complementary skills (so that strong plus strong equals stronger); and not be too mutually competitive (the higher the common competition, the greater the source of tension in the alliance).

As mentioned previously, some alliances come about because of informal industry contracts. There is evidence that a growing number of alliances are now formed as the result of a formal search and evaluation of possible partners by the initiating partner in the alliance. ICL, for example, has a well-defined methodology for discovering possible alliance partners.

How ICL Shortlists Possible Alliance Partners

ICL, the once British computer organization that is now part of Fujitsu, is a member of many joint ventures and collaborations. At one time in the mid-1990s, there were over forty alliances visible at corporate level. They included: Worldwide Multivendor Services, which include ICL/Fujitsu; Bell Atlantic; and Camelot, the organization that operates Britain's national lottery, and teams ICL with Cadbury Schweppes, GTEC, Racal, and De La Tuc.

As a result of its alliance experience, ICL has a mature and effective methodology for selecting alliance partners (see Figure 3.1). The journey from strategic thinking to short-list involves a number of discrete activities. The first step is to think about how strategy could be realized through alliances; to think outside the box. Today's needs may leave you short tomorrow so think ahead five to ten years. An analysis of strengths, weaknesses, opportunities, and threats (SWOT) helps to define the ways in which the organization is geared to carry out its strategy. This analysis uncovers the competence gap that can either be filled through developing in-house resources or through ventures.

ICL collects information about possible venture partners from a number of sources. But what criteria does it use for selection? There are six main criteria:

Figure 3.1
Strategy to Short List Potential Partners

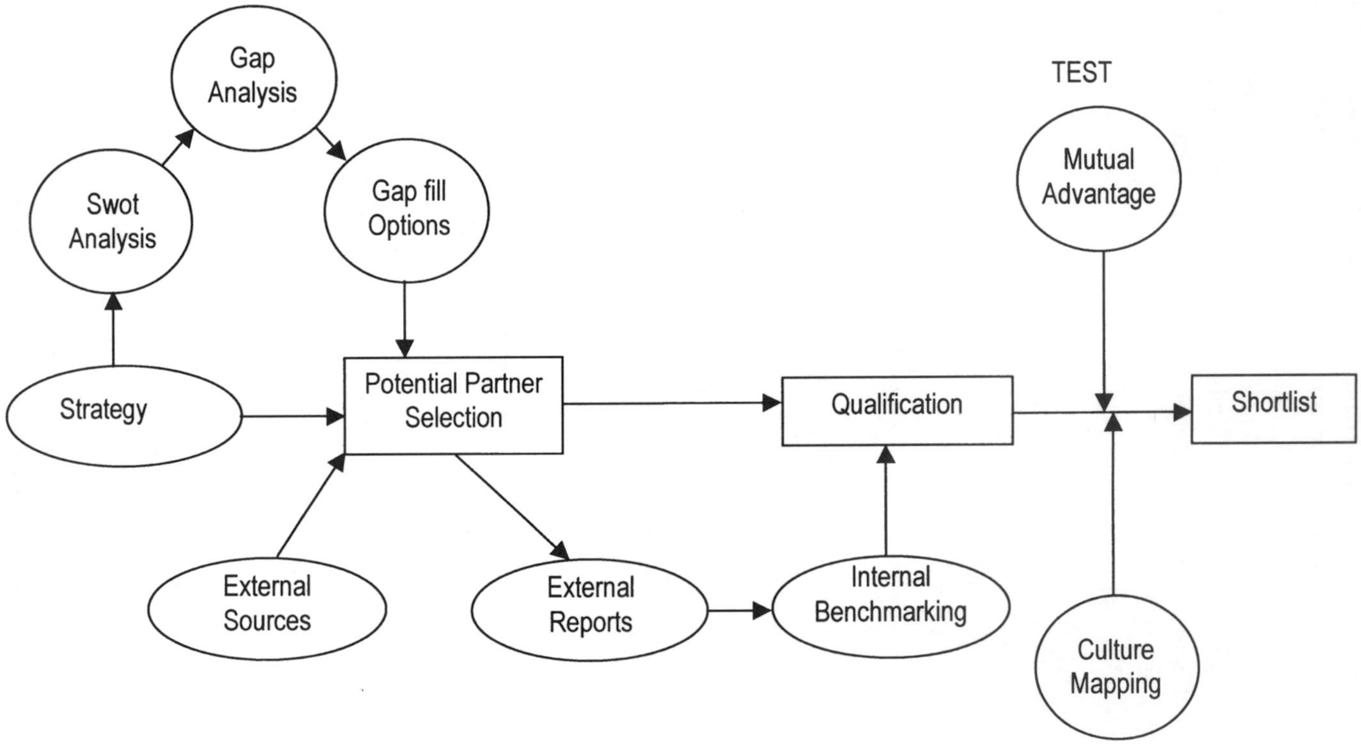

Complementarity: you want your partner to have what you do not.

Low overlap or conflict potential: the magic fit is where it has what you need but there is no competition. If there is no overlap, there is a danger that the two organizations might pass each other like ships in the night.

Financial security: this is important in order to make the venture robust. In its absence, ICL might consider bolstering the partner's balance sheet to provide extra security.

Good reputation: who wants to be associated with anything else?

Synchronous ambitions: The partner's stated ambitions must match your own. This means looking carefully at the end game of the venture. Will both partners be looking to achieve the same results? (In other words, are the strategic intents aligned?)

Compatible business values: It is important to define the ethics of the relationship up front.

Having produced a list of potential partners, ICL then qualifies them using a range of business criteria. The organization is looking for the partner's attitude toword and record of accomplishment in areas that include: empowerment; quality (for example, ISO 9000/14000); customer care; people as an asset; business process reengineering[4] and management of change; time to market; shareholder value; technical standards; program and risk-management methodologies; business planning and control; best of breed benchmarking; arm's length trading and open book accounting; commitment; and existing record of accomplishment in collaborations. This list suited ICL but it is not intended to be prescriptive for other organizations. Having qualified the potential partners through information collected from external reports and internal benchmarking, ICL then submitted them to two further critical tests before they reached the short list.

The first test views the possible "mutual advantage" from working with the potential partners. For example, ICL matched its own core competencies against those of the prospects. It probed the underlaps and overlaps and decided whether a prospect could satisfy its needs without too much potential conflict.

It is also important to look at the venture possibility from the potential partner's point of view. Think through the eyes of your target. What could you bring to his party? There are other questions to answer in testing for mutual advantage. Would there be a balance of inputs, risk, and rewards in the venture? Would there be a balance of power? Can the potential partner be trusted? Would he be likely to do a deal? An important question is: "Are we prepared to concede control?" This can be a sticking point but without it a joint venture can sometimes be a nonstarter.[5]

The second test maps the culture of the potential partner against ICL's own. For example, does the potential partner have a delayered or hierarchical organization? Does it operate management by objectives or based on job descriptions? Does it have a commitment to training and skill renewal? What are its views on standards (which may be critical for some industries)? Does it feature in quality awards? Does it have a service or manufacturing culture? Is it customer or inward focused? Is it receptive to change or does it fear change? Does it have an open or closed culture? There is a need to match up in most of these areas, otherwise there is a risk of conflict.

It is always advisable to put things in writing, no matter how informal the collaborative venture. It would be advantageous to make an outline teaming agreement or collaboration heads of agreement even before approaching the potential partners. It ensures that you are clear in your own mind what you want and it also ensures that you come across as having done your homework to your prospect.

One issue of difficulty for some organizations is finding sources of information about potential alliance partners. There are a number of sources of information about alliance partners to use in the first instance: suppliers and customers (the former is an interesting possibility as a customer may be looking to move upstream or downstream); industry watchers' reports; city analysts' reports; annual and other statutory reports that may be lodged with various government departments and authorities (for example, the body that regulates companies in the countries where the potential partner operates) or information lodged with the various stock exchanges (again where the potential partner may be listed—some organizations are listed on a number of stock exchanges around the world and may have to provide different information to each exchange); corporate, industry and professional bodies' Web sites on the Internet; Reuters and Dun & Bradstreet; trade shows; seminars and conferences; and in-house information sources such as press clippings. While many of these information sources are obvious, not all organizations seem to use them in a systematic way to search for alliance partners.

ALLIANCE FORMATION: NEGOTIATING WITH POTENTIAL PARTNERS

There are no reliable data on how many potential alliances break down during the negotiation stage. However, fair proportions of potential partners who begin talks do not make it beyond the uncommitted conversation stage.

In some cases, this is because both correctly perceive there is little or no basis for a partnership. However, in a few cases, the breakdown may occur because one or both of the partners used ineffective negotiating tactics or their negotiators were not fully supportive of the proposed alliance.[6]

What happens during the negotiation stage can be critical to the future success of the alliance for two main reasons. First, what is decided will color the way the alliance operates, the benefits that flow and the ways those benefits are distributed among the partners. Second, the negotiations often tend to set the tone for the relationship between the partners, for example, whether the relationship is formal or informal, friendly or frosty. There are five critical issues to consider during the negotiation stage.

Build and Understand Strategic Intent

Those organizations that negotiate alliances that last and deliver value almost invariably are open with one another at the outset not only about what they want from their alliance now, but also in the future. They are clear in their own minds about their strategic intent and communicate that openly and frankly to their potential partner.

It follows that when the alliance is strategic, negotiations will usually take place at a senior level. Often senior managers will make the initial contacts, then delegate detailed negotiations to other managers, coming back into the process at the end to finalize agreements.

Negotiate to Cooperate Rather Than to Win

Cooperating rather than winning raises an important cultural issue for managers used to negotiating with customers or suppliers to leverage the maximum advantage from every deal. The purpose of alliance negotiations is to create a win-win deal. If this is not the case, the alliance fails to develop or deliver significant business benefits to both partners and, ultimately, breaks down or fades out. Zeneca and Sumitono Chemicals, for example, had one partner (Zeneca) who felt it had been hard done by the other and was cool on developing the alliance. Zeneca felt that there was an imbalance in long-term rewards. It is perhaps not surprising that the venture remained limited in scope and development.

A former head of mergers and acquisitions at Courtaulds suggested the objective of a partnership framework should not be to shackle the parties and build unfair advantages for one party. That is a sure route to dissolution. The deal must be equitable to both. A framework should articulate the ob-

jectives of the partners, provide means to resolve difficulties, and, ultimately, provide for a smooth dissolution.

The fact that negotiators are aiming for a win-win deal means they must
be capable of seeing both sides of the question. This does not mean they are
"weak" or a "push over," rather it means they have a conception of what
constitutes a balanced and thus strong alliance partnership deal. The people
who do the negotiating should be accountable for the long-term results of
the alliance. To send in a negotiating team and then replace them with a separate management team is a recipe for discontinuity and blurred responsibility.

The person in charge of an alliance should hold the role for a long time.
John Bacchus's sixteen years running the Rover end of the Rover and
Honda collaboration is cited often. The person in charge should also report
to senior managers, usually on the board. If the report is not on the board's
agenda, the alliance is probably operational rather than strategic.

You need to put your very best caliber people on the negotiating team for
two reasons. First, they must be credible to senior managers. Second, they
have to make the deal work. If you cannot get somebody good to lead it, the
alliance probably will not stand up.

Manage Cultural Differences

Due to their nature, forming alliances provides plenty of opportunity for
cultural tensions to arise between the parties. Cultural differences can operate at a number of levels: for example, between organizations in the same
business, between two different industries, or between two different countries. Negotiators need to be aware that cultural differences may need to be
managed at each of these levels. The negotiator not only has to manage cultural differences during the negotiation but also has to create a flexible alliance structure that allows for cultural differences as the two partners work
together into the future. An ideal negotiation environment may be visual-
ized as a series of interlocking political, financial/legal and technical issues
underpinned by culture (see Figure 3.2). The cultural issues include negotiating styles, modes of thinking, trust, and attitudes to change. Everyone expects cultural problems, but no one anticipates just how important they
become.

The key is to find one or two people inside each partner's teams who can
act as informal links even when there is conflict. Once this virtual core team
is in place, it can then be used to help manage the process and ensure that
communication channels are kept open. However, a warning: A high degree
of trust and integrity between the members of this core group is essential.

Figure 3.2
How Factors in an Alliance Interact

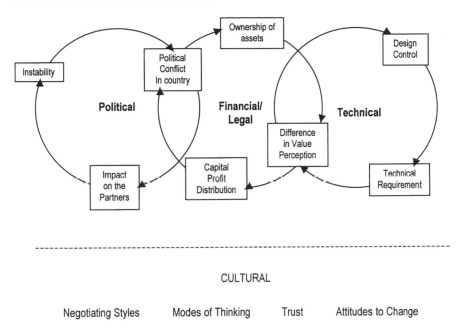

Consider All the Angles

Some alliances fall over because not enough care is given to deciding the terms of the agreement at the outset. This is often despite the fact that lawyers will have worked on the deal for weeks, if not months. For example, in the New Holland-Andersen Consulting joint venture, managers sketched out the main parameters of the deal within two months, but lawyers took four months to encapsulate these in a contract that both parties were happy to sign. In this case, there is every indication that all the angles have been catered for, but other alliances fall short.

Virgin Group avoids many of the problems of inadequately formulated partnerships by putting considerable up-front effort into considering the range of situations that could occur during the lifetime of the alliance. When companies undertake a joint venture, they have to be incredibly clear to all parties involved. It must be clear with each partner what the priorities are, and the time and resources each is prepared to commit to make the venture work.

At Virgin an enormous amount of time is spent defining what will happen in any one of a large number of different contingent situations affecting either of the parties. For example, if party A wants to do X, party B can do Y.

The range and purpose of possible partnerships and alliances are so great it is impossible to generalize about the contents of any partnership agreement. A comprehensive detailed agreement should contain the following elements:

- Scope and objectives of the alliance;
- Resource to be allocated by the partners;
- Definition of duties of the parties involved;
- How the alliance is to be managed;
- Patent, intellectual property and publications policies;
- How to resolve conflict;
- Milestone points (for example, when decisions about new capital are to be taken);
- Built-in flexibility; and
- Exit terms.[7]

Value the Contributions and Benefits

There is a wide range of different approaches to the valuation of contributions and benefits in the alliance mentioned in this report. The approaches range from the formal and carefully structured to the informal. For example, the Royal Bank of Scotland and Banco Santander took a simple 50:50 rule to their collaboration. They jointly own banking operations in Germany, Belgium, and Portugal. In addition, each bought a small stake in the other at market prices. In terms of benefits, each earns its own fees from the arrangement and although most of the early benefit in this flowed to Banco Santander, as the collaboration developed the balance of benefits equalized. Other ventures, however, structure the contributions and benefits in an almost infinite variety of ways.

A warning needs to be given, as valuing respective contributions to an alliance is an uncertain business. However, there are a number of principles that are of use to giving guidance:

- The benefits should be considered as well as the asset-based costs. This is an important aspect because business values should derive from the synergies the partners bring to the alliance;
- The strength of respective need affects bargaining strength. For example, an IBM or an ICI would theoretically be able to cut a tough

deal with a smaller organization. However, the two caveats to this are the need to make sure the deal is a win-win for both sides and how much the larger organization needs what the smaller has to offer; and

- The uniqueness of an asset, such as a brand name, creates a premium value that only emerges during the negotiations. For example, what is the value of Virgin putting its name on Cott Corporation's cola formula? A drink called Cott cola would hardly have drinkers queuing at the bar.

A number of important parameters the organizations need to consider during valuation and benefit negotiations are:

Equity shares: Easily calculated using techniques familiar in acquisitions. But the synergies from the alliance may enhance the organization's equity value over its stand-alone operations;

Assets: Again, there are several ways of valuing assets as in acquisition situations. However, the value of the assets employed in an alliance may be greater than if they were employed separately. In other words, the synergy creates value;

Expertise: This is difficult to value as it is hard to measure. Expertise may be treated as though it were a consultancy asset. For example, Honda charged Rover on a per diem basis for consultancy on quality manufacturing techniques;

Contract network: This is extremely difficult to value although it is often an important element in partner selection;

Market access: This is important in partner selection. If existing sales are put into an alliance, they can be valued on a discounted cash-flow basis;

Brand names: In a few alliances, for example, Virgin's with Cott Corporation, Norwich Union and others, this is vital. Although accountants are currently debating different ways of valuing brands, the final value is often determined by negotiating among partners; and

Technology transfer: A time basis is needed where organization A charges organization B on a per diem rate. An alternative is a royalty scheme on sales using the technology. Another alternative would be a capital value based on forecast future benefits. Or a combination of the first three is also possible.

ALLIANCE IMPLEMENTATION: THE CRITICAL SUCCESS FACTORS

Research into strategic alliances has uncovered an uncomfortable truth—a high proportion either end in outright failure or, at best, fail to deliver the business benefits expected. With alliances, it seems, the devil is in the detail. It is a question of mastering all (or at least, most) of the success factors in the implementation of the alliance. But just what are these success factors?

There are fourteen common success factors in alliance implementation. In a successful alliance, managers will give attention to the following activities.

Manage Strategic Relationships

Too many organizations enter alliances with the management mind-sets they developed to handle mergers and acquisitions. However, acquisitions are about transactions where alliances are, or should be, about strategic relationships. If you take a transaction based set of phenomena and throw them on strategic relationships, you will miss much of the strategy and all of the relationship.

Alliances are not structures as much as processes. The successful alliances make major adaptations over time as three phenomena occur: the strategic environment shifts; the operational environment shifts; and the people relationships shift. In a dynamic alliance, these three shift most of the time and the management team is able to adjust to the shifts and see how shifts in one influence the other two.

Mesh Different Cultures

Successful alliances provide a good fit between the partners on three dimensions: strategy, chemistry, and operations. If the first two do not fit perfectly, there is not much point trying to make the operational fit work. For example, without good human relationships, the operational fit could never work. Alliances would always run up against cultural problems.

However, if the first two fit, then the operational fit is not necessarily easy but certainly "do-able." That is because the operational fit constantly needs adjustment in culture, attitudes, behaviors, and ways of working. It should be easier to overcome cultural differences between international organizations in the same industry than between organizations from different industries in the same country because global industries share issues, problems, and values more than countries.

Involve Top Managers

Quite simply, without senior management involvement the alliance is not strategic. Many alliances are announced but never formed because they lack the top management support to overcome all the difficulties that must be faced during negotiation and implementation. This means that middle management must gain buy-in from senior managers before trying to negotiate and form an alliance.

One key reason why an alliance needs top management support is because only the most senior managers, chief executive officers (CEOs), managing directors (MDs), and general managers have the authority to signal the key strategic and cultural shifts that may be needed to move the alliance forward. This means that senior managers must meet regularly, at least once a year,[8] and in some cases more often.

Create Internal Teamwork

It is essential for all those negotiating and implementing an alliance to work as a team and to "own" the success that flows from it. In too many alliances, the people who negotiate the alliance then hand it over to a different implementation team. This creates gaps in commitment to the alliance. People support what they help to create so it is important for them to keep their involvement.

It is also important for lawyers involved in negotiations to understand the very special quality of an alliance agreement. Lawyers typically push for clearly defined alliance structures. However, you cannot answer the structure question inside an alliance until you have defined the strategies, processes, functions, and organizational design issues that are involved. In fact, a benchmark study reported in Lynch seems to suggest that the role of lawyers is to prevent failure, but they cannot achieve success.[9] The important management point: Have everybody connected with the alliance implementation working as a team and understanding everybody else's role and contributions.

Assign Alliance Ownership

This is tied to the question of appointing an alliance champion. The relevant operational unit of each partner should own an alliance. In addition, there should be a champion, often one manager below the top manager, who acts as the visionary and is passionately committed to the aims of the alliance. Finding a suitable champion is not always easy. The best are often risk takers and have more entrepreneurial flair than many other managers.

Understand the Complexities of Alliance Structure

In successful alliances, the implementation teams have understood the complexities of different alliance structures and chosen the most appropriate parameters for their own alliance. These teams need to understand that complexity runs across different dimensions. For example, it is possible to choose from a range of different kinds of alliances such as collaborations, joint ventures, equity investments, and so on. It is also possible to define an alliance by its purpose, such as marketing, R&D, or distribution. A further dimension is time.

An alliance may be designed as a short-term bridge, for example, to transmit capabilities between two organizations as an interim mechanism for testing the water, or as a long-term commitment. It is important for both alliance teams to have a clear understanding of all these dimensions.

Choose the Right Partner

Here there is a great deal of work in searching for potential partners and winnowing them down to a short list (see the ICL example). However, before making a final decision, it is vital to conduct a wide-ranging due diligence exercise. Too many organizations are not clear about the strengths and weaknesses of their partners. The due diligence exercise should have a wide range covering the kinds of matters that would normally engage the attention of lawyers and accountants.

However, it is equally important to conduct due diligence on the "soft" issues. This covers such issues as the values of the partner, the longevity of staff, the integrity of staff, and so on. About one-third of due diligence should be with the legal and accounting issues and two-thirds with the softer factors such as people and culture (both national and corporate).

Allocate Quality Staff

Many organizations do not allocate their best staff to alliance implementation and management. This finding applies to the United States, and to a lesser extent British alliances. By contrast, Japanese organizations invariably allocate their star performers. One reason for the failings of British and

U.S. alliance makers is that, too often, high flying managers see alliances as a distraction from a career path.

Too often, organizational personnel and human resources policies encourage the career distraction perception or, at best, do nothing to remove it. By contrast, working in an alliance is considered a smart career move in Japanese organizations. The failing among senior Western managers is that they do not see alliances as a major strategic weapon to design a future for the organization. Once top managers make this perceptual leap—the role of alliances in the organization's success—the status of the managers running the alliances rises rapidly. Another critical factor is that an organization is likely to derive long-term benefits from the alliance with its best managers at its heart.

Reduce Alliance-Implementation Time

Time taken to negotiate and implement an alliance can run from weeks to years. There are forces in the business environment that make rapid alliance formation more important. For example, product-design-cycle times and product life cycles are rapidly shrinking, especially in high technology industries. Given that many alliances are focused to address product development and product launch issues, it is important for participants to create the alliances more quickly, but not at the expense of the other critical success factors.

Develop Competencies in Alliance Management

Organizations that have been successful in harvesting benefits from alliances have usually developed core competencies in alliance management. Indeed, this was a key corporate core competence for the Virgin group, which manages its growth through alliances and outsourcing. Competencies in alliance formation and management include such factors as using best practices and processes, having integrated business teams, being able to learn from alliances, and being able to disseminate learning throughout the organization.

No more than half a dozen of the 300 organizations in a study by Lynch had "really good" core competencies in alliance management. In those that had good core competencies, the managing director and the board of directors had explicitly formulated a strategy of growth through alliances and had committed the skills and resources to make it happen.[10]

Create a Center of Alliance Excellence

Those organizations that succeed better with alliances often create a center of alliance excellence within the organization. Frequently, the business development group develops proficiency in alliances. In some cases, there is the possibility of tension between a strategic planning group and a business development group. The alliances that worked well in practice are often driven from the business development units. Someone is needed who can think strategically but who has enough nuts and bolts experience to make the alliance work in real life and not just on paper.

Consider the Wisdom of Minority Investments

Partners to an alliance need to give careful thought to whether minority interests should play any part in the alliance. A minority stake, while sometimes a token of commitment, is rarely an important success factor in an alliance. In the Royal Bank of Scotland/Banco Santander alliance, the minority stakes held by each bank in the other have been key to developing the business benefit from the alliance. A note of caution is required if an equity investment is made, the partners need to be clear about the rights and obligations that investment brings. In the bank alliance just mentioned, for example, both parties set out rules about maximum holdings and divestments.

Recognize the True Levers of Control

Both British and U.S. alliance partners tend to see finance and ownership as key instruments of control in alliances, which is why most take the mergers and acquisitions rather than the alliance path as their preferred expansion route. Japanese organizations, however, tend to see the main levers of control in an alliance as operations and culture. Control prevents failure but does not yield success. Are lawyers and accountants experts in control systems or success systems? Giving attention to operations and culture are the features that build alliance success and help to shape it in the direction the partners want.

Devise Metrics to Assess Success

Few alliances have succeeded in measuring the contribution of partnership activity in any but the crudest financial terms. One means is to measure around five elements of a strategy: financial positions; market position; innovative capabilities; organizational improvement; and competitive advantage. Precise measurements for each alliance will differ but they are likely to focus on issues as varied as cost improvement, customer satisfaction, market share, product quality, and organizational effectiveness. The challenge for alliance partners is to develop metrics that enable them to capture the impact of the synergies from the alliance.

ALLIANCE CONSIDERATIONS

The chemicals and industrial materials group[11] is a pioneer in using alliances. Its ventures stretch back over forty-five years. Yet, the organization is agnostic about its benefits. Any proposal to the board for an alliance is subject to high scrutiny.

Successful ventures have resulted in access to the Japanese markets and new technologies for their product ranges, as well as to marry its fiber expertise to its partner's knowledge of absorbent materials. One outcome: the super-absorbent diaper. The group sees seven main rationales for entering alliances: to access new markets; to access new technologies; to use excess capacity; to acquire management skills and local know-how; to overcome financial limitations on expansion; to meet local statutory participation requirements; and to conduct a staged acquisition or disposal. They believe the main advantages of an alliance over an outright acquisition are the lower cost and risk and the possible integration risks arising from an acquisition. In some cases an acquisition is not feasible.

Yet, there is also a downside to alliances. The biggest dangers are the risk of a cultural mismatch, the complexity of the structures the ventures sometimes produce, their occasional lack of flexibility, and the fact that they are inherently unstable. This organization, like so many others involved with alliances, uses the marriage analogy. What hope would you give to a marriage that circumscribed areas of cooperation, allowed other affairs, and defined the terms for a divorce settlement at the outset?

Many of these problems can be addressed by the following four-stage approach at the time of entering an alliance:

1. Define clear objectives for the venture. This means understanding the purpose of the venture. For example, is it to create horizontal integration or gain access to upstream or downstream activities? Risk is also defined and limited.

2. Establish criteria for the kind of partner wanted. Issues to consider here include cultural compatibility, financial strength of the partner, and its potential technical and market contribution.

3. Assess the contributions to the venture of itself and its partner. This includes the type of contribution—for example, existing assets or business, intellectual property, expertise, market positioning or cash—and how that contribution can be valued.

4. Establish an appropriate structure for the alliance. The objective of an alliance framework should not be to shackle the parties or build unfair advantages for one party, but should articulate the objectives in such a way that it smooths difficulties and avoids disputes.

Structuring the venture is a critical factor in ensuring its success. There are two options. The contractual route is better used for ventures designed to have a short time scale or a limited purpose. The equity route is for ventures designed to last for a long time and with substantial or complex objectives. It is also advisable to avoid structures that result in resort by the parties to deadlock mechanisms as this will only serve to promote confrontation between the partners. As a result of alliances being inherently unstable, the partners must be compatible and the venture structure must be able to absorb the daily knocks and adapt to changing market circumstances.

NOTES

1. L.G. Mattsson (1988), "Interaction Strategies," paper presented at the American Marketing Association's Summer Marketing Educator's Conference, San Francisco. Other definitions include "a strategic alliance is a close, intended long-term, mutually beneficial agreement between two or more partners in which resources, knowledge and capabilities are shared with the objective of enhancing the competitive position of each partner." M. A. Milgate (1999), "Conditions for the Effective Formation, Management and Evolution of Cross-Border Alliances," unpublished Master of Commerce (Honours) Thesis, University of Western Sydney–Nepean, Rydalmere.

2. D. Lei (1993), "Offensive and Defensive Uses of Alliances," *Long Range Planning* 26 (4):6.

3. In 1993 a Honda dealer placed an advertisement that claimed: *"The largest selling Accord, the 2.0 iLS at £14,995 undercuts its near identical sister car, the Rover 620 Sli . . . and the Rover 620 is not available with a driver's side airbag."* A hasty retraction followed, even though a dealer placed it, because the advertisement breached the agreement that neither partner would criticize the other in their common markets.

4. Be warned as this may not produce the desired results. See J. Micklethwait and A. Wooldridge (1996), *The Witch Doctors: What the Management Gurus Are*

Saying, Why It Matters and How to Make Sense of It (London: Heinemann), for an exposé of the behind-the-scenes issues of this fad of the 1990s.

5. Not only is it important to consider any ability or willingness to concede control, but also to what level of control should be considered. The ability to recover control should be included (if there is an ability or willingness) as a safety measure in case things go wrong and should also be included in any discussions on this issue.

6. I worked for an organization in Australia where the managing director gave incredibly motivating speeches about partnering and creating win-win situations for the organization and the client. But then he gave no resources—extra staff or leeway with the other responsibilities those involved had to carry out, deadlines, budget targets, and so forth—to make it happen, so negotiations just died. Then he blamed the people concerned, saying they had made errors or had gone beyond their levels of authority.

7. Given that people like to focus on positive outcomes dealing with the ending of an alliance where the desired outcomes of the partners have been met and the alliance has served its purpose only poses the problem of how to repatriate the successful employees involved with the alliance back into the parent organization. However, if the alliance did not meet the objectives of the partners, other problems arise (blame, accountability for the problems, and so forth). When the joint venture between ICI and EniChem, European Vinyl Chlorides (EVC), had become successful and ICI was restructuring, EVC no longer fitted into the ICI portfolio. It was then decided to float EVC on the stock market. ICI sold down its hold to become a major shareholder with the float and eventually sold the remaining shares it held. This is one way to end an alliance, especially when one partner is still interested in retaining its interest in an arms-length entity.

8. Some may suggest that this is acceptable but if a day is a long time in politics, as the saying goes, it is also a long time in the marketplace. Quarterly or even bimonthly meetings may be a more appropriate frequency if the alliance is really strategic.

9. R. P. Lynch (1993), *Business Alliance Guide* (New York: John Wiley).

10. Ibid.

11. The organizations involved with this example have requested anonymity.

4

STRATEGIC OUTSOURCING PARTNERSHIPS

OUTSOURCING: FROM TACTICAL TO STRATEGIC

When the Boston Consulting Group (BCG) conducted a survey of more than 100 organizations, outsourcing practices in the United Kingdom in 1991,[1] it concluded that most organizations outsourced mainly to reduce overhead and short-term costs. BCG discovered that, consequently, most organizations' outsourcing was piecemeal. The outsourcing resulted in patches of over capacity scattered at random throughout the organization's operations. It concluded that the piecemeal outsources end up with large numbers of subcontractors, which are more costly to manage than in-house operations that are individually less efficient. Even worse, by not providing adequate monitoring and technical backup, some organizations lost their grip on key competencies they needed for the future.

Research conducted since the BCG study suggests that there has been some movement toward a more strategic grasp of the possibilities of outsourcing, but that too many organizations still see it as a tactical activity to deliver cost reduction or cope with capacity peaks. Some indications of the reasons why organizations outsource were given in a Coopers and Lybrand survey[2] that found that 70 percent said outsiders are more efficient; 45 percent said outsourcing helped them focus on their own products; 42 percent said it helped to gain benefits at less cost; 41 percent said outsourcing drained fewer investment funds; and 21 percent said outsourcing removed some regulatory burdens.

In some areas, IT for instance, the move toward outsourcing has quickened from a canter to a gallop. For example, in 1994 PA Consulting, in their UK IT Sourcing Survey, found that in a sample of 250 of the United Kingdom's largest organizations, the number that had outsourced or were considering it had risen to 80 percent.[3] However, those organizations that have developed a strategic grasp of the purpose of outsourcing and have implemented outsourcing programs with management skill are reaping considerable benefits that sharpen their competitive edge.

For organizations such as Marks and Spencer in the United Kingdom or in Nike in the United States, outsourcing is part of an overarching business strategy designed to leverage their core competencies for maximum business benefit. Outsourcing can be an important component in a winning business strategy. However, it also has its downside, for example, in creating supply vulnerabilities or transaction costs, which can undermine those benefits.

There seems to be some correlation between success and those organizations that regard outsourcing as a partnership activity and, thus, retain a close interest in the ongoing management and development of the partnership. Those organizations that regard outsourcing as a way of shifting out troublesome tasks win fewer benefits. The exemplar organizations, however, look on outsourcing as a way of leveraging off the core competencies of their partners as part of a strategy to move their organizations toward the best of everything paradigm. For example:

- Marks and Spencer works closely with its outsource manufacturers on design, product development, product quality, manufacturing and packaging techniques, and a host of other issues. The retailer aims to develop these manufacturers into long-term partners and, although relationships are sometimes tempestuous, it usually succeeds.

- Ford Motor Company worked with outsourcing partners on its "best in class" benchmarking studies of 400 subassemblies that were included in its Taurus/Sable models in the United States. As a result of this exercise, it found that some of its own quality practices were below those of important suppliers. One result of outsourcing was to raise internal quality standards.

- Nike outsources almost all of its manufacturing. Yet it has built a reputation as the quality supplier of sports shoes. Part of its success rests on an intensive ongoing program to work at upgrading the capabilities of its suppliers.

In the most outstanding cases, organizations view outsourcing not only as a way of leveraging their existing core competencies (and strengthening their position in current markets), but also as a way of accessing the competencies of outside suppliers to enter new markets. New Holland Logistics, for example, has outsourced the European logistics of its spare parts operation as a joint venture with Andersen Consulting. It anticipates that this will enable it to build new competencies in logistics services and so enter the market in its own right as a logistics service organization.

Since there are clearly wide disparities in the success achieved with outsourcing, what factors contribute to success?

CREATING AN OUTSOURCING STRATEGY

Those organizations that make a success of outsourcing do two things better than others. First, they see outsourcing as part of a holistic strategy rather than a tactical response to production or supply difficulties or skills shortages. Looked at another way, the successful organizations have a clear understanding of the part outsourcing can play in their value chain—for example, in R&D and marketing in Nike's case—and how they can leverage off the core competencies of outsourcing suppliers in other parts of the value chain. This is essentially a long-term view of outsourcing as a strategic weapon in the battle for competitive edge.

Second, the successful organizations have a culture that accommodates and welcomes outsourcing. At Marks and Spencer managers live in a culture in which it is natural to work with outsourcing suppliers to achieve business objectives. Managers in these organizations have not necessarily turned their backs on vertical integration. Rather, they have a clear vision of the respective roles of vertical integration and outsourcing, and they understand how the organization's own core competencies help to define the natural boundaries between activities that should be outsourced.

Consequently, outsourcing is not viewed as a kind of second-best option to "doing it ourselves." Instead, it is an operationally and culturally integrated part of a business strategy designed to achieve sustainable business advantage. Following is an example of how one successful strategic outsourcing organization, Nike, has approached this process.

Nike's Outsourcing Strategy

Strategic outsourcing is at the heart of the business success of Nike, the phenomenally successful sports shoe organization. Nike's core competences are in the research, design, and marketing of sports shoes. Almost all of the manufacturing is outsourced to a range of different suppliers. Sports-shoe manufacturing, apart from being a ferociously competitive business, is also increasingly complex. The level of "technology" in a sports shoe is increasing all the time. In addition, the pace of design means that new ranges of shoe must be brought to market in ever-shortening time spans. Nike markets more than 400 models. Finally, as a fashion product, the skill in marketing Nike shoes is a critical success factor.

Soon after forming their organization, Nike's founders, Philip Knight and Bill Bowerman, decided that the R&D and marketing issues contained enough complexity in themselves without the additional problems of manufacturing. Nevertheless, Nike's success rests on a highly developed approach to outsourcing that is designed to build a genuine partnership between the organization and its suppliers. Indeed, Nike specifically eschews words such as "suppliers" or "contractors" in favor of calling the organizations that manufacture the shoes, many of them in Southeast Asia (Vietnam for example), "production partners." There are three kinds of partners:

1. **Production partners.** These organizations manufacture Nike "statement products," which tend to be the latest high-fashion and most expensive products. These shoes are both technologically advanced and less price sensitive than most of the other models. Nike aims to provide production partners with a steady stream of orders that generally vary by no more than 20 percent a month. The partners themselves subcontract the nonproprietary components in the shoes to other local suppliers. Production partners typically produce 20,000 to 25,000 pairs of shoes per day.

2. **Volume producers.** As the name suggests, these producers make the shoe models that sell in bulk. Generally, the producers also manufacture shoes for other organizations. Nike accepts this as necessary to provide the economies of scale and scope and flexible production that it seeks from its volume producers. This is a necessity because the shoes are sold on the price-sensitive part of the market. Nike expects volume producers to absorb seasonal fluctuations in production as monthly orders can vary by more than 50 percent. Volume producers typically produce between 70,000 and 85,000 pairs of shoes a day.

3. **Development sources**. These are young organizations, often located in emerging industrial countries such as China or Indonesia, that produce shoes by local technology means exclusively for Nike. These partners produce price-sensitive products at the low end of

Nike's range. Sometimes the developing sources have a link with a developed partner as part of a learning program that Nike stimulates in these organizations. Overall developing sources produce only low volumes of product and are driven by orders that depend on demand.

Nike's strategic outsourcing program is underpinned with four important principles:

1. **Partnership building.** Nike adopts policies that are designed to nurture partnership between itself and its manufacturers. For example, it has an "order reliability" policy that ensures a steady flow of orders and, thus, reduces risk for the partners. Nike stimulates cooperative development with its partners through regular structured exchanges of information. Its culture is to be both open and honest in all dealings with partners in order to foster trust. Finally, it pays its bills on time, thus providing financial stability for partners, many trading in the cash-starved developing world.

2. **Expatriate program.** A key feature of Nike's approach is to become closely involved in the manufacturing management of each partner through its own permanent on-site representative. These Nike "expatriates" then remain with a partner for several years and help foster the close partnership links. The expatriates help plan production, keep partners informed of relevant R&D programs, and work with the partner in implementing and enforcing quality management programs.

3. **Market protection.** In working so closely with its partners, Nike has helped to create highly effective sports shoe manufacturers and is anxious as to whether to extend their own value chains directly into Nike's own markets. In other words, Nike takes specific actions to ensure the partners do not become direct competitors. The strategy behind this is to ensure Nike itself adds considerable value through preproduction R&D and product development and postproduction marketing and image building. Nike's branding and market share deliver considerable value and provide deterrence to any partners tempted to enter the markets directly.

4. **Shared development.** Nike manages to involve important partners in development of new products by harnessing not only its own, but also the manufacturing and materials competencies of its partners. This strategy reduces some of the investment needed to bring new

products to market, because the partners invest in some of the new plant and machinery needed to manufacture the products.

These policies propelled Nike to the number-one spot in the world's sports shoe market. The organization now has annual revenues of more than U$9.5 billion.

SUCCESSFUL OUTSOURCING

The essential precondition of making a success of outsourcing is to develop a holistic view of the role of outsourcing and supporting that is compatable with a developing outsourcing culture. Nevertheless, beyond this critical point, there are other issues to address.

Criteria for Outsourcing

The central reason for outsourcing from the BCG study—saving on overhead cost—still holds good for many organizations. Yet, money savings are essentially a tactical rather than strategic reason for outsourcing.

By contrast, the strategic case for outsourcing rests on a two-pronged argument. First, it enables the outsourcer to leverage off other organizations' competencies in areas where these are more highly developed. For example, Autoglass is leveraging off CSC's competencies in information technology. Second, it enables the outsourcer to increase focus on its own internal competencies that provide it with its important competitive edge. The argument is that this frees management to focus on the core business. However, it is possible to overstate this argument because many of the most successful outsourcers retain a level of management involvement and decision making in some outsourced activities.

Where outsourcing can increase focus is the investment devoted to core activities. In many cases, outsourcing removes the need for investment in peripheral activities, passing that responsibility to the outsourcer. For example, Argyle Diamonds in Australia, one of the world's major diamond producers, outsources the earth-moving operations involved in mining for the diamonds (which removes the need for investment in the expensive equipment), housing and food services for mining workers, and much of the distribution. As well as avoiding substantial capital investment, Argyle Diamonds is also accessing "best-in-class" services from its different suppliers.

Given that an organization has accepted the two central underpinnings of a strategic (as opposed to tactical) outsourcing strategy, how should it decide whether to outsource an activity? Quinn suggests a series of seven sequential questions that need to be answered before a final decision is taken:

- Do we really want to produce the good or service internally in the long run? If we do, are we willing to make the back-up investments necessary to sustain a best-in-world position? Is it critical to defending our core competences? If not,
- Can we license technology or buy expertise that will let us be best on a continuing basis? If not,
- Can we buy the item as an off-the-shelf product or service from a best-in-world supplier? Is this a viable long-term option as volume and complexity grow? If not,
- Can we establish a joint development project with a knowledge supplier that ultimately will give us the capability to be best at this activity? If not,
- Can we enter a long-term development or purchase agreement that gives us a secure source of supply and a proprietary interest in knowledge or other property of vital interest to the supplier and us? If not,
- Can we acquire and manage a best-in-world supplier to advantage? If not, can we set up a joint venture or partnership that avoids the shortcomings we see in each of the other questions? If so,
- Can we establish controls and incentives that reduce total transaction costs below those of producing internally?[4]

These questions not only lead the potential outsourcer through the issues he needs to consider in choosing a supplier but also implicitly raise some of the questions he must answer if he is subsequently to manage an outsourcing partnership satisfactorily. Yet, although answers to these questions help to frame an outsourcing strategy, there is still the question of selecting specific outsourcing suppliers.

Selecting Outsourcing Suppliers

Quinn sees the selection of an outsourcing supplier being governed by two variables: the degree of strategic vulnerability in the activity; and the potential for competitive advantage from outsourcing it.[5] The higher the competitive potential and strategic vulnerability, the greater the need to keep sourcing in-house (see Figure 4.1).

Figure 4.1
Outsourcing Options: Make, Buy, or Ally

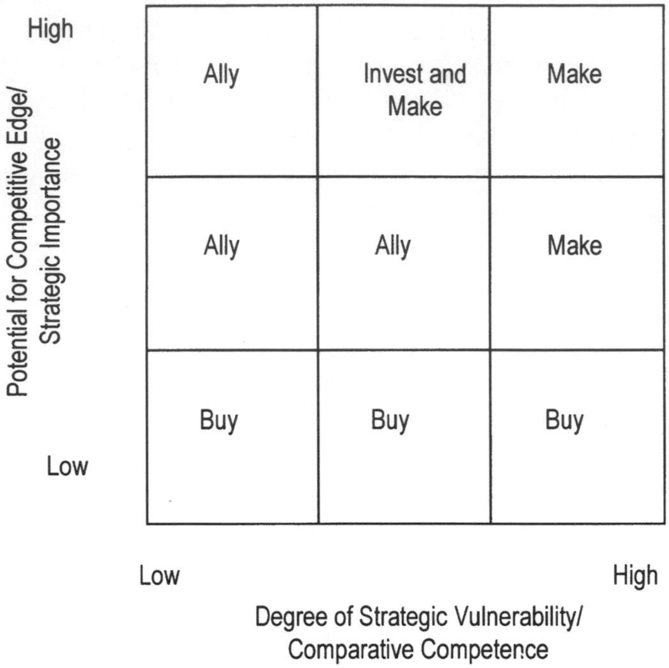

Ally	Invest and Make	Make
Ally	Ally	Make
Buy	Buy	Buy

High / Low — Potential for Competitive Edge/ Strategic Importance

Low ———— High — Degree of Strategic Vulnerability/ Comparative Competence

Source: Adapted from Quinn and Hilmer (1994) and Child and Faulkner (1998).

The methods used to choose an outsourcing supplier are governed by two important variables. The first is whether the function to be outsourced is strategic (for example, manufacturing key components) or tactical (for example, office cleaning or catering). The second is how many potential outsourcers are available.

In terms of strategic outsourcing, most effective users place one critical issue at the top of their selection agenda. Autoglass wanted to access the best thinking as it turned its IT operation into a strategic resource to underpin improved customer service. The same criterion was at the core of New Holland's selection of Andersen Consulting as its partner in the European logistics joint venture. New Holland had competencies in the spare parts business but it needed access to excellent capabilities in business-process innovation and information technology to develop the logistics operations.

The Autoglass case study describes how it used a structured approach to select its outsourcing supplier from a short list. However, plainly every organization will adopt the selection methodology and criteria that are most appropriate in its own particular case.

Managing the Supplier Relationship

The scope and methods of managing the relationship with the outsourcer very according to the strategic importance of the partnership. Less management involvement is needed in a relationship of low strategic importance. However, as we have seen, strategic outsourcing partnerships require a high degree of management involvement. Organizations such as Marks and Spencer, Apple Computer, and Nike devote considerable efforts to manage their outsourcing relationships. It could be argued that this somewhat negates the central reason for outsourcing—that it helps to focus management attention on the core business. In fact, although this is true, the greater benefit is an organization's ability to leverage not only from its own core competencies but also from that of its strategic outsourcing partners.

In managing outsourcers, buyers adopt a range of tactics. New Holland, for example, formed a joint venture with Andersen Consulting to bring together two sets of competencies in its new logistics operation. The venture is controlled by a board consisting of four New Holland and two Andersen Consulting directors. Nike has developed a complex range of procedures for managing its many supplier relationships, which it categorizes into three types. An important figure of its management is the expatriate program that places Nike managers on long-term assignment in outsourcing suppliers. The Nike example describes the sophisticated policies Nike has developed to manage alliance partners.

An important feature of many outsourcing relationships is a shift in the methods of managing from operating by command to operating by contract. This is such a fundamental shift that it can cause considerable difficulties in the operation of the outsourcing arrangement unless its implications are thought through in detail at the outset.

In the worst cases of operating by contract, managers find that the outsourcer is unresponsive to detailed day-to-day requests, or that special requests increase the size of the bill. For example, when Unilever outsourced its head office IT in the mid-1980s, it ran into problems. The contract had been struck in general terms, the supplier found itself making little money as a result of the deal, and, consequently, imposed stiff charges in "gray" areas of the contract.

Autoglass, who faced the shift from managing by command to managing by contract, believes the secret of managing successfully is to understand requirements in detail and negotiate the contract carefully. It took a great deal of time and effort in constructing a contract that was very flexible. Virgin found that it needed to be clear with its partner what the priorities were and the time and resources it was prepared to commit to making it work.

However, the attitude of the outsourcer is also important. An outsourcer with a locker-room lawyer mentality is likely to make it difficult to manage by contract where the contract provides for flexibility. The bottom line: Check out the outsourcer's attitude and be confident that it will be flexible before signing the contract.

Measuring Outsourcing Performance

Two important points need to be made about measurement of performance in the area outsourced. First, without an appropriate measuring regime in place it will be impossible to judge the effectiveness of the outsourcing partner. Second, some of the most valuable gains from strategic partnerships are not susceptible to precise measurement, for example, developing new competencies or acquiring organizational knowledge. What then should be measured and how? There are two issues in the performance measurement regime: charging structure and service-level agreements. From the outsourcer's point of view there needs to be clear linkage between the two.

It is impossible to generalize about charging structures except to say that in the simplest of outsourcing arrangements charges can be based on a flat fee, whereas in most arrangements they will be based on a tariff of charges or a per unit delivered basis.

The service-level agreement needs to define exact levels of service against a base line. The base line is normally a measurement period, generally of three to six months, immediately before the outsourcing arrangement comes into play. It is essential that the base line measures be taken and agreed upon by both parties before the outsourcing agreement starts to operate.

It is very difficult, although usually very desirable, to build incentives into the agreement for exceeding service-level agreements. Conversely, there should be cash penalties for nonperformance of service-level agreements. However, it is important to make sure that any incentives are structured so that performance is not skewed to hit certain targets at the expense of others. The New Holland-Andersen Consulting agreement, for example, provides for Andersen Consulting's costs to be met, but its profit margin comes out of any savings the new organization makes on managing stock against a base line. Savings will be shared between New Holland and Andersen Consulting in the ratio of 70 percent to 30 percent in the first three years and 80 percent to 20 percent for the remaining four years of the seven-year contract.

The Downside of Outsourcing

It is impossible to recognize that outsourcing is not risk-free. There are plenty of tales of organizations who have regretted it. The functions they outsourced range from manufacturing components through running IT to managing the staff canteen. Nevertheless, the successful outsourcers manage the potential downside of outsourcing. Four critical issues are: loss of key markets; loss of competencies; loss of cross-functional synergies; and transaction costs.

Loss of Key Markets

The loss of key markets is a real risk for organizations that outsource all or part of the manufacturing of the their product. There is danger that the outsourced manufacturer could enter the market at a future stage in its own right. For example, in the United States, Schwinn outsourced the manufacture of the frames in its bicycles to a Taiwanese organization, Giant Manufacturing. After a few years, Giant entered the bicycle market in its own right, greatly damaging Schwinn's business. This situation poses twin problems. The outsourcer not only gains a rival that has learned from it, but also loses a source of supply in which it has invested many years of effort.

Outsourcers that guard against this danger successfully erect a "strategic block" between their suppliers and their customers. Often the strategic block is the core competencies of the organization. For example, Nike's core competencies are in R&D, marketing, and branding of its products. Although Nike outsources manufacturing of its shoes, these competencies provide a significant barrier to manufacturers entering a highly fashion-conscious market in their own right.

Other outsourcers use more blunt strategies that include spreading the manufacture of components and subassemblies among a range of suppliers to owning the machinery that the outsourcing partner uses to manufacture the required parts. This is an effective, if short-term, way of pulling the plug on an unsatisfactory outsourcing supplier.

Loss of Competencies

Loss of competency is a critical issue. As mentioned previously, those contemplating outsourcing should define its competencies and ensure they remain in-house. However, might outsourcing other activities reduce peripheral but nevertheless useful skills? There is certainly a danger of this in a

poorly managed outsourcing relationship. However, in an effective partnership in which the outsourcer is alive to the learning possibilities of the relationship, it is possible for the outsourcer to sharpen peripheral skills. In
this sense, outsourcing provides an opportunity for organizational learning.
This was certainly the case for Ford in its benchmark study of suppliers for
the Tarus/Sable project.

All outsourcing arrangements are different. However, the experience of
Autoglass shows both how to choose an outsourcing partner and how to
work with him in a way that delivers genuine business benefit. Although
Autoglass does not regard information technology as a core competence, it
could develop a strategic dimension for the future in helping its own company to deliver the world-class service to which it aspired. Autoglass
wanted its outsourcing partner to bring best-in-breed IT skills to the table.

In choosing an outsourcing partner, Autoglass defined a set of criteria,
then weighted each of those criteria to reflect its importance in the financial
decision. Using this technique, a balance-weighted criteria matrix, each criterion was given marks out of a possible ten to reflect its importance. Then
that mark was squared to identify a score and the scores for each criterion
were added to produce a total. The marks were first totaled for the criteria
one to seven below, which established a quality threshold for contenders.
Two of the five contenders were eliminated at this stage. Then the marks for
criteria eight to ten were added in to establish the over-all winner. The criteria and their weighting were:

1. Commitment to implement urgently needed system (ten marks).
    Evaluated by studying the number of programmers with the spe-
    cialist skills available from each outsourcer;
2. Software competency (ten marks). This is important to rectify
    failures in the in-house organization;
3. Cultural fit (nine marks). Autoglass is a "people-centered" orga-
    nization and the chosen partner "had to speak the same language";
4. Contract conditions (nine marks). This referred to the general
    flexibility and responsiveness of the organization;
5. Hardware competency (eight marks). This was evaluated by in-
    specting clients of each the contenders;
6. Knowledge of Autoglass requirements (seven marks). Autoglass
    was looking to see how effectively requirements were translated
    into plans;

7. International capability (four marks). In the long run, Autoglass may want to work with the chosen supplier in other countries;

8. Cost (seven marks). Autoglass appreciated that it had to pay for world-class quality;

9. Client references (six marks). Autoglass took up these with each of the final three contenders; and

10. Contract length (five marks). How long Autoglass had to sign up for was an issue, as well as the break-points on the contract.

As a result of this analysis, Autogalss selected CSC. The contract was for ten years with reviews at three and seven years. Service-level agreements were included in the contract terms.

In the short term, outsourcing will bring stability to the IT function. In the medium term, outsourcing will help IT systems to become an enabler of new business developments, for example, by facilitating business process design. In the long term, CSC could become the worldwide IT partner for Autoglass.

Loss of Cross-Functional Synergies

At a time when many organizations are reengineering their activities to create cross-functional business processes, does it make sense to outsource parts of those processes? Is there a risk of an organization losing cross-functional synergies by outsourcing key functions? Again, it is dangerous to generalize, but this will not be the case in well-managed outsourcing arrangements. Using the wide range of technological enablers (see Chapter 7) it is possible to reengineer business processes across organizations as well as across functions within the same organizations. Moreover, where an outsourcer brings new capabilities, the synergies could well be enhanced. This seems to be the case at New Holland, where Andersen Consulting's skills in business process innovation is developing a Europe-wide "virtual warehouse" capability for New Holland Logistics.

Transaction Costs

As mentioned previously, effective outsourcing does not necessarily remove all management responsibility for the function. Effective outsourcers spend considerable time managing their outsourcing relationship and there are transaction costs in this activity. Those costs need to be included in the cost-benefit analysis conducted before outsourcing any function. However,

often a true analysis of the in-house costs of the activity will reveal the benefits to be gained from outsourcing, notwithstanding the transaction costs.
Problems arise, however, when an outsourcing relationship starts to go
wrong. In this situation, the amount of in-house management time devoted
to resolving difficulties rises dramatically and can outweigh the benefits of
outsourcing. This was one of the problems Unilever encountered when difficulties arose in its outsourced IT. Unilever also found difficulties in bringing IT back fully in-house because many experienced staff had left. A key
lesson here is to have in mind a clear and viable exit strategy at the outset
should the outsourcing deal fail to deliver benefits.

When Things Go Wrong

Reca and Zieg illustrate an example from Fairfax County in the United
States of what happens when things go wrong and there is fault on both
sides.[6] In 1994, the county sought to contract out one of four garages that
provided maintenance of vehicles operated by the county. The maintenance
of 1,300 school buses is one of the principal services of the garages. The
county chose the West Ox Road garage because it had a mix of vehicles that
the county saw as providing the most challenging option for the new contractor.

The contract had two incentive components for the successful tenderer.
A target cost was established for each year of the contract. This was the
maximum amount that the county would pay. Any savings achieved below
the target cost would be split 40 percent to the county and 60 percent to the
contractor. As an incentive to minimize the number of buses that were not in
operation, the contractor would be fined U$800 per day for each bus that
was inoperable for more than twenty-four hours.

In January 1994, Fairfax County awarded the U$11 million three-year
contract to Johnson Controls and the contract commenced in March 1994.
In July 1994, Fairfax County canceled the contract. While Johnson Controls claimed three reasons associated with the problems (poor maintenance
scheduling, repairs not being performed before contract commencement,
and overly critical safety inspections), it was also apparent that Johnson
Controls did not have sufficient skilled staff to perform all the necessary
work.

Reca and Zieg identify a number of reasons for the contract's failure that
lie with the county as well as with Johnson Controls. The county failed to
obtain consensus among the county supervisors that the outsourcing of this
highly visible service was the right decision. The county did not fully consider ways to reduce any transfer risk. Johnson Controls only gained access

to the county's records two months before the commencement of the contract and the transfer commenced in the middle of the school year; this resulted in Johnson Controls having no adjustment time. Finally, the incentive scheme was impotent because the county had previously identified and removed much inefficiency in the operation of the garages. This meant that it was difficult for Johnson Controls to receive any bonus by performing under the target cost. This shows the importance of the incentive mechanism for contractors and the implications when the incentive mechanism goes wrong.

SERVICE-LEVEL AGREEMENTS

The Johnson Controls example shows it is imperative to look at service-level agreements and the expectations of the parties involved with the outsourcing process. When you decide to establish a service-level agreement (SLA), where do you start? What questions do you ask? Whom do you ask? Alternatively, do you ask any questions at all? Frequently, SLAs are visited upon users, without consultation, by the outsourced group that is supposed to serve them, but that is not how it is supposed to work. At least, the users do not think so. We will look at these issues from the perspective of networked desktop users. While it is a generic example, there is information that can be applied across any function of an organization that is outsourced. The example is not hardware or software specific because users are not interested in what the platform is; they are interested in whether the platform will do the job. The SLA should reflect that interest.

So what is a good SLA? First, some definitions. A *service-level agreement* (SLA) is a contract between a service provider and a service user. The SLA defines the expectations on both sides of the outsourcing agreement. The SLA is typically composed of a statement of measurable outcomes and a greater or lesser number of prescribed activities, that is, things that must be done to achieve a measurable and acceptable result. In the case of the desktop environment, the *service provider* is the IT department. This may be an in-house organization or an organization external to the service users' organization. *Service users* are the desktop computer users who require the support of the applications they use to carry out the business aims of their organization.

In order to define an SLA, *the user requirements* need to be identified. Desktop users have certain requirements of an IT system which have nothing apparently to do with the complexities of IT. They want the system to be there when they switch on their screens. They want the printer to print when they press the right key. They want to be able to get help when they need it.

They want quickly fixed problems, one way or another. After identifying the user requirements, we need to define how we will know they have been satisfied. In order to do this we first define performance indicators, then performance standards, and then mechanisms to measure the satisfaction of the standards.

The *performance indicator* is the gauge or measure against which the service provider's performance will be assessed. Tell a desktop user that it is the network component of response time that causes slow responses and not the data storage response time and they will mostly look blank. Users are not interested in response time per se. The performance indicators they are interested in are consistency, availability, and useability.

The *performance standard* is that standard the service provider must achieve against the indicator if he is to be deemed to be providing an acceptable service. The performance standards do not have to be in milliseconds. The performance standards thatdesktop users need have more to do with comfort zones than anything else and they are quite hard to quantify. In the rest of this chapter, we shall work toward quantifying them. The examples are from real situations and represent typical user expectations. It is important that the performance standards are realistic in terms of their ability to be measured. That is, it is inappropriate to require, for example, that the service provider achieve a certain percentage success rate for the activity where there is no mechanism in place for measuring or confirming that the success rate has been achieved.

THE TEN COMPONENTS OF A DESKTOP ENVIRONMENT

In a desktop environment, the ten typical components of the service required are: help desk, user support, IT inventory management, backup and recovery, business continuity, change management, maintenance contract and software license administration, personal computer (PC) product support and printing support, network and server support, and software support. Of these, only the first three have any real visibility to the users. The others are almost, but not quite, transparent. We will start with the help desk, which is often the only interface the desktop user has, or needs to have, with the service provider.

Help Desk

The help desk should provide the single point of contact between the users and the service provider for all user problems and service requests. The service provider should provide a help desk service for responding to, resolving, tracking, progressing, and escalating all reported problems and service requests related to computing hardware and software systems. The help desk must be open and staffed during basic service hours on all local business days. Users must have access to help desk on-site support. Telephone support may be provided from an offsite location.

The main purpose of the help desk in the users' eyes is problem resolution. The satisfaction of service requests comes second, except when it comes first! The performance indicators must match the users' requirements. The main features of the help desk, therefore, are responsiveness, or the speed with which calls are answered by a help desk operator; and effectiveness, or the time taken to solve a problem or satisfy a user request.

The standards of responsiveness and effectiveness can be stated as minimum required levels of achievement. Bear in mind that a 100 percent achievement is unlikely, since not every problem is immediately solvable. It is also generally true that the higher the desired rate of achievement, the more it is likely to cost. Thus, performance standards should be a reasonable match for the users' real expectations of the service. For example, a help desk operator must answer 95 percent of calls within thirty seconds; must provide initial resolution action within fifteen minutes of call receipt through either telephone advice at the time of the call or a visit by help desk staff to resolve problems (for example printers, application error, reported virus infection, installation and movement requests); if resolution is a workaround, must initiate problem escalation; must resolve 90 percent of problems within 7.5 working hours of call (as reported by problem tracking system).

There is no point in defining performance standards unless there is some way of measuring the results. For this requirement, the logical place to measure the results is at the help desk, through the tracking of calls and subsequent actions. Reporting from the tracking system will indicate whether the desired level of service is being achieved. A problem and service request tracking log should be kept to track every step of problem resolution or service request actions. Comprehensive and frequent reports need to be generated to allow performance monitoring. Reports on problem escalation activities are necessary to ensure that user priority has been satisfied.

User Support

Instead of answering questions or fixing problems, this is the pro-active business of making sure the user has the right level of access to the system and understands how to use the available facilities.

All users must be provided support in the use of workstations and other user equipment (printers, modems, scanners, etc. etc, and user software and applications during basic service hours. The performance indicators reflect the users' expectations of the support function:

Administer access control systems such as the registration of new users, changes to user profiles, and general assistance to users with access problems;

Prevent virus infections and deal with them efficiently when they inevitably occur;

Define user training requirements and coordinate training delivery;

Prepare and distribute documentation on the use of IT systems and software; and

Issue change advice notices to users on impact of system changes, scheduled outages, and other interruptions to service.

Examples of performance standards are:

Complete new user access to systems within four working hours of help desk receiving authorized request;

Complete removal of users from all systems on receipt of separation notification from personnel department on user's last workday;

Users are competent in the use of new and existing systems as measured by no increase in the level of queries;

Users are able to schedule work around interruptions in service as measured by the number of complaints about access; and

Ninety percent of support requests are satisfied within the agreed timeframe (as reported by problem tracking system).

The measurement mechanism should maintain a problem and service request tracking log to keep track of every step of problem resolution or service request actions. It should also provide comprehensive and frequent reports to allow performance monitoring.

IT Inventory Management

Control of inventory should provide services to support the effective deployment of the PC inventory in line with agreed and documented business needs. This includes:

Establishing and maintaining records of hardware holdings by owner, type, model, options fitted, and maintenance history;

Coordinating future requirements and reconciling with current holdings to form the basis for acquisition planning;

Capacity monitoring and management for memory, disk storage, and networks;

Preparing and maintaining an IT upgrade and replacement plan consistent with a strategy of upgrading technology to maintain compatibility with accepted industry standards;

Monitoring inventory of PC replacement and consumable items (e.g., batteries, cables, mice) and notifing the installation when supplies must be ordered in order to maintain the required level of service;

Performing movement and installation of existing PCs, printers, scanners, modems, and other PC equipment for direct connect or where network cabling is already in place;

Performing movement and installation of existing PCs, printers, scanners, modems, and other PC equipment where network cabling is not already in place;

Setting up PCs, in accordance with agreed time frames, in training rooms for training sessions conducted by installation staff;

Monitoring inventory of printer consumable items (e.g., paper and printer cartridges) and notifing the installation when supplies must be ordered;

Building, delivering, and installing new equipment; and

Disposing of obsolete or unwanted equipment.

While inventory management covers a multitude of activities, what the user sees is just the tip of the iceberg. Therefore, the performance indicators are quite straightforward. For example, the deployment of the PC inventory should be conducted in line with agreed and documented business needs so requests for new or upgraded equipment can be met within an acceptable timeframe.

In this example, the performance standards will depend upon what is contained in the "agreed and documented business needs." The definition of the standard can refer to this documentation even if it does not yet exist, because it will be an "agreed" standard. Examples of these are: meet the agreed performance standards 95 percent of the time as measured over a six-month period; adhere to IT upgrade and replacement plan and all changes agreed with contract/SLA manager; and users are satisfied with the execution of the IT upgrade and replacement plan.

Measurement mechanism should include as a minimum: monitoring of inventory management records; audit of inventory management data, including acquisitions and disposals; and annual user satisfaction survey.

Backup and Recovery

User service is effectively transparent to the user, so long as nothing goes wrong. The only real interest the users have is that their data do not get lost and that any interruption to service because of an unforeseen error is minimized. Therefore, the stated user requirement is to ensure that suitable backup and recovery processes and procedures are in place to recover all or any portion of the data on individual platforms supporting IT facilities.

The arrangements behind the satisfaction of the requirement must: minimize the risk of loss and/or corruption of data, and maintain its integrity; minimize the risk of total denial; incorporate recovery procedures that minimize the disruption to user operations or degradation of IT support; minimize the flow-on effect of technical failures that occur in areas that are outside the service provider's responsibilities; and recover data as required to satisfy associated client service-level targets.

Since performance indicators are effectively transparent requirements, the user will only be affected by a lack of performance. A lack of performance will influence the availability of the system. Therefore, the performance indicator is simply *availability*. The performance standard will put a value on that availability, always remembering that the more that is expected, the more costly it will be. That is availability of . . . percent or better. The measurement mechanism for availability is the subject of the second part of this section of the chapter, so we will leave it for the moment and run through the other SLA components.

Business Continuity

Business continuity is the users' view of what disaster recovery is about. The users' requirement is not to plan for contingency or recover from fire, flood, or whatever; it is to keep on working. Therefore, the requirement is very similar to the backup and recovery requirement.

Suitable business continuity processes and procedures must be in place to recover all or any portion of the data or individual platforms supporting IT facilities. To achieve this, the service provider must establish, document, test, and ensure contingency, continuity, and disaster recovery arrangements for

the users' applications, data, facilities, and equipment. As with the previous requirement, and all the other requirements that follow, the performance indicators,
standards, and measurement are connected with the availability of the systems.

Change Management

Change management is about ensuring the integrity of the information
systems while, at the same time, keeping them up to date and error free.
Change management should be completely transparent to the users so the
requirement is simply stated: Provide a change management service to ensure the ongoing integrity and reliability of the information systems.

Change management includes such things as: the analysis and evaluation
of the impact on organizations of IT-related changes and restructuring; development of change management programs to ensure user acceptance and
smooth, efficient, and effective implementation of changes; and administering change control processes to ensure that changes to the information
systems are complete, tested, and documented.

Maintenance Contract and Software License Administration

This user requirement is something that needs to be done, but it is not
something the user wants to worry about. The activity is essential to supporting the availability of the environment. This component of service will
also administer and maintain IT warranties and support agreements with
external suppliers.

Maintenance contract and software license administration includes:

Establishing and maintaining software issue and license records on
PC software installations and de-installations;

Carrying out annual contract reviews;

Managing ongoing contract variations;

Reviewing, administering, and maintaining ongoing software licenses for all software operating systems and products; and

Reviewing, administering, and maintaining ongoing maintenance
agreements for hardware and software products.

PC Product Support and Printing Support

User requirement for product and printing support is to provide repair
and maintenance to facilitate the reliability of the PC and printer configuration. PC and printing maintenance includes the following: correction of

identified problems; provision and maintenance of an incident logging system to log and track all PC problems; preventative maintenance; provision of additional maintenance or upgrades necessary to maintain existing functionality; and testing of upgrades before their release into production.

Network and Server Support

User requirement for network and server support is to provide hardware and software maintenance to facilitate the reliability of the network and network facilities server platforms. Network, hardware, and software maintenance includes the following: correction of identified problems; provision and maintenance of an incident logging system to log and track all network and server problems; preventative maintenance; provision of additional hardware and software maintenance or upgrades necessary to maintain existing functionality; and testing of upgrades before their release into production systems.

Software Support

This user requirement provides support and maintenance procedures for user/application software. Support and maintenance includes: release management, including installation and de-installation; software maintenance necessary to maintain existing functionality; small program enhancements; documentation management; security management; and maintenance of the PC standard operating environment (including builds).

STANDARDS OF PERFORMANCE

Standards of performance for IT support are about *when* and *what*, not about *how* and *why*. In addition, before it is worth asking questions about *what* the performance should be, we need to find out *when* the performance is needed. That means we have to find out when the user expects to be able to use the application.

Service hours can include any or all of the following three components:

Basic service hours required for all applications on a normal working day:

8 A.M. to 6 P.M. 1800 local time. A normal working day is any day of the week other than a Saturday, Sunday, or local or national public holiday.

Additional service hours:

The service provider is to make the supported configuration available to the users for all applications on a normal working day outside the basic service hours, as follows: 4 A.M. to 8 A.M. local time; 8 P.M. to midnight local time; and on Saturdays and Sundays excluding national or local public holidays, as follows:

9 A.M. to 5 P.M. local time. The help desk and user support are not required during additional service hours.

Extensions to service hours:

When requested to do so, the service provider is to provide IT support for periods beyond the basic or additional service hours, whichever the case may be. Where possible, the service provider is to be given a minimum notice of two normal working days for such a request.

The available hours outside the service hours may be utilized by the service provider—provided that processing schedules are met—to perform backups, to undertake hardware upgrades and maintenance, and to install and test system and application updates, new releases, modifications, and new developments.

USER-BASED AVAILABILITY MEASUREMENT

The successful conduct of IT support is largely determined by the availability of the applications to users. The importance of this is reflected in the measurement of availability. The user-based approach allows the installation to focus its availability measurement on the real issue of the availability of the system to the user to do useful work. It allows the service provider to focus its efforts on the provision of user service for that purpose.

The priority of a problem is determined first by the priority of the application and second by the number of users affected. That is, one user's inability to access a first priority application will normally have a higher priority than five users' inability to access an application designated as third priority. In cases where application priority is not an issue, if one user's PC or printer is down, the service provider will attempt to minimize the loss of down time by restoring the functionality of the system to the user. If many users are down, the service provider will focus on fixing, or circumventing the major problem first, since the number of users affected multiplies the problem.

If there is any substantial clash of priorities, the service provider will be required to consult with the installation in order to decide the order in which problems are to be resolved. This approach is to the benefit of the installation and to the service provider, both of whom will have the same goal. Measuring availability at the help desk is the most effective way of fairly measuring the achievement of the goal and puts responsibility for prompt and accurate reporting on the user, and prompt attention to the problem on the service provider.

Definition of Availability

During Basic Service Hours

Availability is measured at the user's PC or printer and is based upon help desk statistics. The statistics are to be used to identify: the time a problem is reported; the determination that the problem is a hardware or software failure (rather than user induced); and the time the problem is resolved (either a workaround or fix to restore user productivity). Down time is measured as the time between the problem being reported and the time the functionality is restored to the user's satisfaction.

Exceptions. A PC is only considered to be down if hardware or software problems make the application unavailable to the user. Time spent answering a user query about how to use particular features of the application does not constitute down time. A printer is only considered down if hardware or software problems make printing unavailable to the user. A printer that has run out of paper or toner is not considered to be down unless paper or toner supplies are unavailable to the user. The user is then responsible for replenishing paper or toner in the printer.

Measurement of Availability

The required standard of availability is 99 percent, measured as follows:

$$\frac{T \times P - D \times 100}{T \times P} = \quad \%$$

where:

T = Total available time in basic service hours

P = Potential number of business users who could access the facilities

D = Total downtime reported by users

Additional Service Hours

During basic and additional service hours the service provider is also to measure the availability for each of the system component types, and for each of the production, testing/development, and training environments. Availability is measured as follows:

$$\frac{T - D \times 100}{T} = \quad \%$$

where:

T = Total available time in additional service hours plus basic service hours

D = Total downtime = Total component downtime

The service provider is required to measure and report availability on a weekly basis for each component of the system (PC, printer, LAN, server, etc.). Where the availability of any component falls below 99 percent, the service provider is required to provide an explanation and, where appropriate, a plan to avoid future occurrences of the exception.

APPLICATIONS

While the stated requirements define user expectations of the IT delivery platforms, an SLA should also describe the service levels required for each application, highlighting any special requirements. First, ask the users what applications they use. Very often, the service provider is not aware of what is going on the platforms he supports, and users tend to have a very different idea of what an application is. For example, the top two priority applications for users in a recent exercise were word processing and printing. The service provider had thought the priority was a homegrown business management system!

General

When writing an SLA it is important to anticipate as far as possible the effects of any predictable variation in the service required. We may not know exactly the size or scope of the variation, but we can identify the likely variations and plan how we will handle them. The two most likely variations in the user requirements are to do with the volume of business, as follows.

Online Transaction Types and Volumes

The service provider is to achieve the specified online response times for the applications, provided the installation operates within the transaction types and volumes specified in the SLA. Where the installation exceeds or is likely to exceed the specified types and volumes of online transactions, procedures set out in the SLA for review of the service provider's performance may be utilized to temporarily vary the required standards of performance and to adjust the capacity provided by the service provider to meet the demands of changed types and volumes of online transactions.

Concurrent Users

The service provider is to achieve the specified online response times provided the installation operates within the number of concurrent users listed in the SLA. Where the installation exceeds or is likely to exceed the specified number of concurrent users, the procedures set out in the SLA for review of the service provider's performance may be utilized to temporarily vary the required standards of performance and to adjust the capacity provided by the service provider to meet the demands of changed numbers of concurrent users.

Application Priorities

The service provider should prioritize the main user systems/applications/facilities currently in existence, then use the priority table as a guide to problem solving priorities where multiple concurrent problems have occurred. In particular, priority in responding to help desk requests should take account of the relative importance detailed in the priority table.

SYSTEMS	IMPORTANCE
Word processing	First Priority
E-mail between all offices	First Priority
Printing	First Priority
Application 1	Second Priority
Application 2	Second Priority
Application 3	Third Priority

A brief description of each application should be provided so that the performance requirements mean something to both sides of the agreement, for example: word processing or purpose. Word processing is central to the work undertaken by the installation and is undertaken on portable notebooks, stand-alone desktops, and PCs connected to the LAN. Documents stored on file servers are potentially shared among several users.

Service Required

The service provider will be expected to: provide help desk services; maintain the availability of supporting hardware; provide user assistance in using word processing software and hardware; maintain existing macros and templates; and undertake minor programming tasks such as macro and template development on request.

Software

Word processing and related office software.

Hardware

The availability of word processing is dependent on the following hardware and facilities: PC; LAN; and file servers.

Growth

Growth of approximately 20 percent per year is expected.

Follow this service-level agreement for every single application that has a user. One unhappy user can upset the whole apple cart.

CONCLUSION

In conclusion, we have covered the ten main areas that affect desktop SLAs, how to define performance indicators and availability, and how to apply the result to the important applications. There is just one thing, one important thing, left to do. We have to negotiate the agreement. In the next chapter we will look at how alliances and outsourcing are changing the traditional approach to management.

NOTES

1. Details of the survey from Boston Consulting Group (1991), Devonshire House, Mayfair Place, London.

2. Coopers and Lybrand questioned 392 chief executives of fast-growing companies in the United States. Details from Coopers and Lybrand (1994), 1 Embankment Place, London.

3. PA Consulting Group (1994), *UK IT Sourcing Survey 1994* (London: PA Consulting Group).

4. J. B. Quinn (1992), *Intelligent Enterprise* (New York: Free Press).

5. Ibid.

6. J. V. Reca and K.C.J. Zieg (1995), "Privatization," *National Contract Management Journal* 26 (2):51–64.

5

NEW MANAGEMENT DISCIPLINES

The drive toward the lean organization, facilitated by alliances and outsourcing, produces a kind of organization very different from the traditional vertically integrated organization of the past. As previously discussed, there is no one paradigm, but the kind of structures that are evolving create new types of relationships between managers within each organization and between managers in those organizations that form alliances or use outsourcing arrangements. Many of the disciplines that served managers so well in the vertically integrated organization—the ability to complete a well-delineated part of a standard task or work toward unambiguous goals, for instance—are less valuable in the new lean enterprises.

But that is not all. Not only are some old skills redundant, but also a whole raft of new skills are required by the managers who will become leaders in the new lean organization. These skills derive from the fact that managers find themselves performing different kinds of tasks, with different objectives, in a new working style set in a novel business culture. Womack describes it as a career in the lean organization "consisting of solving increasingly difficult problems in a multiskilled group."[1]

This is a challenging future for many managers; some might even call it frightening. However, it can be tackled by overhauling the organization's style and culture to create what de Geus and Senge have termed the "learning organization."[2]

DISCIPLINES FOR ALLIANCE AND OUTSOURCING MANAGEMENT

It is too glib to talk about new management disciplines in a vacuum. The lean organization creates new organizational forms. It is important, moreover, to understand the underlying issues that create the demand for these new management disciplines. Three critical issues underpin the management discipline agenda:

- Managing multiple relationships;
- Cooperating and competing simultaneously; and
- Learning from alliances.

Managing Multiple Relationships

One theme that emerges from the growing body of research on alliances and outsourcing is the growing complexity of the network of strategic alliances and outsourcing arrangements that leading organizations are building. ICL, for example, had over forty alliances visible to the board and acknowledges that there are many others negotiated at lower levels of the organization. It seems clear that a consequence of this is that managers must become more skilled at managing and negotiating many multiple external relationships. This raises a number of important but subtle management issues.

There is, of course, nothing new in managing relationships with outside suppliers and customers or, for that matter, with other business partners. However, the complexity of these relationships is changing as they increase in strategic significance. Henderson has argued that major organizations are increasingly structuring what could be termed a "portfolio of relationships."[3] For example, they may have market contracts, performance contracts, specialized relationships, and strategic partnerships.

Rather than thinking of all these relationships as independent, managers should recognize that the relationships form a portfolio much like a financial portfolio. Managers have to recognize that they need to manage each type of relationship using different management processes and mechanisms. Further, the portfolio itself may have characteristics that are beyond the characteristics of each individual relationship.

In some respects, the work of Henderson,[4] Henderson and Subramani,[5] and Henderson and Venkatraman[6] have synergies with the findings of Lynch (see Chapter 3) on strategic alliances.[7] Lynch suggests that processes are more important in managing strategic alliance relationships than structure, although structure plainly has a part to play.

Henderson[8] suggests that managers need to address three critical business-process areas in managing a portfolio of relationships. He defines these as operational control, boundary management, and information and technology enablers (the latter will be dealt with in Chapter 7).

For example, when it comes to operational control, two of the processes that must be managed are performance measurement and risk management. The way these are managed, for example, in a straightforward "market contract" (through compliance tracking and acceptance testing) is different from a "strategic partnership" (through defining business goals and managing risk through experiments and learning). Similarly, a performance contract and a specialized relationship both have appropriate techniques for managing performance and risk.

How does this work in practice? Consider an organization like General Motors. It has hundreds of contracts with component suppliers that fall under the market exchange criteria. It monitors performance of these suppliers through measures such as on-time delivery and reject rates. It manages the risk through acceptance testing of batches of components.

On the other hand, the organization also has a strategic partnership with Toyota. It manages the policy of this at senior management level and monitors its value through the organizational learning it derives from the alliance. For example, through the Nummi joint venture with Toyota, General Motors learned about Toyota's production systems, its quality assurance methods, its supplier relationships, its approach to production engineering, and its "gradualist" management style.

Henderson's thinking carries through to what he terms the "boundary management" of relationships.[9] This deals with issues such as who is to manage the relationship and how the organization will link its business processes with its different partners. For example, in traditional market exchange, the person managing the relationship performs the role of buyer. Business processes between buyer and seller might be facilitated through automated interfaces such as EDI-driven invoicing.

In a strategic partnership, senior executives manage the relationship at the policy level. For example, a committee that includes the chief executives of both banks manages the Royal Bank of Scotland and Banco Santander alliance. Many organizations are intuitively leaning toward the kind of management disciplines needed to manage these multiple types. For example, Eastman Kodak and Rover tackled the issue in different ways.

However, many organizations still seem unclear about how the development of new relationships fundamentally changes the roles and responsibilities of managers. In fact, Snow, Miles, and Coleman[10] suggest one paradigm for considering the new role of managers is as "brokers." In their broker role, managers operate across rather than within hierarchies, assembling from their own organization and from outside sources.

Managers as brokers perform three important roles. First, they act as architects, designing the network or alliance and identifying the component parts that are needed to form it. The key quality needed to perform this role is the vision to understand how new competitive advantage can be harvested from disparate resources that have never been brought together before. In the strategic relationships, this visioning role often takes place at or close to chief executive level. For example, it was the recognition within Rover that it could not find all the resources it needed in-house to develop its next range of family cars that started the search for a business partner.

The second role for the manager as broker is as leader of an alliance network. In this role, the manager selects those staff that will perform different functions within the alliance, designs in conjunction with other partners the business processes that make the alliance work, and accounts for the performance of the alliance. Here, the manager is acting as an organizer and results are often achieved through using negotiation and persuasion, rather than through the more traditional command and control mechanisms used in a conventional management hierarchy. For example, John Bacchus played the leader role on Rover's side in its alliance with Honda. But he empowered and encouraged managers at the working levels to make decisions and resolve problems.

Finally, the manager as broker acts as a caretaker for the alliance. The essence of this role is to keep the alliance moving forward, seeking out new opportunities, and, thus, retaining the enthusiasm of its partners, rather than allowing it to suffer atrophy. In the caretaker role, the manager must judge the performance of the alliance and make judgments about the business benefit flowing from it to the partners. Based on those judgments, the manager should devise ways of developing the alliance to the mutual benefit of both parties and then persuade their own managers to sanction the actions necessary to move the alliance forward. In performing this role, the manager will need finely tuned political skills.

In a significant number of alliances, managers not closely associated with an alliance expressed reservations about the benefits gained. In fact, often it seems that managers not close to alliances take a one-sided and ultimately short-sighted view of alliance benefits. It is the caretakers' role to open their eyes to the true business benefit and so win approval and enthusiasm for further developments.

Cooperating and Competing Simultaneously

Of all the factors in alliances, the one that causes most tensions is the fact that many combine both cooperation and competition. Among alliances, this is especially true in the case of the alliance between Eastman Kodak and Canon and the alliance between Rover and Honda. Yet, both these alliances were long running and the parties to each claimed they won considerable business benefits. Therefore, it must be possible to operate an alliance in a way that manages the tensions that inevitably arise when organizations co-operate and compete simultaneously.

Two factors need to be in place in order to manage the tensions. First, each alliance partner needs to be clear about its strategic intent for the alliance and to communicate that intent to its alliance partners. As noted in Chapter 3, the strategic intent encapsulates the partner's ambitions for the alliance. Strategic intent, therefore, sets the agenda of issues that the partner wants to address as the alliance develops. It is important for alliance partners to have congruent strategic intents for the alliance, even it the ambitions for what they hope to gain from the alliance are radically different. This is important because it creates a common shared agenda that provides a strong framework within which the inevitable tensions can be managed.

Moreover, the partners need to be open with each other about what they expect to gain from the alliance. Where there are hidden agendas, suspicions are invariably fostered and the strength of the alliance is undermined. The alliance is then less able to manage the tensions that arise within it. For example, Eastman Kodak and Canon were open about their own reasons for wanting to enter an alliance. Eastman Kodak wanted access to a range of small- to medium-sized copiers to sell to its corporate customers, Canon wanted access to the corporate marketplace.

In addition, each organization had different competencies in copier technologies—Eastman Kodak in belts, Canon in drums. Their alliance strengthened the competitive position of both organizations, but they still competed against each other. One of the ways to cope with the cooperation/competition paradox is to spell out very clearly at the outset which are the areas of competition and which are for cooperation.

Rover and Honda had to cope with the same paradox in their alliance until it ended after sixteen years. Overall it had worked but there had been disputes along the way. Again, laying out some ground rules for managing cooperation and competition simultaneously eases the tensions. For example, although both organizations were selling cars that were "sisters under the skin" in the same markets, the two agreed that they would not attack each other in advertisements and promotional material. However there was an occasion when a Honda dealer ran a knocking-copy advertisement. This ruffled the feathers in the Rover camp, but because both organizations moved quickly to defuse the situation, the alliance suffered no long-term damage.

Many of the organizations that manage to cooperate successfully acknowledge that it is a skill that does not come naturally to most Western managers. It is more natural in Japan and Korea, for example, where *keiretsu* and *chaebol* create frameworks for cooperative management. In this situation, skills at negotiation and persuasion are important, but so also is the ability to understand the other side's point of view and to take account of that when framing possible decisions. In addition, cultural issues are important, especially for alliances that cross industry boundaries or countries.

Some organizations have trained managers to work in alliances. Often the training specifically focused on issues such as negotiating agreements to create win-win situations and to understand the different culture of the alliance partner. For example, while Rover did not give its managers any formal training in alliance management techniques (they learned their skills on the job), it did provide extensive briefings on its partner organization, Honda, and on dealing with Japanese business customs and practices. At Eastman Kodak, training staff to understand the different culture of its partner, Canon, was also on the agenda.

Another way to manage the tensions caused by simultaneously cooperating and competing is to create a framework in which managers on both sides adopt the kinds of attitudes and behaviors that are likely to reinforce the success elements of the partnership. For example, when disputes occur in a one-organization management hierarchy, it is common for them to be referred up to the next level for resolution. Although this approach can be adopted in an alliance, it is destructive to the cohesion of the alliance because it institutionalizes and exacerbates conflict.

In several alliances, the decision-making processes were designed to force managers to take every possible step to reach agreement before passing it "upstairs." In the Rover Honda alliance, Rover tried to instill a culture among its employees to solve problems at the level they occurred, and if the problems were pushed to a higher level, the problems were often pushed back down to their originating area.

There is a truth that every alliance manager needs to take to heart: *Sometimes you just have to give in.* Some alliances create a gatekeeper. While the primary function of this role is to control the information flow both ways in the alliance, a secondary purpose is to manage any conflicts that arise. What also seems clear is that those organizations that develop "new world" managers raise their chances of succeeding in an alliance. The managers have already acquired a range of new skills that serve them well in the negotiation, implementation, and operational stages of the alliances.

Eastman Kodak, a market leader in the high-volume reprographics market, formed an alliance with Canon, who at the time was the second-largest company in the low- to medium-sized product range. From Eastman Kodak's perspective, the alliance, which built on a tactical partnership formed in 1985, had three main purposes. These were leveraging core competencies, achieving scale economies, and creating improved value for customers, shareholders, and employees. Since working with Canon, Eastman Kodak has learned much about the management discipline needed in an alliance. Three success factors in the alliance were identified: communication channels; roles and responsibilities; and training.

Communication Channels

The two partners set up an alliance management team that worked as a coordination body to ensure a smooth implementation of the alliance so that the goals could be obtained. On the Eastman Kodak side, the team included representatives from manufacturing, development, marketing, and an alliance specialist already working with Canon. As Canon and Eastman Kodak are also competitors, any weakness in Eastman Kodak's communication channels could be used by Canon to its advantage. The maintenance of the information flow ensured that the alliance achieved all the desired performance objectives.

The first step was to find out how Canon worked. Eastman Kodak and Canon are similar complex organizations with a centralized responsibility for planning, development, and manufacturing and decentralized marketing. To ensure the success of the teams developed to work together on product development and manufacturing, it was necessary to go down to each function responsibility and authority within the organization. This revealed that similar functions involved different levels of responsibility in each company. A result of the analysis of the partner organization in parallel with Eastman Kodak's own structure enabled the management team to establish the right communication channels at each relevant level in the organization.

A critical feature of the management of information flow was the establishment by Eastman Kodak of three "gatekeepers." These covered information flows on, respectively, high-volume copiers, medium-volume copiers, and color copiers. Only the gatekeepers were authorized to pass technological information to Canon. There were two benefits from this approach. First, it ensured that Canon only received precise information, information that Canon could use to make decisions. Second, it made sure that Eastman Kodak controlled what information was given away. Information exchange was carefully documented.

Roles and Responsibility

Eastman Kodak never tried to establish an all-encompassing set of rules to cover the alliance. That would be an impossible undertaking. When the communication network was finalized and the appropriate points of contact defined, the analysis of the roles and responsibilities of each function resulted in a written summary so that each person within the network could play an active role in driving projects. Although the partners operated with a number of points of contact for operational matters, there was a single point for problem resolution or for initiating new projects.

The alliance was successful for Canon and Eastman Kodak because coordination made sure that all information going out was correct, and delegation made the alliance run smoothly. One important point was the role of the respective general managers in all of this. It was important that they not be involved with the day-to-day operations of the alliance. It was also important not to bring general managers in on a situation that still had unresolved conflict. When they did enter, all conflict was resolved; they could sign the documents, and the alliance could get on with doing what it was formed for.

Training

Eastman Kodak found that training managers in alliance management and, especially, the cultural issues in dealing with their Japanese counterparts proved a critical factor in the success of the alliance. Eastman Kodak organized training sessions and group discussions to develop the ability to understand cultural changes and to benefit from them rather than consider them as problems. There are many examples of how mastering this cultural gulf helped Eastman Kodak managers forge stronger relationships with their opposite numbers in the alliance. For example, one Eastman Kodak manager took a large vase as a gift for his opposite number in Japan. The Japanese manager was delighted. The large vase had occupied half of the Eastman Kodak manager's suitcase. To the Japanese, who live in small flats or houses and are very aware of the value of space, this underscored the sincerity with which the gift was given.

Ensuring the success of programs within an alliance relies mainly on people. Enabling communication channels, contact points between the partners' organizations, training people to understand cultural differences, and alliance objectives are all fundamental steps in the implementation process to derive all the value expected from the alliance, to grab new opportunities, and to deal with unexpected issues.

Learning from Alliances

Building an ability to learn from alliances is arguably the most important challenge facing managers, for there is a teasing duality in alliances. On the one hand, it provides opportunities to acquire new skills, competencies, and technologies. On the other, it can deliver important competencies into the hands of a partner who may be cooperating in one area but competing in another. The alliance has the capability to deliver much, but also to undermine long-term competitiveness. It can be a thoroughbred winner or a Trojan horse.

It is well to understand the possible downside of alliances in order to underline the critical significance of organizational learning. Reich and Mankin warned, "joint ventures with Japan give away our future" back in 1986.[11] Reich and Mankin argued that U.S. (and by implication European) organizations entering alliances with Japan would lose out in the long run because of a key macroeconomic objective of Japanese policy; to keep higher-paying value-added jobs in Japan. They warned that the policy, which has, in fact, gathered momentum since Reich and Mankin wrote their article, for Western organizations to outsource components and subassemblies to Japanese organizations mortgaged the future. Alliances between Eastern and Western organizations increasingly eroded the core competencies needed to be long-term winners in important areas of production. For example, Westinghouse left the business of color television tube production and only reentered it when Toshiba agreed to provide technical expertise. The result of outsourcing production was that Westinghouse had fallen so far behind in technical knowledge it could not catch up on its own.

Lei and Slocum resurrected this theme. They argue that alliances are coalignments between two or more organizations in which the "partners hope to learn and acquire from each other the technologies, products, skills, and knowledge that are not otherwise available to competitors."[12] Lei and Slocum warn that "without clearly understanding and identifying the risks inherent in alliances, collaboration may unintentionally open up a firm's entire spectrum of core competencies, technologies, and skills to encroachment and learning by its partners." The danger is that an alliance can be used to slowly "deskill" a partner unaware of the risks inherent in the arrangement. Lei and Slocum conclude: "Collaboration within alliances leads to a competition both in learning new skills and in refining firm capabilities in other products and processes. Although collaboration and competition do go hand-in-hand, how managers approach this duality will significantly affect the firm's propensity for learning and developing new skills. This is the Trojan horse downside of alliances spelled out with brutal clarity.

What can be done in order to minimize these dangers? Indeed, more positively, what can be done to use an alliance as an instrument of organizational learning? Managers must address three policy issues. First, it is essential to be aware of the strategic intent of any chosen alliance partner. This point has been made before, but it is so important that it must be made again. The impression is that too many organizations enter alliances in order to find a "quick fix" remedy for a business weakness, perhaps the lack of a key technology or access to an important market. In this kind of situation, the longer-term motives of the partner are, too often, not probed carefully enough. Yet, a conscious effort to look at the alliance from the partner's point of view sometimes produces an unwelcome perspective on the alliance.

It is important to be aware that competencies learned in one product or market (where there is no interpartner competition) can sometimes be transferred to other products or markets, where competition between partners is intense. For example, General Electric Corporation (GEC) originally entered an alliance with Samsung to produce microwave ovens. Samsung learned about the consumer goods market from the alliance and now competes against GEC with a wide range of products. This is not to suggest that alliances should be avoided, but to state that the downside of an alliance should be as realistically weighed in the balance as its potential benefits.

Second, managing the flow of information in an alliance is a critical issue; and it is just as important to manage the in-flow of information as to manage the out-flow. Some alliance partners are reasonably effective at controlling the flow of information, such as technical information, out of the organization. They are less effective at stimulating an inward flow and, then, using the information to promote learning throughout the organization. There is some strong evidence that Japanese organizations are more effective at organizational learning than Western organizations. This may be a result of the Japanese cultural influence of people and organizations being ashamed to seek help from those outside the family or organization. They may see it as their duty to learn these skills as fast as possible. Honda was more adept at learning than Rover during the early stages of their alliance, though Rover eventually acquired skills toward the end.

Some successful alliances, for example Eastman Kodak/Canon, use the gateway principle to control the flow of information. However, the most valuable long-term organizational learning comes not from the formal information changes, which are more easily managed and documented, but from the informal interchange of information that takes place between staff working in an alliance. Again, Japanese organizations overall seem to be more effective at learning from this informal information exchange.

Finally, it is important to institutionalize organizational learning from an alliance. The most effective users of alliances do this, but other organizations are less focused on the need for organizational learning. It is easier to institutionalize learning if part of the strategic intent of the partner is to learn from the alliance and this is spelled out from the beginning. Nevertheless, the organization must also train managers to learn from alliance partners and create both formal and informal flows so that information is disseminated through the organization.

A COMPETENCIES CHECKLIST FOR THE "NEW WORLD ORDER" MANAGER

It is very difficult to generalize about the skills needed by managers working in alliances, partly because every alliance is different and partly because there is an infinity of possible roles and responsibilities in alliances. Essentially, developing new management skills is a change management issue. The experience of a building society provides some useful pointers.

When the society set up its branch network, it devised a set of competencies for the ideal network group manager. For each competency, the managers were invited to assess themselves against a seven-point scale with four positioning points along the scale. For example, on decision making, managers assessed themselves on the scale against these statements:

- At point one: makes practical decisions by following precedents and policy, seeking advice where appropriate;
- At point three: makes nonroutine decisions for self and others by clarifying situations and verifying information;
- At point five: decides between available options by considering broad cost, benefit, and risk implications; and
- At point seven: takes decisive action by balancing options in the context of business objectives and values.

The other competencies against which the managers assessed themselves were: dealing with different views; focusing on quality; change orientation; resilience (drive, commitment); setting objectives; motivating others; monitoring; planning; innovating; influencing; working with others; developing people; communicating; empowering; customer focus; commercial awareness; and problem solving/analysis.

NOTES

1. J. P. Womack (1992), "The Lean Difference," *Prism* (First Quarter): 105.

2. See A. de Geus (1997), *The Living Company* (London: Nicholas Brealy); P. Senge (1990), *The Fifth Discipline* (Milsons Point: Random House Australia); A. de Geus (1988), "Planning as Learning," *Harvard Business Review* 66 (2):70–74.

3. J. C. Henderson (1990), "Plugging into Strategic Partnerships," *Sloan Management Review* 31 (3):7–18.

4. Ibid.

5. J. C. Henderson and M. Subramani (1998), "The Shifting Ground between Markets and Hierarchy," unpublished paper.

6. J. C. Henderson and N. Venkatraman (1993), "Strategic Alignment: Leveraging Information Technology for Transforming Organizations," *IBM Systems Journal* 32 (1):4–16.

7. R. P. Lynch (1993), *Business Alliance Guide* (New York: John Wiley).

8. Henderson (1990), "Plugging into Strategic Partnerships."

9. Ibid.; Henderson and Subramani (1998), "The Shifting Ground"; and Henderson and Venkatraman (1993), "Strategic Alignment."

10. C.C. Snow, R. E. Miles, and H. J. Coleman (1992), Managing 21st Century Network Organizations," *Organizational Dynamics* 20 (3): 5–20.

11. R. B. Reich and E. D. Mankin (1986), "Joint Ventures with Japan Give Away Our Future," *Harvard Business Review* 64 (2): 78.

12. D. Lei and J. W. Slocum (1992), Global Strategy, Competence Building and Strategic Alliances," *California Management Review* 35 (1): 81–82.

6

CREATING A PARTNERSHIP CULTURE

Are organizations with a partnership culture more adept at harvesting value from strategic alliances? This important question has seldom been addressed in research. Organizations that build a participative culture, foster teamworking styles, adopt a flexible organization structure, and break down barriers between business functions create an organization that is more fitted to winning the business benefits from alliances. There are a number of reasons for this.

First, a successful alliance rests on the desire of its parties to cooperate. Yet, Western business culture usually fosters competition rather than cooperation. Whereas competition has managers looking to create a win-lose situation, cooperation demands they seek a win-win situation. Indeed, the harsh fact about alliances is that the choice is between a win-win situation and a lose-lose situation, for in a failed alliance both parties miss potential benefits.

Managers from organizations that have developed a partnership culture are more adept at the negotiation and interpersonal skills needed to create win-win situations. As with ABB, for example, they must create win-win situations in their own organizations.

Second, most alliances involve a high element of teamwork at every level of the alliance. Those organizations with a partnership culture often have more experience in the dynamics of teamworking than those from a traditionally organized command and control hierarchy. In order to be successful, alliance teams need to develop a high degree of internal cohesion and motivation. They need to identify with the objectives of the alliance and they must adopt collegial forms of decision making in which mutual respect between team members is important. Again, this kind of experience in an organization gives it a head start when it enters an alliance.

Finally, a successful alliance engenders complete trust between its respective parties. The implication of this is that information is freely shared and there are no private agendas. Again, partnership organizations are better equipped to develop managers who are sharing these values.

- In working toward a partnership culture, three issues need to be tackled:
- Adopting an appropriate organization structure;
- Developing high performance business teams; and
- Equipping managers with partnership and networking skills.

PARTNERSHIP CULTURE: THE ORGANIZATIONAL ISSUES

Much has been written about organizational design and structure over the past two decades and from this it is possible to pick a number of themes that have significance for alliance formation. As good a starting point as any is the organizational theory developed by Gore.[1] Gore's concept of the "lattice organization" has some strikingly simple but revolutionary management principles. No one has fixed or assigned authority. Sponsors rather than bosses guide teams. "Followship" replaces leadership. People communicate directly with one another rather than through hierarchies. People set their own objectives, then make them happen. Tasks and functions are organized through commitments.

Gore's approach is based on two insights about how people work. First, the effectiveness with which people deliver value to their organization has only a little to do with formal management procedures but much more to do with informal methods of working. Gore wrote that "every successful organization has a lattice organization that underlies the facade of authoritarian hierarchy. It is through these lattice organizations that things get done. Most of us delight in going around the formal procedures and things the straightforward way."

The second is about how business teams deliver more than the sum of their parts. Gore again: "The mathematician, engineer, accountant, machinist, chemist and so on provide a combination of capabilities of a much broader scope than the mere sum of their number. This synergism impels us to join together for mutual benefit."

Gore's paradigm is, sceptics might be surprised to learn, not a model for paralysis or anarchy. Gore recognizes that decisions must be made. "Complete consensus is never achieved." He also realizes that this approach requires strong leadership and clear goals. "Stability and long-term constancy require a firm hand at the helm." Gore's thinking has considerably influenced organizational theorists seeking a business model that can promote a partnership culture and managers in some organizations who have worked to create a partnership culture in the past decade. There is no one model that creates this partnership culture. Rather, there are three main models, each of which can achieve similar objectives, and a myriad of variations on those models.

PARTNERSHIP MODELS

Federal Organization

The theory behind this kind of organizational structure, demonstrated effectively, has been influenced by Charles Handy.[2] He has suggested that federal organizations have moved beyond decentralization because the profusion of their business means they cannot understand enough about what these businesses do in order to make detailed operational decisions about them at the center.

At ABB, for example, the former CEO Percy Barnevik recognized this only too well and developed decision making to the lowest possible level. Barnevik is on record as having said that big organizations are inherently negative. "They create so much slowness, bureaucracy, distance from the customers, take away initiative from people and attract the sort of people who survive in a big organisation." Barnevik argued that with more mergers and globalization of business, there must be a "tremendous challenge to counter negative forces and to try to create the dynamics and entrepreneurial spirit of a small company."

Nevertheless, in other organizations, managers who try to run the business from the center eventually lose control dangerously. As Handy has argued, managers try to collect information at the center using new information technologies, such as management and executive information systems. Handy says, "The new technologies that do not fail to stop trying to run everything from the centre that have to begin to let go. Then decentralisation turns into federalism."[3] Handy calls this the "do'nut" organization. However, does the do'nut promote partnership and set the scene for successful alliances?

At ABB, this is plainly the case. The individual business has to cooperate both with its country managers and with the business area managers in order to achieve business objectives. Moreover, the individual businesses are more adept at identifying alliance opportunities and, once formed, harvesting benefit from them.

Cluster Organization

The cluster organization offers an appropriate model in those situations where the business is not diversified but everybody is focused on contributing to solutions for the whole organization. While clusters emphasize the importance of participating in finding team solutions, they also encourage individuals to contribute across teams. In the United Kingdom, organizations including BP and IBM have used the cluster principle in parts of their respective organizations and it was the principle behind the reorganization of the building society in Figure 6.1.

The building society was "disaggregated" into a number of processes, each serviced by a business team. Although each team has its own roles and responsibilities, there was an overlap between them, for example, the direction management process (what a conventional organization would call the board of directors) and the implementation management processes (in the conventional organizations, everything from accounting to marketing). Throughout the organization there are about 500 teams, each of which meets formally once every two weeks to discuss and resolve outstanding issues.

Figure 6.1 shows how a cluster organization works. As the top flat oval shows, the direction and movement of the organization are carried out by a continuous improvement process that works by measuring existing processes and improving upon them. The direction loop feeds the implementation loop, which feeds off a continuous iterative process of measurement and improvement. The large oval below shows how the direction management process interfaces with the implementation management process through a series of clusters. The purpose of the understanding process is to resolve issues that have not been effectively resolved by any of the clusters.

Clusters work best when it is possible to centralize the skills needed to solve particular problems in one or a few places. Although they have considerable potential, the task of moving from a conventional hierarchy to a cluster is a lengthy and often painful activity. On the other hand, a well-bedded-down cluster organization contains people used for problem

Figure 6.1
An Example of a Cluster Organization in the Finance Sector

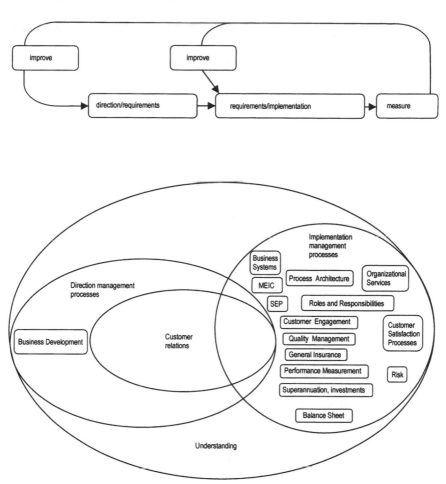

solving who work in unstructured or loosely structured environments and cooperate with others within their own or in other teams to solve previously unseen business problems—skills that contribute to potentially outstanding alliance success.

Starburst Organization

Starburst organizations are rather like a big bang with a powerful core competence at the center (see Figure 6.2). New businesses leverage off this core competence, constantly developing new product lines or services. The

Figure 6.2
The Starburst Organization

New
companies

Second-generation
companies

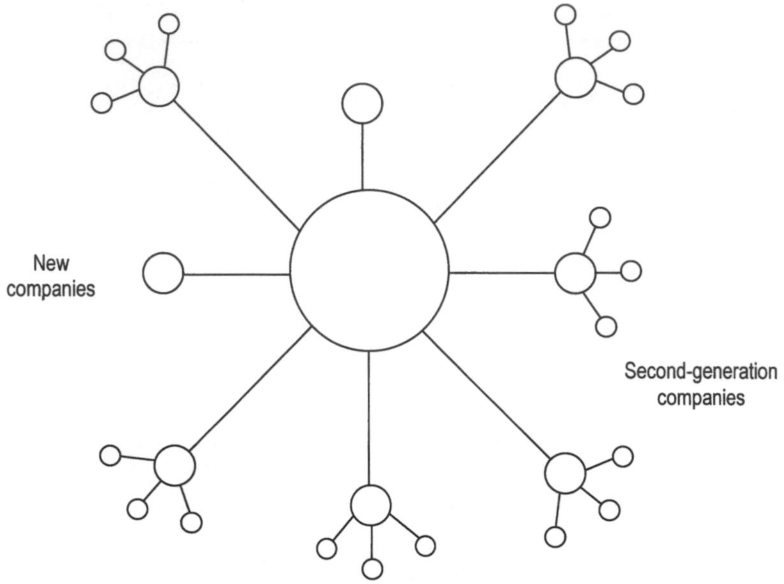

Source: Reprinted with the permission of The Free Press, a Division of Simon & Schuster, Inc. from INTELLIGENT ENTERPRISE: A Knowledge and Service Based Paradigm for Industury by James Brian Quinn. Copyright © 1992 by James Brian Quinn.

secret of their success is to maintain the strength of the core competence, constantly investing in and enhancing it so that it retains the vitality and strength to spawn new products and businesses. There are elements of this approach in the GKN example (see Chapter 2), where there is a central core competence in managing asset-intensive businesses, and in the Virgin Group example (see Chapter 1), where the core competence is an ability to manage high organic growth through alliances and outsourcing. However, a more "classic" starburst approach is seen in an organization such as 3M, which leverages a huge range of products and businesses from its core competence in developing and marketing products based on polymer chemistry technologies.

In a different way, the starburst organization promotes a partnership culture, partnerships between the team that develops the core competence at the center and the teams that develop it into business opportunities in the starburst. There must be considerable trust between the two because neither can manage in detail the work of the other. At the same time, the existence of a highly developed core competence provides a source of potential value to alliance partners, while the individual teams provide the application skills that provide practical opportunities for partnering.

This brief discussion outlines three different organizational modes capable of promoting a partnership culture. It is important to stress that there are few right and wrong answers in this area. However, those organizations that maintain a rigid command and control hierarchy are significantly less well equipped to engage other organizations in alliances, create effective teamworking within the alliance, and win major business benefits from it.

DEVELOPING HIGH-PERFORMANCE BUSINESS TEAMS

A critical question for organizations contemplating strategic partnerships and alliances is how can we form high-performance business teams that cross boundaries? As the previous section argued, those organizations that form high-performance business teams within their own boundaries begin with a head start. Usually, they have experience crossing departmental or function boundaries in their own organization. Crossing over the boundary of their own organization is the next step.

Lipnack and Stamp call them "teamnets."[4] They suggest teamnets incorporate two organizational ideas:

- Teams, where small groups of people work with focus, motivation, and skill to achieve shared goals; and
- Networks, where disparate groups of people link to work together based on a common purpose.

When an organization operates like an alliance of 1,300 small businesses, a range of skills and disciplines foreign to the typical ladder-climber in a traditional corporate hierarchy is needed. ABB, the giant engineering and electrical organization, has developed an organizational structure that combines matrix management with empowered business teams. Former CEO Percy Barnevik built an organization he has described as having "no geographic centre, no national axe to grind—a federation of national companies with a global coordination centre."

There are five elements in ABB's organizational structure. The executive committee sets the policy and strategy of the organization and monitors performance. The 1,300-plus operating organizations work through a matrix management structure in which they report to both country and business area bosses. Some of the larger organizations, and none is very large, are divided into profit centers. Within all organizations, staffs are organized into teams.

This structure resolves three paradoxes for the global business:

- Global and local—the organization operates in more than 100 countries and each country has its own country chief executive whose task is to put local interests first. This means building a distribution network that handles all products and serves the customers of all business areas.

- Big and small—the organization has nearly 250,000 employees. Yet, these are organized into 1,300 businesses that are often broken down into profit centers with around forty to fifty people. The business also has about sixty business areas, each with a business area director supported by a small management team.

- Decentralized and centralized—each of the 1,300 businesses has its own president with wide decision-making powers. Barnevik prevented the whole organization from becoming bureaucracy-bound by pushing decision making down to the lowest possible levels. Yet, the central executive committee meets every three weeks, resolves any issues raised by conflicts in the matrix structure, and reviews performance data collected from every one of the 1,300 businesses. Barnevik described the benefits from this approach: "Take a factory in Germany or Athens. The way you operate that as a manager is not much different from other small companies in your area. But there is one big difference from your neighbours. You belong to a big group. While a U$30 million plant is not overly huge, there are 30 others in the group around the world that combined are worth U$1 billion."

This organizational structure creates a demand for new skills and disciplines from the managers who work in it. Business area managers must be skilled negotiators who use targets and influence as motivators rather than budgets and the right to hire and fire. Country managers need the ability to balance the overall needs of the country operation against the sometimes-competing claims of business area managers for resources.

The chief executives of the 1,300 organizations also have a tough challenge. They have to learn how to report to two evenly balanced bosses—the country manager and relevant business area manager. They need the self-confidence not to become paralyzed if they receive conflicting signals and the integrity not to play one boss against the other.

Lipnack and Stamps suggest, "In an ideal teamnet, people work in high-performing teams at every level and the network as a whole functions as though it were a highly skilled and motivated team."[5] They suggest five principles that bind a teamnet together: unifying purpose; independent members; voluntary links; multiple leaders; and interactive levels. Lipnack and Stamps explain, "A teamnet must have a reason to exist (purpose), a critical number of committed participants (members), a rich web of relationships (links), people who assume specific responsibilities (leaders) and connections at many levels in the environment."[6] Organizations that enter multiple alliances, such as ABB, Digital Equipment, IBM, General Motors, ICL, Fujitsu, and Toshiba, are skilled exponents of these teamnet principles. How, for example, do those principles work in Royal Bank of Scotland's alliance with Banco Santander?

- The unifying purpose of the alliance is to provide the banks with a stronger joint presence in European banking.

- The independent members are the large numbers of managers in both of the banks who have bought into its concept and make it deliver benefits.

- The voluntary links are the different relationships that each bank has formed because of the alliance; for example, with each other's customers and with other banking organizations because of its Interbank On-Line Systems project.

- The multiple leaders are the managers who make the alliance deliver results. Those leaders include, of course, the chief executives of each bank (as well as the departmental heads in each bank whose contacts with opposite numbers foster business opportunities) and the "gateway" managers who provide a focus for alliance activity and help smooth away problems as they arise.

- The interactive levels follow naturally from the multiple leaders. The alliance operates at head office, departmental, and, on occasion, branch level. The two banks are coupled in the alliance at multiple levels using both regular and ad hoc teams of managers.

How can the teamnet principle work to increase the chances of success in a partnership or alliance? Lipnack and Stamps suggest that if a group of people can answer the five questions affirmatively, it has "teamnet potential," the power to make a success from a boundary-crossing alliance. The questions are:

Does your organization have a clear purpose? In the case of an alliance, this means defining the strategic intent of the proposed alliances. All members of the team need to understand the strategic intent, otherwise they will be pulling in different directions or no direction at all.

Are there other people besides you working toward the purpose? In an organization, one visionary might see the need for an alliance, but unless other important personnel are brought on board, it is unlikely to float. Bringing on board other people gives the alliance idea power within an organization.

Do you have sufficient communication and relationships among you to achieve the purpose effectively? The group with the alliance vision needs to interact both within itself and with others in the organization. When a group starts to gel with a myriad of relationships exchanging ideas, it starts to build momentum and move forward.

Is there more than one leader in the group? Lipnack and Stamps argue against the common wisdom that one leader is best. Two heads, or more, are better than one, they say. Defining the purpose of a complex alliance takes leadership from more than one source.

Can you "look up" and see that your organization is part of a larger one? Can you "look down" and see the smaller parts that make up your organization? The team that makes an alliance work with a partner will usually be situated somewhere in the middle of the organization. It needs to win support from teams both above it and below it. It also needs to help foster the multiple links at different levels that are the key to acquiring the organizational learning from an alliance, which is so important.

It is important to understand that the effective use of internal teams does not guarantee success in partnership and alliance ventures. Nor is it possible to quantify with any precision to what extent it raises the chances of succeeding with partnerships. However, it seems abundantly clear from many researchers that internal teamworking skills often adapt effectively in alliances.

SKILLS FOR THE NETWORK ORGANIZATION

Whether it is called federal, cluster, starburst, or anything else, many managers increasingly find themselves working in a network organization. As previously noted, the culture and style of these organizations are radically different from a traditional command and control organization.

Charan conducted a four-year study of network organizations and concluded that they were "faster, smarter, and more flexible than reorganizations or downsizings—dislocating steps that cause confusion, sap emotional energy, and seldom produce sustainable results."[7] Charan suggested that a network "reshapes how and by when essential business decisions get made."

> It integrates decisions horizontally at the lowest managerial levels and with superior speed. In effect, a network identifies the "small company inside the large company" and empowers it to make the four dimensional trade-offs—among functions, business units, geography, and global customers—that determine success in the marketplace. It enables the right people in the organization to converge faster and in a more focused way than the competition on operating priorities determined by the imperatives of meeting customer needs and building concrete advantage.[8]

However, making a network organization work effectively demands a new range of skills from managers. It is suggested that the network organization manager needs to focus on a two-level skills framework. The first level focuses on skills managers need to develop and leverage their networks. The second level addresses the *core personal networking processes* involved in developing and leveraging the network (see Figure 6.3).

FIRST-LEVEL SKILLS

Knowing the Network

In order to operate successfully in the new boundaryless organization, most individuals need, literally, to develop a new mental map of how their organization functions. Functional managers are often either ignorant or naive about how other parts of the organization work. Yet, if they are to cross boundaries within their own organization they need to adopt a more worldly wise attitude to it.

Organizations such as ABB that have moved toward the network approach find there are no short cuts to tackling this issue. However, clear

Figure 6.3
Framework for Development of Personal Networking Skills

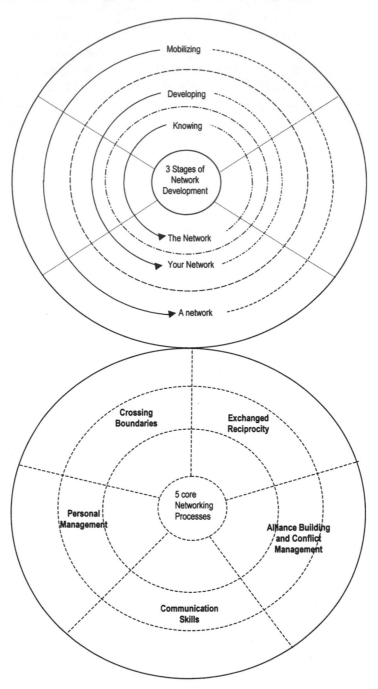

Source: Colin Hastings, New Organization Consulting, *from The New Organization* by Colin Hastings (Maidenhead: McGraw-Hill, 1996), 73.

leadership is essential and Barnevik adopted the principle of "over communicating" to ensure that managers and staff at all levels are infused with information about how the organization is working.

Developing Your Network

There is an uncomfortable truth about network organizations. The reality of organizational networking is that:

- It is frequently difficult to get things done;
- It makes considerable demands on individuals;
- It requires balancing constant trade-offs and contradictions;
- It creates stress;
- It is riddled with conflict above the norm; and
- It requires individuals to embrace complexity and see the whole picture.

The harsh fact is that network organizations are demanding environments in which to work.

There are a number of actions that can reduce the potential for conflict and stress. First, decision making has to be pushed to the lowest possible level of the organizations, as at ABB. Then managers at higher levels should accept the decisions made and judge performance by results. Second, senior managers should create a culture in which staff are encouraged to make their own decisions. This approach may easily underpin the more traditional decision-making culture. It encourages staff to develop the confidence to solve their own problems. Third, the network organization must foster a collegiate style of decision making. Involving a range of concerned people in decision-making processes can be slow.

An example of an organization that has reaped clear business benefits from developing a network is Dun & Bradstreet Europe. The organization operates a "development network" that evaluates and monitors new business information products and customizes existing products. According to Charan, who included the organization as one of the ten in his study, Dun & Bradstreet Europe "has faced the tensions that afflict so many cross-border and cross-cultural organisations." Dun & Bradstreet Europe centralized databases and technical staff, a sensible move, but it made it more difficult to adapt products for different European markets. The solution is the development network. This is "designed to make those trade-offs more quickly and more skilfully." Charan says it is

> neither a new layer of bureaucracy nor a means to wrest power from the functional organizations. Rather, a core of 12 or so key players meet weekly to monitor the performance of the development process, identify barriers, and devise ways to remove them. One of the networks's first steps was to create an investment-management function responsible for specifying which projects get done, in what order and how quickly—in ways that meet the needs of customers and countries but that also reflect corporate goals and strategies.[9]

Mobilizing the network

Mobilizing the network involves cashing in the benefits of the first two stages where the people who have got what you want and those who need what you have are identified. However, this is also where staff, who were used to being compliant in the command and control hierarchy, need to become more assertive. The critical culture shift here is in finding resources rather than being handed resources. One key to this, successful practitioners discover, is in creating excellent information flows throughout the organization.

For example, Digital's VAX Notes computer-conferencing system enabled staff to find resources, skills, and knowledge anywhere in the world. Some major consultancies, such as Price WaterhouseCoopers and Andersen Consulting, also leverage their organizational knowledge using similar systems. ABB has a well-developed information system called Abacus, which is designed to provide the executive committee with the information it needs to make "globally sensitive" decisions.

SECOND-LEVEL ORGANIZATIONAL PROCESSES

Crossing Boundaries

Boundary crossing takes place at a number of levels, not only the physical boundaries of departments or operating units but also the psychological limitations and status boundaries. These status boundaries are as important as the psychological ones, for they provide staff with the confidence to cross-corporate boundaries and operate on unfamiliar territory.

The ability to do this within an organization prepares people for doing it between organizations in the course of forming and operating partnerships and alliances. For example, many of the alliances discussed in this book involved organizations operating in different countries and cultures. Repeatedly, mastering the cultural differences was a key to making these alliances work smoothly. Yet, achieving this requires an ability to understand other cultures, points of view, and ways of working. It involves crossing many of these "softer" kinds of boundaries that are discussed in this chapter. The issues involved with cultural mismatches will be dealt with in more detail in Chapter 10.

Exchange and Reciprocity

This is an understanding of the processes of cooperation. Successful network organizations work through negotiation and persuasion rather than instructions and orders. In ABB, for example, business area managers have no power of "hire and fire" over staff in the 1,300 operating organizations; that is a power reserved to the operating organizations' chief executives. They must work through persuasion and agreed target setting. At Digital, the culture expected people to share information proactively with others, and this is underpinned with technology that promotes active information sharing.

Alliance Building and Conflict Management

Much of the progress made in network organizations comes from the creation of internal alliances. This requires ability to create not only a sense of but actual common vision among employees, to be able to negotiate and resolve conflicts relating to different objectives and means of achieving these objectives, as well as collective problem solving in order to find ways of achieving different objectives simultaneously.

Stability and long-term constancy require a strong hand at the helm. Organizations that had mastered these skills within their own organization were in a strong position to deploy the same skills in forming and managing alliances. They often came to an alliance situation better understanding the dynamics of partnership organizations than managers from command and control hierarchies did.

Communication Skills

In listing this as one of the five processes, it is not only in terms of the need to communicate information in network organizations but also of the skills needed to communicate information effectively. There is a significant knot of both culture and competence issues tied up in this problem. To begin with, the culture must encourage, even mandate, people to share informa-tion. Second, it must provide them with the competencies to do so. This could include skills as basic as learning to exchange information by tele-phone with people in other parts of the world. At a more sophisticated level, it involves developing competencies in a wide range of information-shar-ing technologies, including electronic mail, computer-conferencing, and video-conferencing. Yet, even in the network organizations, managers and staff are often left to acquire and develop many of these skills on their own initiatives with little or no formal training.

Personnel Management

Since organizational networking inherently contains conflicting de-mands and priorities, it can produce work overloads and stress. Staff work in a demanding environment in which they must review and assimilate a vast amount of information as a result of the information sharing culture. Staff in networking organizations will need to understand their own reac-tions to and strategies for coping with stress.

There is a danger in being overprescriptive about the skills that managers need in an organization that operates as a network of one design or another and fosters partnership. It does seem, however, that staff at all levels need to adopt attitudes and behaviors that are radically different from those encour-aged in a hierarchal command and control organization.

NOTES

1. W. L. Gore (1985), "The Lattice Organisation: A Philosophy of Enter-prise," *Networking Journal* 1 (1) (Spring/Summer): 24–27.

2. C. Handy (1989), *The Age of Unreason* (London: Arrow Books); C. Handy (1992), "Balancing Corporate Power," *Harvard Business Review* 70 (6): 59–72; C. Handy (1994), *The Empty Raincoat* (London: Hutchinson).

3. See Handy (1989), *The Age of Unreason.*

4. J. Lipnack and J. Stamps (1995), *The Teamnet Factor* (Essex Junction, VT: Oliver Wright Publications).

5. Ibid.

6. Ibid.

7. R. Charan (1991), "How Networks Reshape Organization—For Results," *Harvard Business Review* 69 (5):105.

8. Ibid.

9. Ibid., p. 106.

BUILDING ALLIANCES: THE TECHNOLOGICAL ENABLERS

THE ROLE OF INFORMATION TECHNOLOGY

Information technology has played some role in many alliances and outsourcing arrangements. However, the importance of IT in alliances varies dramatically from one situation to another. In an organization such as Texas Instruments, for example, IT plays a role at several different levels in building links between alliance partners. Texas Instruments uses IT in creative ways to add value to many of the partnerships it creates. On the other hand, IT is not a critical success factor (although it is a useful enabler) in the alliance between Royal Bank of Scotland and Banco Santander.

IT is playing an important role at two levels. First, it plays a part in leveraging the core competencies of the partners in an alliance. Second, it facilitates communications and information exchange and, in fewer cases, adds value to the alliance.

IT and Core Competencies

Apart from the question of using technology to enable links between alliance partners, IT has an important role in underpinning and developing the core competencies that often form the foundation of solid alliance partnership and plays this role in two ways.

First, it facilitates new business processes that an organization uses to leverage the full benefits from its competencies. A good example of this is the spare parts European systems that New Holland Logistics implemented in its depots. Importantly, the systems facilities new processes were designed as part of a business reengineering exercise. These processes speed fulfilment of customer orders while reducing stock holding by moving New Holland Logistics toward what it calls a "virtual warehouse" in which an order from anywhere in Europe can be filled from any depot, transparently to the user. The virtual warehouse concept is, in fact, a neat way of encapsulating the logistics and service competencies at the heart of New Holland Logistics.

Second, IT provides a powerful tool to promote organizational learning, the process that is often at the heart of developing new or existing competencies. ITs are used both to assemble and analyze information and to disseminate it through the organization. The use of IT both to compile and analyze raw data and to enable people to access it has a qualitative effect.

Again, an example to illustrate this point was Digital Equipment's VAX Notes computer-conferencing system that contained a vast amount of information—about 6,500 conferences in which Digital's 65,000 staff participated. These conferences provided an invaluable archive of organizational knowledge that enhanced Digital's core competencies as well as provided a means of leveraging that knowledge in order to serve customers. In this case, VAX Notes provided both the means by which knowledge can be collected and the tool that encourages Digital's staff to share their knowledge with others in the organization.

There are particular imperatives if technology is to be used to enhance and reinforce core competencies. The technology needs to enable the users to leverage not only their values but also their personal skills to the greatest possible extent. It must capture the maximum complexity possible in repeatable solutions. There may also be a need to change the underlying processes focusing on the value-added content. There are echoes of these ideas in the New Holland and Digital examples mentioned before. Systems such as these also provide technological handcuffs for those staff whose own skills add most to the organization's competencies.

For example, management consultants accessing the knowledge database at Price WaterhouseCoopers know it would be much harder to work outside the organization without that resource available. Developing IT systems enhances core competencies. While being simple to access, the technology's innards must be sufficiently complicated and well protected, making it nonportable and unique so that loss of access to it will genuinely inhibit essential individuals from leaving.

However, only a minority of organizations are using IT extensively and creatively to enhance and exploit their core competencies. Too often, IT is applied in a fragmentary way to operations without enough thought as to its strategic possibilities. Where this is the case, senior managers need to consider IT's present role and develop a new mission for it.

IT and Strategic Alliances

Every alliance involves sharing information and the most successful use IT to share information effectively. In the early 1990s Konsynski and McFarlan saw "reciprocal skills in information technology" as an important issue in "information partnering." They suggested that competence in areas such as telecommunications, database design, and programming must be "reasonably sophisticated" in all partners, and "at a very high level in the partner that is playing a leadership role in developing the information platform." Konsynski and McFarlan argued that "minimally, all participant companies should be able to manage communications networks, have very high standards of internal quality control, at least with respect to data handling, and be accustomed to working with very large databases." They noted that "many companies that have initiated electronic data interchange agreements have been shocked to find partners unable to assimilate even modest data technologies and applications."[1]

The debate is moving on and the more recent research has focused on the relationship between different types of partnership and a range of technological enablers. Henderson argues that the kind of information used and the most appropriate technological enablers will be determined in part by the nature of the alliance. For example, Henderson saw the main focus on information being rather different depending on whether the alliance is a simple market exchange (where information centers around prices and trends), a performance contract (where information focuses on "outcome metrics"), a specialized relationship (where information measuring, for example, shared processes is often important) or a strategic partnership (where key information often centers on sharing proprietary knowledge).[2]

Similarly, the kinds of technology enablers used are influenced by the nature of the relationship. Henderson cites the use of order-entry systems and EDI in market exchanges, management support systems in performance contracts, shared files in specialized relationships, and systems to underpin new products and processes in strategic partnerships.[3] Of course, Henderson is only citing examples but they underline the different kinds of relationships between alliances and technology enablers that are possible.

In the previously mentioned alliances, technology often played an important role in building information links between the partners, and only occasionally a critical role. Generally more important were the strategic, cultural, and human resource elements of the alliance. In the Royal Bank of Scotland/Banco Santander alliance, for example, the two partners exchange information by telephone, e-mail, and fax. They also occasionally use videoconferencing to hold meetings involving managers in the United Kingdom and Spain. However, these are no substitute for face-to-face meetings. Technology is no substitute for building an alliance based on a sound business strategy and solid human relationships. Its role is simply that of "enabler."

There was a similar picture in the Rover/Honda alliance. Sophisticated information technologies played little part in the success of the alliance. However, at the time that the alliance was formed and started to develop, the main technology used to aid communication was the fax machine. The other technology that Rover and Honda found useful was the printing whiteboard. This allowed the Japanese to note their action points down one side and the British down the other side of the board as the meeting progressed. They both went away from a meeting with a printed version of what each had to do.

In these and other cases, easily accessible technologies such as e-mail and fax are the essential enablers of the alliance. It is possible to argue that these alliances would function less efficiently or effectively without these technologies, but it is stretching the point to suggest that they underpin the success of the alliance.

However, should alliances be looking to leverage more value out of the technologies that are now available? There are both danger and opportunity in this search. The danger is that the alliance becomes too focused on the technologies used to make it work at the expense of the critical success factors of the alliance:

- The strategic intent of the partners;
- The means of achieving the business objectives; and
- The creation of organizational learning from the alliance.

The purpose of using technology is to enable these and other activities, not to dominate them.

Nevertheless, there is a case for suggesting that some alliances do not look widely enough when searching for technological enablers to support their partnership activities. For example, more significant than the useful but essential low-level stories of IT in use previously mentioned, there are a few examples of technology being used in alliances to provide extra competitive edge, and this potential should not be ignored. For example, Texas Instruments made its highly sophisticated (and expensive) proprietary computer-aided design software available to customers such as Ericsson, Apple Computer, and IBM who wish to work in partnership to design application-specific integrated circuits.

Another organization that made its proprietary software available to business partners was Eurodollar, a car rental organization. For some major customers, Eurodollar provided a car-booking screen from its own software as a window in customers' own computer systems. These two examples show how thinking "out of the box" can enable an organization to use technologies in imaginative ways that build partnership links. They are also good examples of organizations creating effective "technological fit" with their business partners.

In general, creating a technological fit between partners in an alliance should not be a major issue. In some technologies, for example, e-mail and EDI, there has been considerable progress toward standards in the past few years. This makes the creation of interenterprise information links generally a technologically easier process than when Konsynski and McFarlan were developing their ideas on information partnerships.[4] Where issues of "technological fit" exist, they tend to disappear as technological standards develop.

In general, most organizations focus on only a limited range of technologies as enablers of partnership information links. However, it is also clear that there is a much wider range of technologies that could be used as enablers in alliances. Some of these, along with their alliance enabling potential, are discussed in the following section.

PARTNERSHIP ENABLERS: TECHNOLOGIES TO CONSIDER

It is very difficult to draw any sensible boundaries around which technologies might be used as an "enabler" in a partnership or alliance, partly because the purposes of alliances are so varied and partly because the range and scope of technologies is so great. The following list, which is supported by some examples and descriptions, is primarily for nontechnical managers; IT specialists will find this familiar territory.

Application Software

By sharing proprietary application software, an organization can add value to its partnership with an important customer.

Automatic Teller Machines (ATMs)

Familiar in the walls of banks, these are a practical example of how banks cooperate to compete. By sharing ATM networks, the banks provide a more extensive network at a lower capital investment cost.

Bar Code

Familiar at the supermarket checkout, the bar code is also an effective way of quickly transmitting information between business partners. For example, in the United States parts suppliers for Ford attach bar codes to the side of packaging. This means that parts can be processed through Ford warehouses without any accompanying paper documentation.

Client/Server Computing

A computer system splits an application into parts that are executed in different places. In practice, this often means that clients in different places access central files from a server. Client/server provides a useful model for distributed computing and for creating networks that link different locations that can be in different enterprises. Although the model is simple, the tasks of making it work in practice can be complex with a host of issues, including the security and integrity of data, which must be resolved.

Computerized Reservation Systems

This is an example of how a mixture of network and database technologies can create a powerful competitive tool shared by partners. Major computerized reservation systems, such as Galileo and Amadeus, are shared by alliances of airlines, hotels, and car rental organizations that win business from customers who purchase a combination of all services.

Databases

Sharing information from databases seems to be one of the major growth areas for alliances. There are several ways of using them. For example,

Texas Instruments allows its distributors to access a database of up-to-date price and stock information about microchips. In this way, the distributors can prepare quotations more quickly for their own clients. There is considerable potential for alliance partners to build share databases of information containing a wide range of different data such as customers, products, patent, quality, and so on.

Electronic Data Interchange (EDI)

This is direct computer-to-computer exchange of information for a wide range of transactions including purchasing, distribution, accounts payable and receivable, and increasingly, a wider range of information including stock control and quality. The use of an EDI has grown rapidly in the past decade, stimulated partly by the emergence of the United Nations sponsored EDIFACT standard, and partly by the insistence of many large manufacturers that suppliers exchange information using an EDI. For example, ABB's Abacus management information reporting system is based on an EDI. Abacus allows information on performance standards to be presented in a common and structured way throughout the group.

E-Mail

This relates to software and communications technologies that enable messages and computer files to be transmitted from one computer to another. The widespread use of the X.400 standard means that previously incompatible e-mail systems are now able to interconnect. E-mail will probably become, after the telephone, the most important interenterprise communication technology in the next decade (as well, of course, an intraenterprise technology). The most wanted features in e-mail are:

- Directories to make accessing other users and services easier: Users see the implementation of X.500, which provides A worldwide "white pages" of user contacts, as "crucial." X.500 holds more than just e-mail addresses. It is, effectively, an enterprise-distributed database and client/server system that can also hold such organizational information as fax and telephone numbers, postal addresses, annual reports, and even personnel files.
- Mobile e-mail functionality: This demand is stimulated by the more than 20 percent of workers who are mobile at some time, including "corridor cruisers" such as production managers. The most

prevalent mobile mode is the user with a laptop/notebook computer servicing two or more locations, such as work and home.

- Rules and agents: Many users are already concerned about the growth of "junk e-mail." However, as legitimate e-mail grows, users will need effective filters such as rules and agents so that productivity improvements made possible by e-mail do not disappear through a rise in the work needed to manage it.

- Improved bulletin boards: These offer the ability to post broadcast messages without cluttering up e-mail in-boxes or creating information overload.

Groupware

Groupware is an omnibus term for a combination of technologies that enable people to work more effectively in teams. Although there are several different taxonomies of groupware, the term is generally reckoned to include mail and messaging systems (generally based in some form of e-mail), information sharing and workspace (similar to Lotus Notes and other systems such as VAX Notes), workflows software used to pass electronic documents and information through a business process to different people, and group decision support systems (which help a team of people to make decisions).

Networks

"Networks" is the catch-all term for the telecommunications highway over which information transmitted from a wide range of devices travels. Local area networks (LANs) connect devices in close proximity to one another, generally in the same building. Wide area networks (WANs), either public or private, connect devices over a large area, conceivably the whole planet. "Bridges," "routers," and "gateways," can connect both kinds of networks. A special type of network that provides an extra service in addition to basic transmission capacity, for example, EDI or e-mail, is called a value-added network.

Open Systems

Open computer systems are those that are independent of vendors' own standards and that promote interconnection and interoperability. The rise of open systems during the 1990s, including adoption of the concept by major computer industry players such as IBM and Unisys, has eased some of the problems of linking systems between organizations. However, there are still many other issues, for example, in sharing or combining information from databases, which often complicate the task of sharing information between alliance partners.

Teleconferencing

Teleconferencing is not a substitute for all face-to-face meetings but it is likely to grow as it is recognized as an effective way to communicate between alliance partners, as well as internally with other parts of the same organization, its current main use. There are three main categories of teleconferencing:

- Audio and audiographic conferencing: At its simplest level, this is a conference call; at a more sophisticated level, a conference call backup on which the participants can work at the same time on text or graphics interactively at their different locations.

- Interactive videoconferencing: This enables participants in a meeting held at two or more locations to see and speak to one another. Videoconferencing technology is moving into its third generation. The first consisted of specially equipped videoconferencing studios. The second, now growing, is the "rollabout," a videoconferencing unit that can be pushed from office to office and plugged into the phone lines. The third generation, now entering the marketplace, is desktop to desktop videoconferencing where sound and vision are delivered through a personal computer or workstation.

- Business television: This is a satellite-delivered private television service in which a program is initiated at one location and broadcast to multiple reception sites. In theory, viewers can raise questions with the main speaker by telephone. In practice, the amount of interaction in business television is limited.

As mentioned in Chapter 1, there are six building blocks needed to help an organization become lean. These have now all been covered. In the next few chapters we will look at some of the negative issues associated with the outsourcing process and the alternatives that an organization may have, as well as looking at the impact of cultural mismatches for both alliances and outsourcing.

NOTES

1. B. R. Konsynski and F. W. McFarlan (1990), "Information Partnerships—Shared Data, Shared Scale," *Harvard Business Review* 68 (5): 114–120.

2. J. C. Henderson (1990), "Plugging into Strategic Partnerships: The Critical Connection," *Sloan Management Review* 31 (3):7–18.

3. Ibid.

4. Konsynski and McFarlan (1990), "Information Partnerships."

8

DISADVANTAGES OF OUTSOURCING AND THE ALTERNATIVES

This chapter discusses some of the negative aspects of outsourcing and some alternative approaches that might be taken by an organization. The problems that have been reported when organizations start down the outsourcing path have stemmed from a variety of causes, partly determined by why outsourcing was chosen, and partly by how it was put into effect. If organizations have failed to solve a problem themselves and as a solution transferred it elsewhere, they have tended to find that it has remained difficult. Meyer suggests that in some cases outsourcing is simply a matter of paying someone else to experience the pain of managing a dysfunctional function, rather than trying to figure out how to make the function healthy again.[1] This is a costly form of escapism that sacrifices a valuable component of business strategy for short-term convenience.

There are other difficulties that have resulted from inadequate or faulty decision making (that is, choosing the wrong activity to outsource) or poor preparation (entering an incomplete contract). These problems will be grouped together not by their cause but by their effect.

Contractual difficulties cover a range of predicaments. At the most extreme have been legal disputes with the current or ex-contractor, or with a third-party client. Disagreements with contractors can occur over such things as the terms of the contract (whether they are being met, whether additional monies should be paid, over the ownership of information, and so on). These can reach a point where the client or contractor wishes to cancel the arrangement. Even when it is accepted that the contract terms are being met, clients may wish to exit from contracts because of their deleterious effects, or simply to alter direction or regain flexibility. For example, a U.S. mining company, Freeport McMoran, canceled a ten-year U$200 million deal with EDS because Freeport McMoran wanted to change technology.

Perhaps more worrisome for clients are lawsuits, brought by end users in situations where the client thought he had passed responsibility on to the contractor. One could envisage a variety of situations where claims could be made, for example, food poisoning by a catering contractor or maladministration by a relocation agency. To avoid these difficulties, careful monitoring of the contractor's performance against the contract is necessary. Some organizations have felt that this has spawned a new bureaucracy and tied up managerial time.

Szymankiewicz reports a survey that shows that only 36 percent of logistics managers are satisfied with contractor management.[2] Problems identified include:

- A complete failure to perform, for example, saw an organization bring an entire logistics operation back in house after a near breakdown of the service;[3]

- Poorer service performance than anticipated, or inability to meet expectations of improvement. An example of this is where graduate recruitment was outsourced, but the standard of candidates referred for final interview was unsatisfactory;

- A lack of contractor innovation or creativity reported in an IT survey, where 40 percent of the sample were dissatisfied.[4] Even outside high technology areas, there have been similar complaints;[5]

- The disadvantage of being tied to arrangements that turn out to be inflexible and cannot respond to changing business circumstances, especially deteriorating conditions. More often, inflexibility is a problem in areas where the technology is immature (particularly true in IT) and changing fast. This difficulty can be exaggerated if a long contract has been entered into. The client can fall behind in the market if the contractor does not enhance its technology. For example, Victor Products, a U.S. automotive parts supplier, found itself with outdated logistics technology and lost market share as a result.[6] Or the client who signed a ten-year contract for mainframe services that meant that when migration to client/server technology occurred it was at a higher cost than justified;[7] and

- Failure to understand the complexity of the task or its connections to other systems. A United Kingdom food company is reported to have had these difficulties with a new automation system because the links to purchasing and inventory control were not made.[8]

These problems are exacerbated by lost expertise with the result that managing the contractors is extremely difficult. This has happened because insufficient capability has been left behind on transfer and/or the responsibility has been switched from the original service provider to the purchasing department. For example, BUPA had to reappoint one of its fleet managers to manage an external contract because of an inability to handle day-to-day operations without specialist support.[9]

The opposite problem can occur if there is residual control over the contract from the previous managers who have ideas of the standards they expect and are frustrated with the delivery by the contractor. This may result from false expectations of what the contract is intended to provide, due to ignorance of the standards set. This can be even truer for user groups who generally are very demanding of service irrespective of cost and may expect a level of service that was never provided in house. Even without cost issues, end users may have objections to dealing with third parties whose response may well be conditioned by contractual terms, particularly where the specification is sufficient to meet their needs. For example, some specialist IT users may find that the contract does not cover aspects of their work and that the contractor support is less amenable or competent than previously. This type of problem arises if the users and contract managers are not party to the terms of the deal. It is particularly aggravating to clients if the rationale behind outsourcing was to make the contractor responsible for managing uncertainty and solving problems. One CEO responded, "They [complained] about IT before outsourcing, they [complain] now—but at least it's costing me a lot less."[10]

Employee difficulties tend to occur at the time of contract transfer but can be more persistent. The types of issues that have arisen include: terms of transfer; selection for transfer; consultation and negotiation particularly with trade unions; subsequent resourcing problems; and comparison of terms and conditions between those affected. These issues will be dealt with in more detail later, but here we may note that, whether in applying Transfer of Undertakings (TUPE) in the United Kingdom or in the quite different legal environment of the United States, legal disputes have occurred. In particular there have been notable cases concerning employee rights to consultation over a transfer, the transfer terms, and selection procedures. In the United States there have been lawsuits involving ex-Kodak employees and ex-Blue Cross/Blue Shield employees in transfers to DEC and EDS respectively. The employees were successful in the latter case to the tune of U$7 million.

Unexpected costs may arise because of a failure to analyze fully precontracted-out services and costs, making a poor estimate of the initial contract price. Moreover, the existing service may not have been fully documented in the contract. Even meeting intended services may involve extra charges. One organization found it was paying more in excess charges than in its fixed monthly price because the contract was inadequately drawn up. This is particularly true if the aim is to ensure flexibility in delivery. These costs can escalate if the implications of change were not recognized in the contract; for example, a change of spreadsheet package may seem trivial to the client but is a cost to the contractor who will pass it on. Finally, if the contractor does not meet user needs, costs may arise when users bypass the contract through the development of their own systems or arrangements. Beyond the service aspects, it may be that the costs of monitoring the contract and managing its control features have not been taken into account.

Another cost implication that organizations seem to neglect is that of overhead allocation. If an activity is outsourced, it will no longer bear its share of overhead (unless this is built into the contract). Consequently, the remaining services have to shoulder a bigger burden, worsening their cost position and making them candidates for contracting out.

Szymankiewicz suggests that the lesson—that contracting out involves different management skills and is not an abrogation of management responsibility—is one that is being painfully learned.[11] The type of skills that may be lacking include: third-party negotiation skills; contract management; interpersonal skills; inability to manage differences (for example, between own and contractor employees); people management skills (for example, developing team spirit in a group with a variety of employment relationships); and integration skills to manage services coming from several sources.

Poor communication between the parties is often a significant issue and tends to be worse if activities or management is dispersed, for example, if contractor management is off site. Problems can occur through such things as:

The client failing to inform/consult internal users of implications of change;

Contractor not advising client of difficulties or opportunities;

Client not telling contractor of revised specifications;

Failure to delineate the boundaries between contractor and client responsibilities;

Dismantling management information systems, thereby making it harder to inform senior management of contractor performance; and

Problems with the security or confidentiality of information.

Some commentators on the contracting out of services and alliances have gone beyond these complaints to make a fundamental case against outsourcing, certainly once it goes further than the clearly peripheral activities. Their principal objection is the loss of competitive advantage that may occur. As illustrated in Figure 8.1, they see a downward spiral, starting with underinvestment due to an overemphasis on cost cutting, and leading ultimately to a reduced capacity to innovate. This sequence is exaggerated where a risk-averse management is too concerned with short-term financial performance and is not sufficiently aware of the invisible assets of the organization or even of how the business works.

A consequence may be that more and more is outsourced or greater and greater reliance is made on partners. The result, it is claimed by some, is in-

Figure 8.1
Losing Competitiveness Through Outsourcing

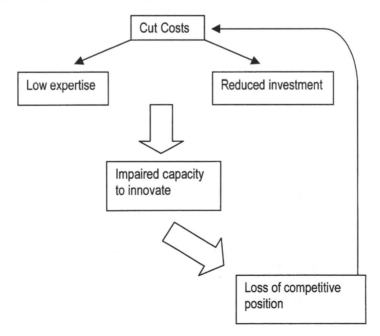

sufficient internal investment and the passing of knowledge and expertise to the supplier who may be able to seize the initiative. This is especially dangerous if the activity is close to important business processes, even if they were regarded as noncore. Illustrating the point is the way some Japanese technology grew on the back of supply contracts from U.S. manufacturers, such as in developing the ability to produce transistor radios.[12]

Proponents of this view believe that the loss felt by organizations through outsourcing is particularly keenly felt in the loss of skills and expertise of staff. Even if not all the key employees leave, the insecurity it creates in the rest of the workforce has to be faced. It means that the organization is less able to do things itself, its ability to change or develop is reduced, and its capacity to reinvigorate itself is damaged if experienced staff have gone. Staff fear that the result will be a hollowed-out organization. Instead, staff have an inclusive employment model in mind, where all are equally committed to the success of the enterprise. Staff believe long-term employment relationships, rather than commercial ones, can accomplish only this when skill development and organizational learning are enhanced.

Without going so far, there are organizations and managers who have pragmatically weighed the pros and cons and are left with doubts as to the benefits of outsourcing. For example, in Szymankiewicz's survey of logistics managers cited service, flexibility, cost, and control as the principal reasons why third-party management was rejected.[13]

Some managers believed that there is a fundamental difference of outlook between the contractor (wishing to maximize profit) and the client (aiming to minimize cost). This distinction means that there never can be a true partnership between client and contractor, and that talk of "strategic alliances" between the two is pie-in-the-sky dreaming. For example, contractors' account managers may be rewarded for increasing their profits by maximizing income from a contract through charging additional fees, rather than by making savings of benefit to the supplier. Instead, the client can develop a dependency on the contractor, who has no ultimate responsibility or liability. It conjures up a picture of the client being at the mercy of the contractor. Clients can find they are being exploited over costs and service, or worse, responsible for liabilities that they did not expect.

This is a problem that some believe gets worse over the duration of the contract. Willcocks and Choi suggest that what often compromises such arrangements in practice is asymmetrical resources, dependence, and power relations developing over time in favor of the vendor.[14] The dependence increases because the client's ability to manage the contract declines, as expertise is lost—the point made previously by the opponents of outsourcing.

Some fear that business performance will suffer. This could be through becoming locked into an inflexible contract, being unable to respond quickly to change, being unable to benefit from cost or technological improvements, and suffering in both the quality of service delivery and bottom line profits. One cause of the deterioration in customer relations is the loss of control over the important interface between supplier and recipient. In passing it to a third party, the organization no longer has direct responsibility. For example, Sony took the view that distribution drivers are the "ambassadors" of the company and should be employed by them.[15]

More fundamentally, there is the fear that outsourcing will bring a loss of competitive edge, not necessarily through poorer performance, but because the corporate offer becomes indistinguishable from that of competitors. Another way of stating this is to say that it is more difficult to sustain the brand image under these circumstances. The organization may be represented by the contractor with the latter's livery, uniform, or logo, thereby belittling the corporate contribution. The alternative is that actions performed by contractors are seen as being wholly the responsibility of the client if the contractor is at fault.

Performance can suffer through the exclusion of those contracted out from full participation in the enterprise. Contractors are not part of the organizational "cultural web" of understanding and shared experience.[16] In tangible terms, this may mean that in the longer term the organization suffers through poor communication, impaired coordination, reduced responsiveness, limited flexibility to adjust, and inferior learning capacity. If contractors are not "part of the loop" they will be less informed; they will be more likely to act autonomously; they have other priorities than the success of the client's business.

There is also loss of control over employee selection and deployment. Though it can be specified in the contract who the key contractor employees should be, in general, resource management is passed to the contractor. Contractors may not provide the same continuity of personnel, again because they have other interests to protect. Nor should it be assumed that the quality of staffing would improve through outsourcing, particularly if a TUPE occurs. Earl quotes one manager saying "all we did was transfer our weaker staff, and then we had to deal with them all over again."[17] Managers may also be trapped into requiring increasingly outdated skills to manage old systems and be unable to provide the expected technological leadership.

Another important issue is the contention—that may or may not be supported by evidence—that better cost and/or service can be provided in, house. This has been the result of many compulsory competitive tendering (CCT) exercises where in-house bids have proved lower than those from external sources. Indeed, it has provoked the complaint from contractors that too few invitations to tender are serious outsourcing exercises, and led the United Kingdom government, for example, to review the CCT process to identify bias against the private sector. Some in the private sector have similarly tested their services by comparison with outside suppliers.

In large organizations, internal suppliers can themselves achieve important economies of scale and exploit considerable buying power. In all sizes of organization, in-house managers know their customers and the context within which they operate much better than outsiders. They can argue the advantage of familiarity and inclusion in the wider formal and informal business processes, as well as perceived increase in flexibility of response. They can argue they are committed to the purpose of the enterprise, not to the success of another organization, and that they do not have to make a profit. There are also the short-term costs of change, as well as the cost of managing the contract to consider. For this reason, some organizations put a benefit threshold (for example, 20 percent cheaper) before considering changing to an outside supplier. It can be claimed that using one's own staff will deliver a better, cheaper product.

ALTERNATIVES TO OUTSOURCING

The concerns described in the previous section may cause managers to pause before proceeding to outsource work. Some may believe that difficulties can be avoided by better contractor performance because of improving the contracting process. Others may see these problems as an argument to be careful about the activities that should be outsourced to prevent important processes or competencies from being damaged.

Outsourcing can be considered alongside a number of alternative mechanisms. These can be: changes to the overall shape and size of the organization; introduction of more flexible work arrangements; and alteration to the means of structuring service provision. Changes can be made to the overall structure of the organization that allow it to meet the same objectives as outsourcing. As Table 8.1 illustrates, reducing the size of the workforce can achieve cost reduction. Devolving decision making, delayering, or in other ways simplifying structures may lead to better, quicker decision making, bringing about improvements in quality of performance. If a service is currently under-used, improved take-up may result from redesigning its organizational form. This may lead to the development of internal contracting.

Besides these changes, there are a number of initiatives that may be taken to improve the contribution of one's current workforce before one moves toward partial or complete externalization. In the models proposed by

Table 8.1
Alternative Source of Service Improvement and Cost Reduction

Principal Motives	Decentralization	Outsourcing	Rationalization
Coast saving	X	X	X
Increased accountability	X		
Reduced overhead	X	X	X
Specialist service		X	
Quality improvement		X	
Improved service utilization	X	X	

Atkinson and Meager[18] and Handy,[19] not only is the peripheral workforce expected to be flexible, but the core group should also be prepared to alter work arrangements. Taken together, the following benefits can be derived from the employer's own workforce: optimization of supply input to meet demand requirement; acquisition of specialist skills; reduction of costs; and improvement in productivity. These advantages should be realized through functional flexibility, temporal flexibility, locational flexibility, and forms of numerical flexibility.

Functional flexibility should result in a more effective internal allocation of labor through better deployment. This is partly an organizational issue (freedom to move labor as required), partly a question of technological improvement, and partly one of training staff to be able to undertake a variety of tasks. The benefit is clearly one of improved productivity, but there is also an investment cost. Outsourcing may have been chosen precisely because management has not been prepared to make this investment, or has been unable to make the necessary changes themselves, perhaps because of employee opposition. It has then been left to the contractor to reorganize because his or her control over the workforce may be greater.

There is a great variety of different types of flexibility achieved through varying working hours. Temporal flexibility offers an advantage for the employee in that it can help meet domestic responsibilities or allow extra income to be earned. Employees often seek it. For example, the principal advantage is to obtain a better match between service or production schedules and employee input, sometimes at reduced cost. The choice of arrangement will reflect work patterns that may be standard or extremely variable.

Some forms of temporal flexibility are traditional overtime, shift working, and part-time working. Others are of more recent origin (at least to a significant extent) such as flextime, flexible working weeks, annual hours contracts, term-time contracts, and zero hours contracts. Employers can achieve some flexibility and reduced costs through locational flexibility. This involves using outworkers, homeworkers, and teleworkers. These arrangements are still relatively uncommon but may grow and are facilitated by technological improvement; by employee interest in meeting conflicting home and work demands, particularly in a tighter labor market; and by employer interest in cutting overhead costs or in achieving flexible deployment.

The employment of those on fixed period contracts or in temporary, seasonal, or casual employment can achieve numerical flexibility. The advantages found by employers include: matching staff to peaks in demand and short-term cover for holiday or sick leave, and to a lesser extent in cover for maternity leave, dealing with one-off tasks, providing specialist skills; and giving a trial for a permanent job. However, employers do not always see benefits. Their reservations in order of importance include the beliefs that temporary workers are less reliable than permanent ones, and they need in-house training.

Numerical flexibility can be extended further; agency or contractor labor is used to top off one's own workforce. It has grown in importance both in the number of agencies and in their self-reported workload.[20] As with temporary employees, they are found in both low- and high-skill occupations. Temporary employees are used to supplement labor in a catering operation and in plant maintenance, but there are also specialists used in, for example, information technology, where they are often self-employed consultants. The advantages and disadvantages of agency labor are the same as for temporary employees in general, though they are particularly useful to support activities (of declining or emerging importance) where internal resources are sufficient or where costs can be reduced because of lower agency pay rates.

Numerical flexibility can be realized completely through outsourcing because the contractor then bears the brunt of supplying appropriate levels of labor to meet work requirements. This may occur even if the management of the work is retained in-house with the contractor responsible solely, and fully, for resourcing. Where specialist skills are required, for example, in pension/superannuation administration, it may have the advantage over using supplementary labor from an agency as better quality of input is acquired. Agencies may not be able to provide trained labor at short notice. In outsourcing, contractors should be able to manage their workforce so that sufficient expertise is always available. In addition, as noted earlier, contractors should be able to achieve higher levels of temporal and locational flexibility.

The employment options may range from the use of own employees only (with varying degrees of flexibility of use), through supplementing them with agency staff, ultimately to contracting out the whole operation where only third-party staff are used.

RESTRUCTURING SERVICE PROVISION

Besides this variety of employment options, there are also various organizational steps that precede outsourcing that nevertheless go beyond the traditional deployment of employees. (see Figure 8.2).

The first variation is to set up an in-house service provider (also known as insourcing). This has the advantage of identifying clearly how much the work costs, particularly if activity-based costing is used. It establishes more clearly what the real demand for services is, if they are paid for as used. Moreover, with service level agreements, it allows more precise specification of what is expected of the provider by the user. Insourcing is, in other words, a move from soft contracting where controls are informal and social, to hard contracting where controls are formal and explicit.

Not surprising, insourcing is sometimes used as a precursor to full outsourcing, as it enables management to negotiate an appropriate contract through a better understanding of the costs and capability to evaluate bids. Alternatively, and more motivating for employees, in-house departments have been allowed to compete with external contractors. Some senior managers have used the threat of outsourcing quite consciously as a spur to improved performance and reduced costs, and thereby achieved savings that were previously unobtainable.[21] Under CCT, in-house bids have proved successful. However, it has been argued that this has often been at some cost in terms of wages (loss of bonuses rather than reduced base pay), job loss, and changes to working agreements to increase productivity.[22]

Figure 8.2
Organizational Deployment Options

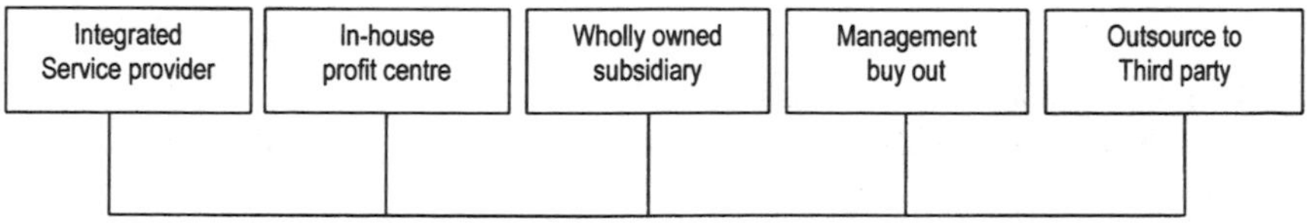

Integrated Service provider	In-house profit centre	Wholly owned subsidiary	Management buy out	Outsource to Third party

One issue that needs to be addressed is whether users must take the services of the in-house provider, or can they shop around externally. The former is a real test of the value of the service offered. Similarly, will the service provider equally be able to bring in work from outside? If not, it may be felt unfair to judge the performance of an internal operation against external competition, if the insider cannot act in a commercial way. However, some concern may be caused to management if this results in unwelcome exposure or risks to security and confidentiality. There are also concerns about managing conflicts of interest between internal and external customers.

To clarify this situation, some companies have taken the next step of setting up the service provider as a separate company, for example, Barclays Bank Operations, a wholly owned subsidiary providing IT services.[23] The decision to make this move is likely to be judged in terms of corporate benefits in management and finances. Whether it actually makes it easier to take on work from outside the organization is a moot point. If the service provider remains on company premises, as is likely, the risks are probably unchanged. We may be talking about perceptions regarding exposure that are part of an adjustment process from the traditional to the new arrangements.

Going one step further, the activity can be sold to one's own employed and established as a separate company. It then contracts to provide the service, but as a truly external operation. The differences between a management buyout (MBO) of an activity and outsourcing is purely one of ownership. Yet, it probably has a psychological as well as practical significance. MBOs allow continuity of service by people who are known to the client and who know its business. In that sense, it is closer to insourcing. The decision to sell the equipment and transfer the work is again a management judgment of the financial and corporate advantages. It also accepts that the new organization will want to extend its business elsewhere and this may in fact be the primary reason to allow separation.

An alternative model is the example of Philips that went into a joint venture with the Dutch software company BSO, to form a new company to provide software development for itself and externally. This gave Philips a secure supply for software and support from staff it knew, at a lower cost, and BSO received a wider customer base and expertise.[24]

NOTES

1. N. D. Meyer (1994), "A Sensible Approach to Outsourcing," *Information Systems Management* 11 (4) (Fall): 23–27.

2. J. Szymankiewicz (1993), "Contracting-out or Selling-out?" *Logistics Focus* (December): 2–5.

3. See M. Rock (1995), "In, Out, Shake It All About," *Director* (August): 34–54.

4. S. Smith (1996), "Better Out Than In," *Computer Weekly* (23 May): 30–31.

5. See Szymankiewicz (1993), "Contracting-Out."

6. R. A. Jacobs (1994), "The Invisible," *National Productivity Review* (Spring): 169–183.

7. See M. C. Lacity, R. Hirschheim, and L. Willcocks (1994), "Realizing Outsourcing Expectations," *Information Systems Management* 11 (4):7–18.

8. See M. C. Lacity, L. Willcocks, and D. F. Feeny (1996), "The Value of Selective Outsourcing," *Sloan Management Review* 37 (3):13–25.

9. See Rock (1995) "In, Out, Shake It All About."

10. See Lacity, Hirschheim, and Willcocks (1994), "Realizing Outsourcing Expectations," p. 13.

11. See Szymankiewicz (1993), "Contracting-Out."

12. See R. A. Bettis, S. P. Bradley, and G. Hamel (1992), Outsourcing and Industrial Decline," *Academy of Management Executive* 6 (1): 7–22.

13. Szymankiewicz (1993), "Contracting-Out."

14. L. Willcocks and Chong Ju Choi (1995), "Co-operative Partnership and 'Total' IT Outsourcing," *European Management Journal* 13 (1):67–78.

15. Business Europe (1993), "Pros and Cons of Third-Party Distribution," *Business Europe* (December): 7.

16. See G. Johnson (1987), *Strategic Change and the Management Process* (Oxford: Blackwell Business).

17. M. J. Earl (1996), "The Risks of Outsourcing IT," *Sloan Management Review* 37 (3) (Spring): 28.

18. See J. Atkinson and N. Meager (1986), *New Forms of Work* Report 121, IMS.

19. C. Handy (1989), *The Age of Unreason* (London: Arrow Books).

20. See Atkinson and Meager (1986), *New Forms of Work.*

21. Lacity, Willcocks, and Feeny (1996), "The Value of Selective Outsourcing."

22. See T. Colling (1993), "Contracting Public Services: The Management of Compulsory Competitive Tendering in Two County Councils," *HRM Journal* 3 (4):1–16; Industrial Relations Services (1995a), "Contracting-Out and Contracting-In Covered by TUPE," *IRS Employment Review* 515 (February): 8–13; and Industrial Relations Services (1995b), "EOC Highlights the Gender Impact of Compulsory Competitive Tendering," *IRS Employment Review* 515 (June): 14–16.

23. B. Rothery and I. Robertson (1995), *The Truth about Outsourcing* (Aldershot: Gower).

24. See Willcocks and Chong (1995), "Cooperative Partnership."

9

ALLIANCES AND OUTSOURCING IN THE PUBLIC SECTOR: PUBLIC MONEY AND PROBITY

"Probity"—What exactly do we mean when using this word? Public administration in many countries is being transformed by the use of contract or contractual models for the ordering of public resources. One aspect of this that has received increasing attention is the "probity" of the tendering processes. The courts, auditors-general, royal commissions, and various other government and private "watch-dog" bodies and the media have all scrutinized tendering processes and in some cases highlighted probity concerns.

Some have claimed that accountants and lawyers have hijacked the word "probity" in recent times. The word has a perfectly clear meaning in common usage. Probity is defined in various dictionaries as "moral excellence, integrity, uprightness, conscientiousness, honesty, sincerity, and as confirmed integrity." In this chapter when we use the word probity within the context of competitive tendering and contracting (CCT), we are referring to "procedural integrity"; that is, that all processes and procedures within the tender will sustain external or independent scrutiny. Some further definitions to this discussion are:

Probity plan: sets out the processes and procedures to be followed by the organization at each phase of the tendering process.

Probity adviser: works with the government body from the beginning of the tendering process to develop and implement the probity plan. The probity adviser should be independent, professional, and commercially competent. The probity adviser will need to have a good understanding of administrative and contract law as well as an awareness of government processes. The probity adviser will typically have an ongoing role (often day to day on large projects) throughout the tendering process, ensuring: adherence to the probity plan, or modification of the probity plan, where appropriate; that individual probity issues are resolved in accordance with probity objectives; that staff involved in tender assessment are appropriately trained and monitored; and that assessment of tender bids is consistent with published tender documentation.

Probity auditor: verifies that the probity plan has been followed. This will usually involve the probity auditor reviewing the relevant documentation after the event and highlighting any noncompliance.

Due diligence: in the context of tendering, the term commonly used to describe the investigation of bidders to ensure both financial security and the integrity of the organization itself. Such a due diligence may include some, or possibly all, of the following lines of investigation: corporation regulatory bodies' searches; business risk analysis; financial stability analysis; litigation searches; bankruptcy searches; credit reference checks; and reference checking. Appendix A contains an example of a typical bidder due diligence checklist.

PROBITY IN GOVERNMENT TENDERING

Three aspects underpin probity (or procedural integrity) in the context of government tendering:

1. The quality of, and adherence to, the funding allocation or tender documentation;
2. The processes to ensure that there is objective and consistent assessment at each phase by appropriately qualified and trained assessors; and
3. Decision making in accordance with legislative or regulatory powers and consistent with four administrative legal principles: only take into account relevant matters; not apply an inflexible policy or rule; not act under the dictation of another person; and not exercise the power for an improper purpose.

Common Probity Objectives

The main objectives for probity when public money is being spent on alliances or outsourcing are: to ensure integrity in all evaluation and selection processes; to ensure all respondents are assessed objectively and consistently and in accordance with the published documentation; to ensure all confidential information is secured; to address any potential, perceived, or actual conflicts of interest; and to promote defensibility of process.

Two Main Limbs—Process and Bidder Investigation

In the context of tendering for major government tendering, probity has two main limbs: the integrity of the processes involved in the evaluation and selection of a successful bidder; and bidder checking/investigation or "due diligence."

Why the Concern with Probity?

Insofar as you are regarded as decision makers in the process, your role will be scrutinized from a probity perspective. There are a number of reasons for the concern with probity including: increased concern with ethics in public life and accountability; increased watchdog/regulator scrutiny; increased media scrutiny; bidder confidence; market confidence; public confidence; distraction from the formal tendering process while defending processes can be very time consuming, costly, and personally destructive for those involved; and defensibility from legal challenges by unsuccessful bidders.

How to Ensure Probity Objectives Are Met

Those organizations responding to invitation documentation may invest significant time and resources in the formulation of their bids. It is essential that the process itself is transparent and that bidders have confidence in that process. If integrity and impartiality are not evident, bidders may be reluctant to make a bid. In that case, competition is likely to be lessened and the best value for money may not be achieved. Transparency in the entire contracting-out process is essential so that potential contractors and members of the public can have confidence in the outcomes. This relates, of course, to the process; not to the confidential, commercial information that the bidders may provide.

No discussions should be held with any bidder about the project, about the nature of any bid, or about the decision-making processes unless provided for in the legislation or the probity plan; and if there are not a large number of resources allocated to the project, at the very least documentation should outline the steps that will be adhered to in accepting and evaluating the bids. For example, an Australian government department called for tenders from accounting firms to conduct a scoping study for the sale of a government-owned business enterprise. It was made clear that there would be a further call for tenders for the sale process, and the firm appointed to conduct the scoping study would need to tender again for that appointment. Upon completion of the scoping study, tenders were called for the implementation of the sale. Some of the previously unsuccessful organizations complained that the firm that conducted the scoping study would have an unfair advantage, because it would be fully familiar with all of the issues relevant to the sale and would surely produce the best response to the request for tender.

The government department invited the previously unsuccessful firms to put questions to the assessment panel in relation to the recommendations of the scoping study. Numerous questions were received and the government department was concerned about the time that would be consumed in answering each question and the adequacy of the responses. Accordingly, the government department invited the previously unsuccessful firms to appoint a representative to read the scoping study and take notes. The result was that the firm that had done the scoping study was unable to secure appointment for the sale process, losing to one of the firms who was unsuccessful in its tender for the scoping study.

Ensuring Integrity in All Evaluation and Selection Processes

The evaluation and selection processes should be documented before bids are received. They should demonstrate how the process would be conducted with regard to probity, transparency, confidentiality, and according to competitive tendering principles. As bidders will have formulated their bids based on predetermined selection criteria, any deviations to those criteria should, at best, be avoided. In the situation where it is necessary to deviate from that criterion, all bidders should be notified. If necessary, all bidders should be given the opportunity and sufficient time to re-submit bids in light of the new information.

Provision of information to all bidders is essential, but care must be taken to ensure no bidder receives, or is perceived to have received, additional information to that which is already publicly available in respect of the tender. A formulated and documented policy should be in the invitation documentation that relates to how nonconforming bids will be dealt.

Often assessment of bids will involve a number of assessment panels. In this situation, there should be a separation of assessment panels. For example, a panel of experts may review financial viability while another will look at those same bids from a design perspective. Assessment panels would commonly not meet and would be quarantined through the evaluation period. Justification statements should be documented by assessors and provided to bidders, successful or unsuccessful, where requested. The assessment of bids should be completed swiftly. Unexplained delays could compromise the perceived integrity of the process.

For example, a consortium tendered to purchase a government-owned printing business. The request for tender included a clause specifying that the successful tenderer would be required to hold prices for some of the services provided by the business at current levels. The consortium said when submitting its tender that it was unequivocally unable to agree to this clause, on the basis that the business was not commercially viable, and some prices would have to rise. The tender evaluation committee rejected the consortium's tender on the basis that it did not comply with the request for tender. The consortium took legal action against the government. The consortium was held to have been misled, because the request for tender did not make it clear that the relevant condition was "a fundamental term and condition that underpins the philosophy and strategy of the tendering process." The judge said that tenderers could be excused for thinking that unconditional acceptance of the clause was not fundamental to the tendering process.

Addressing Any Potential, Perceived, or Actual Conflicts of Interest

Conflicts of interest may arise where those involved with decision-making processes are influenced or appear to be influenced by any personal interests when they are carrying out their responsibilities. Any perceived actual or potential conflicts of interest from those who may be involved in any aspect of the tendering process should be disclosed at the outset. All people involved, directly or indirectly, in the contracting-out process should understand their obligations to disclose any potential or actual conflicts.

No conflict of interest should exist in respect of anyone involved in evaluating bids, and processes should be in place to deal with the potential for such occurrence during the evaluation stage. In cases where an in-house team is submitting a bid, it will be appropriate to isolate those working on the in-house bid from the evaluation team both physically and in relation to the flow of information. Members of the assessment panels should be made aware of the need to disclose any potential conflicts of interest before their appointment. Members should also disclose any conflicts of interest that arise during the purchasing process.

For example, a local council announced that it had arranged with the state government for the funding of an aquatic center in the local council's area and a request for tender would shortly be published. An engineering company contacted the project manager and invited her to lunch, to discuss the progress of the project. The engineering company was concerned about putting the project manager in a difficult position, so it planned a short, inexpensive lunch. Early in the lunch, one of the engineering company's directors remarked that he did not want to compromise the project manager in any way, and said that he would understand if the project manager was unable to give away any details of the project. The project manager responded that she would not be able to disclose details that would not ultimately become generally known when the request for tender was published, and she had no difficulty in giving that information away early to those companies who were sufficiently keen to do the work to seek out details at an earlier stage. The project manager enjoyed the lunch tremendously, suggesting multiple courses and various expensive wines, and the lunch blew out into a long affair. The request for tender was published. The engineering company put in an excellent response, relying in part on information given by the project manager at the lunch. The company was unsuccessful.

Ensuring All Confidential Information Is Protected

Bidders will expect that information they provide in a bid will be kept confidential. In any one tender process, it is likely that two or more direct competitors will submit bids. Commercial imperatives dictate that any information provided in a bid be kept confidential. All information, in whatever form, contained in or relating to the evaluation of bids should be stored securely at all times to prevent access by unauthorized persons. All assessors of the bids should sign confidentiality agreements.

For example, a government agency sought bids for the supply of stationery products. Tender documentation specified that the closing time for the receipt of bids was 4 P.M. Eastern Standard Time. Faxed bids were acceptable. At 3:50 P.M. on the last day for receipt of bids, Bidder X called the government agency expressing a printing problem. The head of the government agency, using his discretionary power, said that the bid would be accepted no later than 5 P.M. The other bids were opened at 4 P.M. At 5 P.M., the bid from Bidder X was received. Bidder X quoted one dollar less than the second lowest bidder who had met the 4 P.M. deadline and was awarded the supply contract.

Ensuring Defensibility of Process

Public sector accountability to the community is an essential and reasonable requirement. Such accountability requirements are designed to save money, resources, and time in the long term and to prevent allegations of corruption, maladministration, and the wastage of public resources. Accountability covers those involved in the tendering process, and ultimately the government, though the responsible minister may be held to account for each stage of the process.

The process should be well documented, consistent, and able to be held up to the most intense scrutiny. There should be a process for receipt, recording, and acknowledgment of bids. Negotiations should be documented. Reasons for selection/rejection of bids should be documented. Documentation should be maintained at all phases of the assessment process. It should give sufficient particulars to enable a full and conclusive audit to be undertaken.

Any deviation from documented procedures should be based on proper reasons communicated in writing, in accordance with probity requirements. For example, in April 1997, an Auditor-General's special report, the result of a performance audit of a metropolitan ambulance service, was made public.[1] Raised in the report were numerous concerns over a lack of integrity in the tendering processes in the ambulance service. A consultant was engaged to undertake a commercial review of operation of the service in a number of stages. Key deficiencies in that tender process and subsequent appointment of the consultants, as identified in the report of the auditor-general, included:

- No evidence to indicate attention was given to potential conflicts of interest, technical competency of the firm, or potential for the services to be provided at a lower price;
- There was an absence of evidence that the proposals received by the other tenderers had been fully evaluated; and
- The initial arrangement with the consultant, without a tender or a contract, was for A\$45,000. The total payments to the firm amounted to A\$1.5 million without any documentary evidence of questioning by management.

The auditor-general found a "continual hands-off approach" by management and suggested that arrangements "at best, involved serious mismanagement or, at worst, constituted corrupt activity."

Ensuring Maximization of Efficiency and Effectiveness

Probity is often seen as potentially at odds with efficiency and effectiveness. This is counteracted by the argument that addressing probity issues can enhance the commerciality of a project for bidders. If fairness and impartiality are apparent and bidders are comfortable with the process, they will be more willing to make a bid and submit future bids. This increases competition. Addressing probity issues can also ensure that unsuccessful bidders, on the grounds of unfairness, do not challenge the tender process. The process should be able to stand up against intense ethical and financial scrutiny. For example, in an auditor-general's report, it was noted that more than A$70 million of government money was expended throughout the tendering and negotiation phase for a major government project and at the end of the day there was very little to show for the time and money.

Bidder Probity Checking or "Due Diligence"

In some cases, such as the awarding of a license to build and operate a casino or a prison, there may be very specific requirements for bidders in terms of satisfying probity checking requirements. In the United States, it is common for bidders to fund the probity-checking process. In one recent overseas casino contract, more than a year was spent on probity checking of bidders and the bidders were required to fund more than U.S. $1 million worth of probity checking. The extent of probity checking would generally be related to variables such as: legislative requirements; value of the project; political sensitivity of the project; risk (financial and other types of risk) transference; security needs; and past negative experiences—criticism by auditor-general, courts, and so forth. Even where the project is not a highly sensitive one covered by legislation it is likely that public/private sector partnered projects will involve a range of probity checks to ensure that a preferred bidder is a viable proponent and able to proceed with the project.

Bidder probity checking could be expected to cover matters such as the following: bidder corporate information (consortium partners, entities, relationships, corporate structure, history, directors' profiles); litigation (historic and pending); key personnel; ownership; financial information; business affiliations; credit rating; any government/regulatory investigation; share structure; business failure; relevant experience claimed; documents from publicly listed corporations lodged with stock exchanges, taxation and regulatory authorities, and so forth.

PITFALLS TO AVOID

The main problems can be summarized under five headings: processes, policies, people, politicians, and paper.

Processes. I refer to processes for the receipt, registration, conformance checking, assessment, selection of preferred bidders and parallel processes for selecting and training all that will take part in the assessment. Some processes are poorly understood or applied by assessors, specifically, processes to ensure that conformance and financial viability checks are appropriately and systematically carried out; that all bid material is read and assessed against published criteria; that any information on past providers is equitably used; and that new entrants have an appropriate opportunity to put their claims. Quality assurance (QA) should be an essential element of the whole tendering process. Definition of the role to be played by the QA team and the appointment and training of additional team members is crucial. The form of all reports from assessors requires significant attention if they are to be defensible.

Policy. Policy concerning tendering is often made "on the run," sometimes well after the bids have been received.

People. Care should be taken to ensure that suitably qualified people fulfill assessment roles. Inadequate training in probity requirements and processes to be followed is sometimes a major handicap.

Politicians. In my experience, some well-meaning though often ill-informed politicians might seek to intervene and lobby public servants on behalf of constituents who are preferred bidders or their personally favored bidders. Preparation of clear guidelines and protocols combined with probity briefings may assist.

Paper. The absence of adequate document management systems combined with the limitations of some registry systems and staff may be significant handicaps. The probity adviser should be confident that all confidential information was secured, or adequately tracked throughout the tendering exercise. The volume and complexity of material that may need to be controlled during the tender exercise mean that appropriate professional assistance and tools must be obtained as early as possible.

CONCLUSION

It is clear that probity requirements are unlikely to lessen. As we scrutinize our public sector processes more rigorously, we as a community want more evidence that decision-making procedures are administratively and legally sound as well as assurance that special information, personal relationships, or political interference does not advantage bidders. Appendix C gives a detailed example of how a major public hospital dealt with an outsourcing project and the associated probity issues.

NOTE

1. Auditor-General of Victoria (1997), *Metropolitan Ambulance Service*, Special Report 49, Victorian Government Printer, Melbourne.

10

MANAGING CULTURAL
MISMATCHES

The intercultural dynamics between two organizations in a strategic alliance are examined in this chapter focusing on the experienced world of boundary spanning personnel. Diagnoses of cultural mismatches are reframed in terms of underlying dynamics of trust. Three possible states are identified and implications for managing cultural interfaces are noted.

The purpose of this chapter is to examine how intercultural dynamics may form between two organizations in a strategic alliance. I focus on the social-constructive and institutional processes that affect the work of boundary spanning personnel at the interface between the organizations. I identify trust as a property of the social system created out of patterns of routine interaction between partners' boundary spanners; trust serves to structure the relations between the organizations. This view of alliance relations enables a reframing of what are often called cultural mismatches in terms of negotiated systems of action which pivot on trust. Finally, I offer three propositions concerning the structuralization of these social action systems at the boundary, which may be useful for future empirical research.

This analysis developed out of a case study of interaction of personnel in two large organizations involved in a long-term alliance on a specified range of services.[1] In this case, destructive conflict emerged as a critical issue among the boundary spanning personnel in the two organizations. The conflict affected the alliance's performance and was serious enough that one of the organizations would have liked to terminate the relationship.

However, due to the economic ramifications of termination, both organizations felt compelled to continue their alliance agreement. In this chapter I have drawn out some theoretical implications raised by that study and explore the underlying dynamics.

The scope of this analysis follows situations in which all of the following conditions apply. Two organizations are involved in an alliance that is continual, ongoing, and important. "Continual" means that the interactions between actors are not sporadic or narrowly bounded but emergent. It suggests that actors may develop a distinctive subjective experience that evolves over time. "Ongoing" means there is no indicated end point and suggests that a desire to sustain the relationship in the future may motivate actors to address conflict situations in ways that enhance rather than destroy trust.[2] "Important" indicates that the relationship has substantial financial and strategic ramifications, and suggests that the actors may be invested psychologically and want to make the alliance work.

The alliance consists of contractual agreements between two organizations, fulfilled by boundary spanning personnel at one or more levels. Boundary spanners are simply those employees in an organization who work routinely with employees in another organization to fulfill negotiated obligations between the two organizations.

Each organization has a strong culture. In one case, a strong culture was thought to contribute to each organization's superior performance in its industry, and produced a strong positive emotional response toward the organization by its managers. Each culture had different norms (for example, high versus low tolerance for ambiguity and conflict), and the differences made personnel in each organization resistant to seeing that other ways of doing things could be equally valid and effective. This in turn produced a strong negative emotional response in its managers toward the other organization. Many kinds of alliances fulfill these conditions. Long-term subcontracting arrangements, alliances to develop new technologies, acquisitions to capture distribution systems, licensing agreements, and other types of "hybrid organization"[3] have proliferated in recent years.[4] The spread of virtual and boundaryless organizations,[5] consisting of ad hoc performance agreements between two or more organizations drawn from a network of loosely allied organizations, may increase the number of situations where the above conditions exist.

Customer-supplier relationships are perhaps the most common type of partnership.[6] In the past decade, stable supply relationships have become popular as a means of buttressing just-in-time inventory management systems and increasing competitive advantage. In the computer industry, for example, computer organizations often sell their hardware to original equipment manufacturers (OEMs) who in turn add value to the hardware and resell it, for instance as a complete data-processing system.

I do not focus on interdepartmental situations in this chapter, although some of the literature that will be cited below necessarily draws on it. Cummings argues forcefully that interorganizational dynamics are qualitatively different from intraorganizational dynamics, because in interorganizational contexts, a hierarchy of authority rarely exists and even a loosely unified normative context cannot be assumed.[7] For example, power and interaction patterns have been found to affect cultural agreement within organizations through their influence on formal and informal status.[8] These connections, however, cannot be assumed for cultural agreement between organizations.

ALLIANCES AND CULTURE, TASK AND TRUST

Developing successful alliances is a sensitive and extended process,[9] which is poorly understood[10] and under-researched.[11] Problems in ongoing dyadic relationships may emerge from issues relating to scheduling, prioritizing, decision-making processes, budgeting and resource allocation, and product and service quality standards. Not all of these issues can be precisely defined in the initial contract establishing the terms of the relationship.[12]

There is a temptation to view such problems as if they were purely task related. The instrumental logic of much of the early interorganizational literature[13] drew attention toward instrumental explanations of conflict—such as incompatible goals, insufficient resources, or inadequate task boundary management—and away from social-constructive or institutional kinds of explanations. Moreover, researchers' tendency to favor coordination of activities[14] implied disapproval of the conflicts that are routine, and in some cases useful, aspects of such relations. This coordination bias is still evident in the strategy literature on alliances, mergers, and acquisitions,[15] where managers are admonished to consider the other organization's culture as an important determinant of a successful encounter and to integrate the two cultures harmoniously. Finally, there was a tendency to treat the organization itself as a purposeful, acting entity. In the case of an alliance, an "organization" would act symbiotically with, or competitively against, another organization.[16]

However, alliances are often complex mixtures of task factors (such as procedural agreements), expressive factors (pride, defensiveness), and symbolic factors (trust, leadership). Many conflicts in alliances are rooted in symbolic or expressive differences[17] such as a preference for formally prescribed reporting relationships over looser, more organic interactions.[18] Such differences indicate cultural mismatches. It is important to explore the underlying reasons for difficulties in alliance relations, and not merely to rely on superficial explanations or to treat symptoms that manifest in poor task performance.

Some more recent research in interorganizational relations has recognized symbolic and expressive issues and their effect on task performance.[19] An important source of this work is the "normative context" of an interorganizational relationship,[20] which defines appropriate behavior across an organization's boundary, and comprises cognitive, expressive, and behavioral dimensions.[21] Normative contexts may range from highly competitive to highly cooperative modalities. Later in this chapter I demonstrate why this concept is crucial to understanding intercultural dynamics.

Conceiving of an alliance as a network of interaction rather than as a structural relation has important analytic implications. For example, the relationship between a supplier and a customer consists of a buying center, a selling center, and the ties between them.[22] The centers consist of networks of employees in a variety of roles and positions in each organization that are involved in transactions with employees in the other organization. The interorganizational network comprised of these centers is dynamic, requires active management, and dislodges the notion that the organization as an entity acts.

In the culture literature, a growing number of studies explore the notion that organizations have multiple cultures.[23] In some cases this is seen as the dominant culture with compatible subcultures,[24] in others as competing and conflicting subcultures,[25] and in still others as the influence of different subcultures on each other.[26] Martin's important contribution was in recognizing that all organizational cultures may be viewed simultaneously as unitary with harmonious shared values; differentiated into stable subcultures; and fragmented into shifting and emergent groupings.[27]

Organizational cultures can consist of both general and specific organizational frames.[28] General organizational frames engender a cultural synergism,[29] which consists of cultural elements within an organization that are broadly shared across functional areas, hierarchical levels, and even subcultures. General frames guide relationships with outside groups. Specific organizational frames are the cultural elements that are not widely shared, but instead are specific to a particular group or subculture.[30] A cultural grouping consists of a shared set of cognitions held by actors about a specific situation,[31] and is consistent with Martin's fragmented perspective in that "the boundaries of cultural groupings are . . . flexible; they may shift. And the membership in one cultural grouping may just be one of several for a person. Because individuals have several frames of reference at their disposal, the salience of these frames may change depending on the issue at hand."[32]

Sackman distinguishes cultural groupings from subcultures that are viewed as having distinctive boundaries (cf. Martin's differentiation perspective). Sackman confined her analysis to intraorganizational situations, but cultural groupings can also transcend organizational boundaries. Distinct cultural elements may build up among the personnel in an interorganizational hybrid.[33] Elements such as stories serve to differentiate the hybrid from its two "home" organizations and "can encourage cohesion among hybrid members and allow them to transcend their parochial loyalties to the partner and act in concert for the good of the hybrid."[34] Lippit and van Til[35] suggest a similar point about competing pressures and divided loyalties with respect to the members of interagency coordinating committees in the nonprofit sector. Moreover, "there may be a culture unique to the relationship" between a customer and a supplier that "would contain interactional habits, norms, roles, and shared worldviews."[36] The concept of cultural groupings can enhance our understanding of how actors from the same and different organizations interact at an interorganizational interface.

The existence of an overarching cultural synergism, or general organizational frame, helps to explain why boundary spanning personnel may both agree and disagree with aspects of their organization's dominant culture and how they might develop some affiliation to an interorganizational cultural grouping. Different groupings with different norms may in fact compete for the attention of those boundary spanners as they try to negotiate their way through various cultural groupings and consider their affiliations with and loyalties to those groupings. For example, boundary spanners may experience a tension between a cultural grouping of people from their employing organization and one of the people from their interorganizational team working on an alliance contract. They may cope with the tension by developing shared cultural cognitions that help individuals to recognize, frame, and integrate meaningful alternatives from an essentially infinite number of possibilities in similar ways. This capacity is a prerequisite for mutual understanding, for communication, and for effective coordination in social systems.[37]

The interorganizational literature's treatment of trust is consistent with its orientations toward decontextualized instrumentality, coordination, and reification. Trust is often seen as an alternative to installing monitoring systems for assuring compliance with a contract and reducing opportunistic behavior;[38] or for breaking down barriers that inhibit economic development[39] or coordination.[40] In this regard, trust is viewed as an expectation rather than an outcome of successful interactions.[41] Trust is positioned implicitly as the residual of risk that cannot or need not be specified in the initial contract or monitored during the term of the alliance. Managers risk investments of information and technology to obtain the "social capital . . . that arises from the prevalence of trust."[42]

The dominant discourse on trust is one of commodities: if the relationship can be filled with more of the commodity called trust, then it can be expected to be more effective. When trust is viewed as an expectation of interactions in a partnership, it is as if trust-as-commodity is an input to a transformation process. This kind of language reifies trust, positioning it as an objective entity, not as a continual intersubjective experience.

Alternatively, if a partnership is viewed as an interaction network rather than as a structural relation, then trust may be viewed as developing in the network because of successful repeated encounters between boundary spanners. For the purpose of this chapter, trust is an emergent, collective property of a network of interaction among boundary spanners from two organizations.[43] This collective property has its antecedents in task-based interactions among those boundary spanners, and also has implications for their subsequent interactions, in so far as trust guides the tone of interactions[44] and enables or constrains goal attainment.[45]

Trust can spread or erode in a network depending on various conditions.[46] For example, task interdependencies and shared technology tend to produce shared understandings about behavioral norms across interacting organizations.[47] This appears to happen because "manufacturers induce suppliers to invest in complementary products. . . . In turn, the marriage of suppliers to manufacturers and distributors forces a convergence of interests that translates into a common world-view."[48] A common view and shared values have been identified as important preconditions for high levels of trust.[49] In addition, expectations of future exchange inspire a greater willingness to share information and to trust the partner.[50] However, the emergence of a common worldview is not ensured. Each organization in an exchange relationship may cling to its distinctive worldview that is consistent with its strategic interests. Just as in many labor-management arenas, such divergence in values in partnership situations might be expected to lead to low levels of trust.

Trust is a dynamic part of the normative context of the alliance. The top decision makers in an alliance may enter the relationship in a cooperative spirit; the expectation is win-win collaboration.[51] Alliances on new products are commonly cited examples of this so-called high trust context.[52] Alternatively, the decision makers may go into the alliance with the notion of a tentative, circumscribed exchange relation and an attitude of wariness and defensiveness toward the partner. First-time purchasing contracts between two organizations are common examples of such low-trust contexts.[53] A normative context of high trust tends toward solidarity between the interacting parties; low trust toward mutual adjustment and compromise; and distrust toward atomism and isolation.[54] Trust functions to structurate relations in a partnership[55] for a similar positioning of cooperation. This is discussed after the case material to be presented.

Some promising foundation works have been laid for a fuller understanding of intercultural dynamics in strategic alliances and in the interorganizational, cultural, and trust literatures. The possibility of an emergent social system, cultural grouping, and normative context at an interorganizational interface directs attention to the subjective worlds of boundary spanning personnel. The literature also points to ways in which boundary spanners might create specific organizational frames at interfaces.

THE CASE STUDY IN CONTEXT

The alliance between the parties[56] was both long term and broad. Each organization had a large number of employees working on the relationship on a routine basis at a variety of sites throughout Europe. Both organizations had strong corporate cultures and were highly successful in their respective industries. One partner had strong mechanistic characteristics (in this chapter this organization will be referred to as Mechanus Pty. Ltd. [Proprietary Limited]), and the other strong organic characteristics (this organization will be referred to as Organus Pty. Ltd.).

An action research project with the partners began when a consultant was called in by the CEO of Mechanus Pty. Ltd. to help the organization deal with conflicts it was having with its partner, Organus Pty. Ltd. The ensuing project focused on resolving chronic problems between the organizations during production problems. The identified task-related problems were raw material availability, technology issues, engineering competence, and documentation deficiencies.

The quality of the relationship would be described as problematic. Both could recount stories of when personnel from the other organization did not follow an agreed-upon procedure, did not perform adequately, behaved uncooperatively, or delayed the correction of serious problems. Mechanus Pty. Ltd. personnel eventually felt there was nothing they could do to get action from Organus Pty. Ltd. Organus's personnel felt that Mechanus's personnel would never be satisfied with their efforts or performance.

Problems and issues became so equivocal that it was difficult to get a handle on what the major problem areas were, what was getting worse, and what was improving. The lack of agreed-upon or appropriate documentation and trend analyses made any position virtually impossible to support or refute. This allowed, and indeed even forced, people to fall back on their opinions, gut level feelings, and historic reactions.

Interestingly, there was evidence that the technical people at the point of interface between business and customers cooperated more effectively and experienced fewer problems than did their senior managers. Both senior managements were committed to addressing the problematic relationship. Previous attempts by the organizations to resolve their differences foundered on issues of style. Consistent with their organic and mechanistic characteristics, Organus Pty. Ltd. was inclined to discuss process as well as technical issues that affected the relationship, whereas Mechanus Pty. Ltd. wanted to stick to the technical matters alone.

A grounded theory approach was used to interpret the data gathered from interviews with key actors and document reviews. Positing a two-level layering of problems, with cultural issues underlying the presenting, made a sense of the situation (technical problems previously noted). The cultural issues identified were differences in decision making, problem solving, conflict resolution, and performance measurement during production problems. The conclusion was that the actors in the Mechanus–Organus relationship were experiencing a cultural mismatch.

The consultant's intervention in this situation consisted of raising the level of cultural consciousness. This involved the consultant first interpreting to key personnel from each organization conflictual situations in terms of the cultural norms and practices, and second, describing more directly to them their own and the other organization's culture.

This approach had an effect. Over time, personnel from both organizations became more receptive to looking at alternative explanations for the other organization's behavior. Once each group of personnel from each organization understood that the technical was interpreted through, and indeed partly shaped by, cultural experience, each group's views of the other were no longer constructed as arbitrary and personalistic.

An important question remains. How did the boundary spanners in Mechanus Pty. Ltd. and Organus Pty. Ltd. make sense of their situation, as the tone of the alliance became distrustful over time? How did they create the spiral of distrust into which they fell? More generally, how do boundary spanners create cultural matches and mismatches, and how do such matches and mismatches affect task performance?

INTERCULTURAL DYNAMICS

In order to get beyond facile descriptions of intercultural dynamics, leaders need to examine the intersubjective and institutional processes that influence boundary-spanning personnel in their work. Behaviorally, an ongoing, continual, and important alliance consists of interactions among boundary spanners, embedded in particular technical and social contexts. In the Mechanus–Organus case, the influence of task-related and cultural factors in the relationship between the two organizations was mutual, and was evident in the data collected. On the one hand, the technical nature of the relationship, and the mismatched reporting structures between the organizations, conditioned the cultural processes between them.[57] On the other hand, the strong corporate cultures affected the task-based relations between and among the boundary spanners by making personnel resistant to alternative ways of solving problems at various sites. However, it was not recognized that a normative context was evolving at the boundary, nor that the normative context was having an effect on the performance of the partnership over time.

Leaders are supposed to create and manage corporate culture to suit task-performance needs.[58] In this sense, culture helps to implement strategy.[59] In the history of the Mechanus–Organus alliance, their respective leaders had paid little attention to the cultural dimension. By ignoring it, they impeded the fulfillment of the strategy that led to the alliance in the first place.

The intentions and objectives that an organization's leadership projects to its personnel affect how its boundary spanners act toward those in the organization's environment. Distinct "social action systems" crystallize when and where interactions become continual. Van de Ven recognized that the social structure among organizations in a social action system is such that the system can *act as a unit*.[60] This implies that many activities in an interorganizational relation cannot be explained simply by analyzing the behavior of member organizations. Collective events arise out of the actions of the social systems and are formally a property of the interorganizational relation itself. [61] To attain its goals as a unit, a social action system adopts a structure and process for organizing member activities.

Social action systems are focused on task accomplishment. However, they are also vehicles for the shared understandings that both signify cultural groupings and mark the normative context of the relationship. Interactions that define a social action system come to "structurate" the relationship. That is, the interactions leave cultural "residues" that build up and become institutionalized. The shared meanings and rituals of the actors condition subsequent interactions as they interact over time.[62] Social action systems enable actors to bring distinctive rules and resources that they have created at the boundary into action.[63] Cultural groupings infuse social action systems to create intercultural dynamics with a distinctive (and evolving) normative context.

Having identified the general character of intercultural dynamics, the analysis proceeds in two directions. A social constructive path examines the working world of boundary spanners as they negotiate it intersubjectively. An institutional path examines the two organizational cultures as emergent wholes. These paths ultimately converge on implications for intercultural management.

While the normative context of the relationship between two organizations influences the behavior and attitudes of boundary spanners, it does not control them completely. Boundary spanners actively perceive and enact their general and specific organizational frames. They are able to reflect on their situation, and this gives them some freedom from cultural straightjackets.[64] What happens at the interface will be a product of prescribed intentions of the top decision makers in both organizations and the emergent negotiated interactions of the boundary spanners (some of whom may be the top decision makers themselves).

The working world of boundary spanners is more complex than that of other employees, "reflecting transactional efficiencies as well as the features of [embedding] social networks."[65] It includes routine access to other organizations, some of their subcultures and cultural groupings, and the working worlds of the boundary spanners in other organizations with whom they regularly interact. It is a mutually defined world because multiple organizations inhabit the same space and each time, through its boundary spanners, tend to

> shape action in accordance with *their* favourite interpretative schemes and thus influence the environment to which others are trying to adapt and react. Environments are enacted by hosts of individuals and organizations each acting on the basis of their interpretations of a world that is in effect mutually defined.[66]

The mutually defined world can mean that boundary spanners, through their recurrent interactions, create space for new cultural dynamics to emerge. This could include those actors' attempts to colonize each other's space by gaining advantage over resource dependencies[67] or over symbols and meanings.[68] In an alliance, differences may exist in each organization's projections of its shared meanings and in the cognitive schema by which each organization's agents, including boundary spanners, make sense of their world.[69] These differences are the cultural mismatches. In the Mechanus–Organus case, a social action system characterized by poor performance, mutual recrimination, and distrust emerged at the interface and became institutionalized. The boundary spanners experienced tensions in their interactions because both general and specific organizational frames conflicted. Before the intervention, they were unable to resolve those tensions and establish task-based norms for their interactions by negotiating mutually acceptable cultural practices.

However, a study in cross-cultural management produced some empirical support for the claim that intercultural negotiation might occur. Brannen and Salk studied the cultural negotiations between two national groups (Japanese and German) in an international alliance in an existing plant of one of the partners in Germany.[70] The two groups continually negotiated cultural outcomes as issues evolved into "issue domains." They found that "organizational culture as a negotiated entity evolves as a dynamic, ongoing, and changing subtotal of interpersonal negotiations around organizational issues as they come up in real time over the course of the organization's history"[71]

Boundary spanners' trust in their partner's employees is an outcome of successful interactions with them, which "lead to social-psychological bonds of mutual norms, sentiments and friendships . . . in dealing with uncertainty."[72] These bonds develop into psychological contracts at an intersubjective level, with implied obligations of the partner's acting with integrity and goodwill.[73]

In sum, at an intersubjective level the interface between Mechanus Pty. Ltd. and Organus Pty Ltd was characterized by boundary spanners exchanging technical information relatively cooperatively in problem-solving situations; interpreting situations (for example production problems) incompatibly in a context calling for long-term reciprocity and trust; being ignorant prior, to the consultant's intervention, of their mismatched cultural frames; and distrusting the motives and behaviors of employees from the other organization. Negotiated cultural practices take place within cultural contexts.[74] Hence, an examination of the cultural features of each organization in an alliance adds to the inter-subjective analysis by showing in what ways or areas the two cultures are structurally compatible or incompatible.

Two distinct processes are embedded in the cultural mismatch between Mechanus Pty. Ltd. and Organus Pty. Ltd.: normative integration and the projection of culture. Normative integration deals with how experience is collectively structured and articulated, that is, how it is codified. This involves formal and informal coordination mechanisms.[75] The literature on the management of culture suggests this can be a conscious or unconscious process. In "strong" cultures, or from a "unified" perspective, leaders use deliberate strategies to mobilize desired employee behavior by codifying their work experience around core values and symbols.[76] In "weak" cultures, or from a "fragmented" perspective,[77] work experience is codified unconsciously and equivocally. Culture within an organization may be more or less integrated from, for instance, its strategic apex to boundary spanners at lower levels (for example, field service representatives).

The second process is the projection of a culture as a gestalt cognitive schema to other organizations during routine transactions. This involves what Boisot[78] calls "an institutional mechanism." Institutinal mechanisms deal with how information is diffused and how diffused information is. The processes of projecting corporate culture to other organizations are less often discussed in the literature and are often unconscious and unintended.

Codification and diffusion may be viewed as dimensions with high and low ordinal values. Combining the two produces a matrix of prototypical "transaction strategies," as shown in Figure 10.1. Boisot uses this matrix to describe different types of cultures.[79]

In the Mechanus–Organus case, the boundary spanners in each organization codified their reality differently as they attempted, individually and

Figure 10.1
Matrix of Prototypical Transaction Strategies

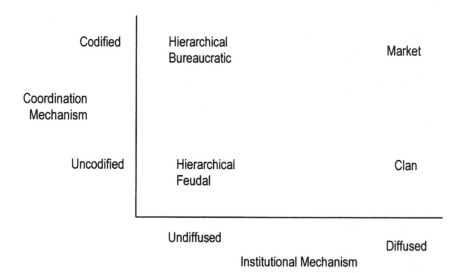

collectively, to make sense of their experience with the other organization. The mechanistic management style and the organic management style reflect this difference.

In effect, the mismatch between the organizations was two-dimensional. First, the organizations had different operating styles internally. Mechanus Pty. Ltd. was a hierarchical-bureaucratic culture; its employees preferred information to be highly codified but undiffused. In contrast, Organus Pty. Ltd. functioned as a clan culture; its employees preferred uncodified, diffused information. The organizations were cultural opposites.

Second, the senior managers of the two organizations held different conceptions of the nature of their relationship. Mechanus Pty. Ltd.'s leadership saw it as more codified, like a licensing agreement; Organus Pty. Ltd.'s leadership saw it as less codified, like a subcontracting agreement.[80] These views affected the frames of reference of the boundary spanners and created dissonance in the enactment of the relationship.

We may conclude that a cultural mismatch may be decomposed into an issue in the coordination of culture within each organization and an institutional problem at the boundary. The institutional problem is more apparent because the conflicts became visible to clients, the consultant, and the boundary spanners themselves. Using Boisot's language one could say the two organizations were reaching for convergence at a relatively uncodified information boundary. As a result of the structural incompatibility in the two cultures, the boundary spanning personnel at several levels in each organization were collectively unsuccessful in this quest. Conflict persisted until the intervention enabled the actors to reframe their experiences.

At this cultural level of analysis, trust is a function of the compatibility of organizational codifications of reality. In the Mechanus–Organus case, for example, the two organizations interpreted the character of the relationship differently. Organus Pty. Ltd. saw it as a sound relationship, which sometimes experienced problems; they codified it as high-trust. Mechanus Pty. Ltd. saw it as a problematic relationship that sometimes because intolerable; they codified it as low-trust. From these different codifications, we can infer that each organization would interpret certain behaviors by the other as opportunistic when in fact they were merely part of its standard cultural script.[81] Before the intervention, misaligned inter-subjective experience helped to produce incompatible cultural patterns at the interface. A normative context of distrust resulted. Subsequent behavior by one organization's boundary spanners, informed by distrustful assumptions about the other organization's personnel, in turn served to reinforce the incompatible cultural patterns.

In sum, the social-constructive and institutional explanations of cultural mismatches in alliances inform each other. Emergent cultural dynamics negotiated by boundary spanners are influenced by institutional factors that are intended to reduce uncertainty and risk.[82]

DISCUSSION

Three assumptions underlie an adequate understanding of cultural interfaces in alliances. First, the meaning of an alliance, as experienced intersubjectively, is socially constructed through the medium of culture[83] and is expressed in emergent cultural groupings.[84] Second, organizations are themselves "social constructs that express a culturally determined cognitive order."[85] Social action systems express these emergent constructions. Third, some, but not total, shared meaning between actors in an alliance is needed in order to make their contractual relationship viable.[86] This assumption is grounded in the self-reported interpretations of the actors in Mechanus Pty. Ltd, and Organus Pty. Ltd. themselves, who saw the conflicts between the two organizations as destructive and draining.

In ongoing, continual, and important alliances, I suggest that a distinctive social action system will crystallize at the interface in one of three ways:

1. As they work on their interorganizational task, boundary spanners from each organization may work out a harmonious working relationship by integrating elements of the two main cultures, as each culture manifests locally (that is, at the boundary). They mutually adjust by reconciling the general organizational frames through deliberation. Brannen and Salk found that "a type of synchronization began to occur" between their two national groups over conflictual issues.[87] The emergent negotiated outcome was often a compromise between the two. Other possibilities include yielding to the cultural practice of the other group, innovating a new cultural practice, and dividing tasks to minimize the need for negotiation. All of these possibilities are harmonizing behaviors and are consistent with low-trust relations.

2. A distinctive kind of culture may emerge at the interface that draws on elements in each organization's culture but is different from either of them. This might be termed an "interculture," and is a distinct cultural grouping.[88] An interculture is grounded in the intersubjectivity reality that emerges from interaction.[89] As a cul-

tural grouping, an interculture enables boundary-spanning personnel in the two organizations to create a specific frame of reference[90] and to codify meaning through norms, symbols, and procedures to guide specific task-related activities. The actors create new cultural dynamics. It is possible for intercultures to emerge in ongoing, continual relationships because the boundary spanners struggle together to make sense of their complexly experienced world. One way to reconcile the tensions in the specific and general organizational frames that they experience is to transform them into something else, an interculture. Their behaviors in this context are consistent with high-trust relations.

3. The boundary spanners may be unable to harmonize elements of the two main cultures in the course of their normal working relationships, and they may be prevented from evolving a distinctive interculture by strong cultural sanctions from their employing organizations. Consequently, they may be stuck. In the absence of other alternatives, this could mean that their frames of reference would become polarized, and they would persist in discordant enactments. The relationship would become sour and a cultural stalemate would result. The social action system would crystallise at the boundary into recurrent patterns of behavior that actors see as destructive, that threatens the viability of the partnership and indicates a normative context of distrust.

Cultural mismatches in alliances have been explained in terms of the dynamics of trust that underlie and evoke them. Trust is shown to function at two levels. First, it functions as a mediator between task performance and cultural norms and practices at the intersubjective level. Second, it is an emergent property of a network of interactions at the cultural level. It can have positive or negative valency. This conceptualization enables us to reconcile the views of trust as an expectation and as an outcome of exchange.[91] A spiral of rising trust[92] can be set in motion when boundary spanners interpret others' behavior as cooperative; this interpretation inclines them to expect the others' future behavior to be guileless; and this expectation is reciprocated. Conversely, boundary spanners can dig themselves into a hole of distrust when they interpret others' behavior as uncooperative, that inclines them to expect the others' future behavior to be vicious, and when this expectation is reciprocated. Such spirals and holes can be inferred from circular models of organizational trust.[93]

CONCLUSION

This chapter has highlighted the bearing of trust on the intercultural dynamics of long-term routine alliances. The approach in this chapter has been to integrate cultural and interorganizational perspectives, and is based on social-constructive and institutional logics. The major conclusion is that structurated processes involving trust can underlie diagnoses of cultural mismatches when conflicts occur at alliance interfaces.

Empirical research that might flow from this approach might proceed along two paths. One path would explore the conditions for expecting harmonization, interculture formation, or polarization, as presented in the three propositions. For example, does the formation of an interculture depend on structural alignment?[94] A second path would examine in a more fine-grained way how actors collectively construct contexts that are conducive to the three intercultural states.

Reexamining cultural mismatches in alliances in terms of negotiated systems of action may help us to understand better the management of intercultural dynamics. Including intercultures and polarized states in the repertoire of possible states of partnerships can help managers and consultants to move beyond the often-facile admonitions to harmonize or integrate cultures at alliance interfaces.

NOTES

1. See M. A. Milgate (1999), "Key Conditions for the Effective Development of Cross-Border Alliances," unpublished Master of Commerce (Honors) Thesis, University of Western Sydney–Nepean, 1999.

2. See W. Powell (1990), "Neither Market nor Hierarchy: Network Forms of Organization," in B. Staw and T. Cummings (eds.,) *Research in Organizational Behavior*, vol. 12; C. Sabel (1993), "Studied Trust: Building New Forms of Co-operation in a Volatile Economy," *Human Relations* 46 (9): 1133–1171.

3. B. Borys and D. Jemison (1989), "Hybrid Arrangements as Strategic Alliances: Theoretical Issues in Organizational Combinations," *Academy of Management Review* 14 (2): 234–249.

4. M. Lyons (1991), "Joint Ventures as Strategic Choice—A Literature Review," *Long Range Planning* 24 (4): 130–144.

5. G. Dess, A. Rasheed, K. McLaughlin, and R. Priem (1995), "The New Corporate Architecture," *Academy of Management Executive* 9 (3): 7–18.

6. R. Kanter (1989), *When Giants Learn to Dance* (New York: Touchstone Books).

7. T. Cummings (1984), "Transorganizational Development," in B. Staw and T. Cummings (eds,). *Research in Organizational Behavior*, vol. 6, pp. 367–422.

8. W. Stevenson and J. Bartunek (1996), "Power, Interaction, Position, and the Generation of Cultural Agreement in Organizations," *Human Relations* 49 (1): 75–104.

9. See A. Buono and J. Bowditch (1989), *The Human Side of Mergers and Acquisitions* (San Francisco: Jossey-Bass); and A. Larson (1992), "Network Dyads in Entrepreneurial Settings: A Study of the Governance of Exchange Relationships," *Administrative Science Quarterly* 37: 76–104.

10. D. Whetten (1982), "Issues in Conducting Research," in D. Rogers and D. Whetten (eds.), *Inter-Organizational Co-ordination* (Ames: Iowa State University Press).

11. See Kanter (1989), *When Giants Learn to Dance.*

12. P. Ring and A. Van de Ven (1994), "Developmental Processes of Co-operative Inter-organizational Relationships," *Academy of Management Review* 19 (1): 90–118.

13. For example, A. Van de Ven (1976), "On the Nature, Formation and Maintenance of Relations among Organizations," *Academy of Management Review* 1: 24–36.

14. See Whetten (1982), *Issues in Conducting Research.*

15. See Borys and Jemison (1989), "Hybrid Arrangements"; Lyons (1991), "Joint Ventures"; and J. McCann and R. Gilkey (1988), *Joining Forces: Creating and Managing Successful Mergers and Acquisitions* (Englewood Cliffs, NJ: Prentice-Hall).

16. E. Abrahamson and C. Fombrun (1994), "Macrocultures: Determinants and Consequences," *Academy of Management Review* 19(4): 728–755.

17. B. Gray (1989), *Collaborating* (San Francisco: Jossey-Bass).

18. See Kanter (1989), *When Giants Learn to Dance.*

19. Larson (1992), "Network Dyads"; Powell (1990), "Neither Market Nor Hierarchy"; Sabel (1993), "Studied Trust"; B. Sheppard and M. Tuchinsky (1996), "Interfirm Relationships: A Grammar of Pairs," in B. Staw and T. Cummings (eds.), *Research in Organizational Behavior*, vol. 18, pp. 85–112; and M. Suchman (1995), "Managing Legitimacy: Strategic and Institutional Approaches," *Academy of Management Review* 20(3): 571–610.

20.–E. Laumann, J. Galaskiewicz, and P. Marsden (1978), "Community Structure as Interorganizational Linkages," *Annual Review of Sociology* vol. 4: 455–484.

21. J. D. Lewis and A. Weigert (1985), "Trust as a Social Reality," *Social Forces* 63 (4): 967–985.

22. M. Fichman and P. Goodman (1996), "Customer-Supplier Ties in Inter-organizational relations," in B. Staw and T. Cummings (eds.), *Research in Organizational Behavior*, vol. 18, pp. 285–329.

23. P. Frost, L. Moore, M. Louis, C. Lundberg, and J. Martin (1991), *Reframing Organizational Culture* (Newbury Park: Sage); and R. Rose (1988), "Organizations as Multiple Cultures: A Rules Theory Analysis," *Human Relations* 41 (2): 139–170.

24. J. Martin and C. Siehl (1983), "Organizational Culture and Counterculture: An Uneasy Symbiosis," *Organizational Dynamics* 12: 52–64.

25. G. Morgan (1997), *Images of Organization*, 2nd ed. (Thousand Oaks: Sage Publications).

26. S. Barley, G. Meyer, and D. Gash (1988), "Cultures of Culture: Academics, Practitioners and the Pragmatics of Normative Control," *Administrative Science Quarterly* 33: 24–60; and J. Van Maanen and S. R. Barley (1984), "Occupational Communities: Culture and Control in Organizations," in B. Staw and T. Cummings (eds.), *Research in Organizational Behavior*, vol. 6, pp. 287–365.

27. J. Martin (1992), *Cultures in Organizations* (New York: Oxford University Press).

28. A. Wilkins and W. Dyer (1988), "Toward Culturally Sensitive Theories of Culture Change," *Academy of Management Review* 13 (4) 522–533.

29. S. Sackman (1991), *Cultural Knowledge in Organizations: Exploring the Collective Mind* (Newbury Park: Sage).

30. Wilkins and Dyer (1988), "Toward Culturally Sensitive Theories."

31. Sackman (1991), *Cultural Knowledge.*

32. Ibid., p. 40.

33. Borys and Jemison (1989), "Hybrid Arrangements."

34. Ibid., p.240.

35. J. Lippit and J. van Til (1981), "Can We Achieve a Collaborative Community? Issues, Imperatives, Potentials," *Journal of Voluntary Action Research* 10 (3–4): 7–17.

36. Fichman and Goodman (1996), "Customer-Supplier Tiers," p. 303.

37. Sackman (1991), *Cultural Knowledge.*

38. R. Gulati (1995), "Does Familiarity Breed Trust? The Implications of Repeated Ties for Contractual Choice in Alliances," *Academy of Management Journal* 38 (1): 85–112; and L. Hosmer (1995), "Trust: The Connecting Link between Organizational Theory and Philosophical Ethics," *Academy of Management Review* 20 (3): 379–403.

39. Sabel (1993), "Studied Trust."

40. Gray (1989), *Collaborating*; and Ring and Van de Ven (1994), "Developmental Processes."

41. Hosmer (1995), "Trust."

42. F. Fukuyama (1995), *Trust: The Social Virtues and the Creation of Prosperity* (Harmondsworth: Penguin Books) p. 26.

43. Lewis and Weigert (1985), "Trust as a Social Reality."

44. S. Robinson (1996), "Trust and Breach of the Psychological Contract," *Administrative Science Quarterly* 41 (4) 574–599.

45. Sabel (1993), "Studied Trust."

46. J. Selsky (1991), "Lessons in Community Development: An Activist Approach to Stimulating Inter-Organizational Collaboration," *Journal of Applied Behavioral Science* 27 (1): 91–115.

47. Abrahamson and Fombrun (1994), "Macrocultures."

48. C. Fombrun (1988), "Conflict and Cupertino in Interfirm Networks," unpublished paper, p. 11.

49. Sheppard and Tuchinsky (1996), "Interfirm Relationships," p. 361.

50. Larson (1992), "Network Dyads"; and Powell (1990), "Neither Market Nor Hierarchy."

51. Larson (1992), "Network Dyads."

52. A. Fox (1974), *Beyond Contract: Work Power and Trust Relations* (London: Faber).

53. Ibid.

54. Lewis and Weigert (1985), "Trust as a Social Responsibility."

55. See Ring and Van de Ven (1994), "Developmental Processes."

56. The parties to the alliance have requested that their identities and industry not be disclosed.

57. R. Luke, J. Begin, and D. Pointer (1989), "Quasi Firms: Strategic Inter-Organizational Forms in the Health Care Industry," *Academy of Management Review* 14 (1): 9–19.

58. E. Schein (1985), *Organization Culture and Leadership* (San Francisco: Jossey-Bass); Buono and Bowditch (1989), *The Human Side of Mergers*.

59. R. Daft (1992), *Organizational Theory and Design*, 4th ed. (St. Paul: West).

60. Van de Ven (1976), "On the Nature, Formation, and Maintenance," p. 2, emphasis in original.

61. E. Durkheim (1947), *The Division of Labor in Society* (Glencoe, IL: Free Press).

62. M. Seabright, D. Levinthal, and M. Fichman (1992), "Role of Individual Attachments in the Dissolution of Inter-Organizational Relationships," *Academy of Management Journal* 35 (1): 122–160.

63. G. DeSanctis and M. Poole (1994), "Capturing the Complexity in Advanced Technology Use: Adaptive Structuration Theory," *Organization Science* 5 (2): 121–147.

64. K. Golden (1992), "The Individual and Organizational Culture: Strategies for Action in Highly-Ordered Contexts," *Journal of Management Studies* 21 (1): 1–20.

65. Seabright, Levinthal, and Fichman (1992), "Role of Individual Attachments," p. 154; see also Fichman and Goodman (1996), "Customer-Suppliers Tiers."

66. Morgan (1997), *Images of Organization*, p. 149, emphasis in original.

67. M. Crozier and E. Friedberg (1980), *Actors and Systems* (Chicago: University of Chicago Press).

68. Rose (1988), "Organizations as Multiple Cultures."

69. J. Shaw (1990), "A Cognitive Categorization Model for the Study of Intercultural Management," *Academy of Management Review* 15 (4): 626–645.

70. M. Y. Brannen and J. Salk (1995), 626–645. "Putting Japanese and Germans Together: Negotiated Culture in a German-Japanese Joint Venture," paper presented at Academy of Management meeting, Vancouver.

71. Ibid., p. 25.

72. Ring and Van de Ven (1994), "Developmental Processes," p. 93.

73. Kanter (1989), *When Giants Learn to Dance*; and Robinson, S. (1996), "Trust and Breach of the Psychological Contract," *Administrative Science Quarterly* 41 (4): 574–599.

74. Golden (1992), "Individual and Organizational Culture"; and S. Robinson (1996), "Trust and Breach of the Psychological Contract."

75. M. Boisot (1986), "Markets and Hierarchies in a Cultural Perspective," *Organization Studies* 7: 135–158.

76. Martin (1992), *Cultures in Organizations*.

77. Ibid.

78. Boisot (1986), "Markets and Hierarchies."

79. Ibid.

80. See ibid., p. 149.

81. Hosmer (1995), "Trust."

82. C. Lane and R. Bachmann (1996), "The Social Constitution of Trust: Supplier Relations in Britain and Germany," *Organizational Studies* 17 (3): 379.

83. Boisot (1986), "Markets and Hierarchies."

84. Sackman (1991), *Cultural Knowledge*.

85. Boisot (1986), "Markets and Hierachies"; see also Crozier and Friedberg (1980), *Actors and Systems*; and Shaw (1990), "A Cognitive Categorization Model."

86. W. Stevenson and J. Bartunek (1996), "Power, Interaction, Position, and the Generation of Cultural Agreement in Organizations," *Human Relations* 49: 75–104.

87. Brannen and Salk (1995), "Putting Japanese and Germans Together," p. 23.

88. Sackman (1991), *Cultural Knowledge*.

89. K. Weick (1995), *Sensemaking in Organizations* (Thousand Oaks, CA: Sage).

90. Wilkins and Dyer (1988), "Toward Culturally Sensitive Theories."

91. Hosmer (1995), "Trust."

92. Fox (1974), *Beyond Contract*.

93. R. Mayer, J. Davis, and F. D. Schoorman (1995), "An Integrative Model of Organizational Trust, *Academy of Management Review* 20" (3): 709–734.

94. See Sheppard and Tuchinsky (1996), "Interfirm Relationships," p. 354; and Stevenson and Bartunek (1996), Interaction, Positions."

11

CONCLUSION: KEY QUESTIONS FOR THE LEAN ORGANIZATION

There are a number of questions that organizations face if they are going to be successful in the new millennium. The more important issues are: What will the important developments be in alliances and outsourcing over the coming years? Are the easy bits of alliances and outsourcing done? In other words, have they reached their peak or will they continue to grow? If there is growth, will it mean denser coverage of the same areas as now, or will new sectors be involved? Will there be a change in the nature of alliances and outsourcing, away from cost as a primary driver to service and simultaneously from antagonistic to cooperative relationships? Is there really a move to strategic alliances and outsourcing or is it a move to operational rather than strategic alliances and outsourcing arrangements? Will there be a tendency toward insourcing rather than outsourcing? Will there be greater variation in the way tasks are carried out, such that arrangements will be more complex than a simple dichotomy between internal and external sourcing? Naturally, it is hard to say precisely what the future trends will be. However, some of the influences on decision making are clearer.

GOVERNMENT

We can expect to see practical changes from government toward a more general alteration in the climate within which business operates:

- A switch from CCT to performance targets in the public sector. To ensure value for money for customers, these measures may stipulate year-on-year service improvements, but leave government departments and agencies free to decide their methods; the introduction of the minimum wage restricting the scope of contractors to cut payroll costs. Important issues are at what level it will be set and how it will be enforced;

- Greater regulation of the terms and conditions of employment of employees and atypical contracts;

- Greater regulation of contractors in certain sectors to meet minimum standards; this is likely to mean that the big sophisticated service providers will flourish at the expense of the cowboy operations; and

- Strengthened rights for trade unions to obtain bargaining agreements with employers if they can demonstrate sufficient membership and support.

EUROPEAN IMPACT

If any of the parties involved with the alliance or outsourcing program have their organizational roots within the European Union (EU), there may be EU legal requirements that impact the operation and/or contractual issues. This may come from two directions—from legislation by the EU itself or from the interpretation of existing law by the European courts, especially the European Court of Justice. Some proposals for change that will be addressed in the short term by the EU that affect alliances and outsourcing are:

to provide a codification of what constitutes an employee transfer;

to restrict coverage, where only an activity of an undertaking transfers, to those where they are part of an economic entity that retains its identity;

to make clear that the directive applies to public or private entities whether they operated for gain or not;

to allow member states to exclude the provisions from certain situations of rescue from bankruptcy;

similarly to allow employees terms and conditions to be changed where the survival of the business is in doubt;

within certain limitations to allow member states to decide who is an "employee" under the terms of the directive;

to harmonize definition of workers' representatives and to preserve their status and function more than at present;

to make the transferor and transferee jointly liable for the rights and obligations of employees so long as the transferor's liability is limited to those that occur in the first year after transfer;

to prevent multiestablishment organizations from avoiding the requirement to inform and consult by claiming that the enterprise in question was not involved in the transfer decision; and

to allow member states to introduce minimum workforce thresholds before there is a requirement to inform and consult.

Several of these changes would have a limited impact. The first three are already covered by European case law. For the rest there is a balance of advantage and disadvantage from the employer or employee perspective. Trade unions would no doubt welcome greater protection than at present. Currently, the continuity of their rights only applies while the transferred undertaking maintains itself distinct from the rest of the transferee's organization. Employers might benefit from greater flexibility in a corporate rescue operation. Contractors or the partner in an alliance might welcome the sharing of liability with clients.

PRESSURES ON EMPLOYERS

It is unlikely that the pressures to reduce costs and maximize productivity in a fast changing, competitive environment will decrease. This will mean that ways of doing business and working practices will constantly be examined. It will result in continuing changes in organizational structure and employee deployment, as well as acquisitions and disposal activities or companies.

Organizations will not be working in either the climate of the 1980s boom or the 1990s recession. There is something of a revolt against the philosophical championing of outsourcing once found in the management literature. This is partly because problems with outsourcing have occurred and have been highlighted, thereby causing some to wonder whether market-determined solutions are always appropriate. This links to the concern that the exclusive emphasis on rational, cost-based decision making neglects the softer issues of culture and employee motivation, which are also seen as important in deriving competitive advantage.

Organizations face a number of paradoxes: they form alliances or outsource in order to save money, yet are worried about being exploited in both financial and nonfinancial areas. They desire alliances or outsource to improve service, but fear that it may deteriorate or that they could be stuck with something that is obsolete. They choose to contract out to avoid the hassle of management, yet they still need to control. Some organizations (such as Virgin and ABB) will not be concerned with these issues; they would argue for strategic alliances and outsourcing by retaining only core tasks. Others who see it as a tactical question will make their judgments on an activity-by-activity basis, being careful not to damage their vital interests. They are likely to be sympathetic to the view that a simple core/periphery model is not without its problems. It is not always self-evident or easy to analyze. Who would think of the payroll system as a core task that confers competitive advantage? This is what a U.S. security company found in attracting quality guards, because the company had a reputation for on-time and accurate payment of wages.[1] Moreover, what constitutes the core changes? For example, automatic teller machines were once a source of competitive advantage but they are now standard practice.[2] Who the core workers are, and their skills, may also change (say through technological developments) as in the move away from big mainframe IT systems. Moreover, noncore activity may significantly affect the core indirectly. Issues of integration and synergy are important.

The move toward alliances aims for a win-win arrangement where both parties benefit. From the client's perspective it seeks to minimize Williamson's concern over opportunism by locking the contractor into a deal, but also satisfies contractor fears by in turn binding the client.[3] Despite the reservations of some, this type of arrangement is likely to prosper in high technology situations, but has also been the basis of many organizations' approach to supply contracts.[4] Appendix D looks at the questions that an organization should be asking of itself as well of those potential alliance partners and/or outsourcing suppliers.

A NEW MODEL FOR WORLD BUSINESS

This book has examined how organizations must, increasingly, focus on their core competencies and leverage more value through strategic alliances, partnerships, and outsourcing. It has explored the ways in which this kind of business activity should best be underpinned with a network organizational structure as well as new management skills and disciplines. What I have been describing is nothing less than a new model for a global business. In this model, an organization typically develops a network of business units, each with a significant degree of autonomy. Increasingly, those units are tied together not through the machinery of a command and control management hierarchy, but more through a sense of shared values and mission.

In the most effective organizations, the business units will have a vision of the competencies that bring strength to the organization as a whole—Honda is a good example—so that those competencies are developed in a way that balances the needs of the different business units. While internally the organization is a network, externally its business units forge a myriad of different relationships through alliances, partnerships, and outsourcing arrangements. The overarching of this is to build excellent performance.

Alliance building is gathering pace. The world's business is moving inexorably toward an arrangement of super-alliances. In these super-alliances, members cooperate with one another, each pooling its own core capabilities to create global leverage in valuable international markets. Increasingly, the core of all major world markets, whether in aerospace, computers, motor cars, construction, food, financial services, leisure, or other industries, is becoming dominated by a small member of such super- alliances in which the lead members are, themselves, usually billion dollar organizations. Those major organizations not on the inside track of super-alliances will find it harder to defend existing markets and penetrate new ones. This is a lesson already learned by the leaders in IT (IBM and Fujitsu), automobiles (General Motors and Ford), and aerospace (Boeing and Airbus Industrie). It is being rapidly learned in other business areas. However, alliance forming is not only a game for giants.

There are also plenty of opportunities for large (but not huge), medium, and small organizations. Increasingly, these super-alliances are becoming the hubs of great global industrial universes. Like a giant sun exerting a huge gravitational pull, the super-alliances are tugging into their orbits hundreds and, in the biggest cases (such as IBM), thousands of smaller organizations which, themselves, form partnerships and alliances or provide outsourcing services for the super-alliances at the center.

There are important implications here for those organizations still confused about their core competencies or unclear about how they should be developed in the future. Increasingly, these new individual solar systems glide through business space seeking out only those organizations with the best core competencies of their type. Excellence is becoming the byword for business performance in every industry, driven by increasingly sophisticated consumers, tougher competition and tighter regulatory frameworks for every major business.

It is the core competencies of the medium-sized and smaller organizations that catch the light from the super-alliances and provide the source of attraction that pulls them into the alliance's orbit. The skills of super-alliances increasingly lie partly in incorporating their own as well as their smaller partners' core competencies into best-in-class value chains that deliver world-class products.

Yet, while the direction is clear, there are still imponderables about the pace of change. For example, it is still not clear what impact the emergence of regional economic groupings like the European Union (EU), North American Free Trade Area (NAFTA) and the Association of South East Asian Nations (ASEAN) will have on the regulatory framework of the world economy. There is the possibility that an unpredictable world event—another oil crisis, another regional war—could have an unforeseen impact on world economic growth and development. There is the danger that national governments in the west could swing back toward protectionism faced with a mounting economic and industrial challenge from the Pacific Rim and China. All these imponderables could upset the pace of change, but not the direction.

The conclusion is that, increasingly, skill at finding, forgoing, and exploiting beneficial alliances as a route to building world-class organization performance will be one of the most valuable of business skills and one of the most critical issues on every organization's business agenda. Is it impossible for a major organization to opt out of this and survive? That looks increasingly problematical.

Hamel, Doz and Prahalad reached this conclusion:

> Running away from collaboration is no answer. Even the largest Western companies can no longer outspend their global rivals. With leadership in many industries shifting towards the East, companies in the United States and Europe must become good borrowers—much like Asian companies did the in 1960s and 1970s. Competitive renewal depends on building new process capabilities and winning new product and technology battles. Collaborations can be a low-cost strategy for doing both.[5]

This 1989 conclusion looks just as true all these years later.

NOTES

1. M. C. Lacity, L. Willcocks, and D. F. Feeny (1996), "The Value of Selective Outsourcing," *Sloan Management Review* 37 (3): 13–25.
2. See ibid.

3. O. E. Williamson (1973), "Markets and Hierarchies: Some Elementary Considerations," *American Economic Review* 63(2): 316–325) O. E. Williamson (1975), *"Markets and Hierarchies: Analysis and Antitrust Implications* (New York: Free Press).

4. K. Sisson (1995), "Organisational Structure, in S. Tyson (ed.), *Strategic Prospects for HRM*, IPD.

5. G. Hamel, Y. L. Doz, and C. K. Prahalad (1989), "Collaborate with Your Competitors—and Win*," Harvard Business Review* 67 (1): 139.

Appendix A

BIDDER DUE DILIGENCE CHECKLIST

1. Company/Consortia Information
   - Name
   - Addresses
   - Telephone and fax
   - Incorporation date and articles
   - Incorporation place and ACN
   - Brief history
   - Related companies
   - Associated companies
   - Net assets movements
2. Litigation
   - Historic litigation
   - Pending litigation
3. Addresses Five Years
4. Personnel
   - List of directors, secretary, executives
   - Former directors
   - Auditors

- Correct consultants

5. Ownership
    - Twenty largest shareholders
    - Beneficial ownership

6. Financial Information
    - Audited financial statements
    - Holding company financial statements
    - Loans
    - Change to financial situation
    - Confirmations

7. Business Affiliations
    - Director affiliations
    - Agencies and branches
    - Agencies
    - Change of name

8. Credit Rating

9. Government Investigation
    - Investigation or charges
    - Corporate regulatory investigation

10. Licenses

11. Corporate Structure
    - Corporate structure diagram
    - Joint venture

12. Share Structure

13. Business Failure
    - Receivership/liquidation
    - Charges
    - Agreement/composition
    - Receiver/liquidator
    - Judgments

14. Relevant Experience
    - Applications
    - References

- Terminated contracts
15. Publicly Listed Corporations
    - Fine, suspension for breaches of rules
    - Media releases
16. Foreign Corporations
    - Last year accounts
    - Last half-yearly accounts

Appendix B

OUTSOURCING AND LOCAL GOVERNMENT

In the postwar years until the end of the 1970s, the provision of public services saw enormous growth driven by the need for social reconstruction. There was political unanimity regarding the requirement for new public housing, schools, medical services, transportation, and the like, and an understanding that much of this should be provided through the medium of public bodies. This process of expansion and development was carried out in an environment of major commercial growth and a volatile market place, involving competition for labor and scarcity of materials.

The strategy adopted by local governments and other public bodies in these circumstances was based on some simple suppositions:

Usefulness rather than any concept of market or profitability should lead service design;

Access to services should be determined by need;

Service provision is about mass rather than individual consumption;

Public ownership and democratic accountability were preferable to market forces; and

Public service should emphasize standards of employment, job security.

The guarantee of appropriateness and quality lay in the professionalism of public sector staff, their sense of vocation, and their spirit of "serving the community." There was little evidence of interest in outsourcing, still less of work actually being carried out externally.[1] This mind-set appeared to be unchallenged by citizens who, as consumers, were relatively passive in their acceptance of the provider model and appeared to concede that the provider knew best. However, as the rise in customer focus and consumer demand grew in other sectors of the economy, so the public sector came under increasing scrutiny.

The change started in May 1979 in the United Kingdom with the election of Margaret Thatcher as prime minister.[2] This was followed by the election of a number of other governments that wished to reduce the size of the public sector, limit public expenditure, gain some control over the activities of public bodies, especially local government, apply a "free market" philosophy to local services, reduce the power of trade unions, and respond to the demand for consumer rights. The impact was felt across the entire public sector. There was and continues to be widespread denationalization of global free trade. There have been market testing and compulsory competitive tendering (CCT). The latter has been applied to ancillary services in many government departments and bodies, but it is the example of CCT in local government on which we will concentrate.

WHY THE NEED FOR MARKET TESTING?

If companies in the private sector were responding to the type of external and internal pressures by contracting out peripheral services, local authorities were being required to contract out what had previously been regarded as core activities in a competitive process. It is important to recognize this distinction. Whatever the reasoning was behind private sector organizations' decisions to outsource, they at least determined their own outcomes. For the public sector, the locus of control is outside the organization: it comes from a central government that would appear to have no faith in the sector's ability to manage the process itself. Nevertheless, some local authorities have embraced outsourcing with much more enthusiasm than others have.

What motivated government to adopt this position and why have some authorities pursued outsourcing willingly? For the governments supporting this, outsourcing was seen as a means of cutting costs and improving efficiency. It fitted with their free-market principles that determine:

The most cost-effective supplier should provide services;

Consumers have the right to choose who should provide a particular service;

Supply should be governed by the rules of price and demand; and

Competition engenders better and more cost-effective service.

The underlying principle was that activities carried out in the private sector were intrinsically more efficient than in public hands. The latter was seen as wasteful of resources because, without the spur of competition, there was no incentive to restrain costs or maximize efficiency. This was an issue of particular importance with government's aim of restraining public expenditure in order to reduce taxation and liberate the wealth-producing part of the economy. Successive initiatives by government have sought to open up certain activities in the public sector to market forces and confront the providers of local services with a new set of accountabilities. This implied a clearer separation between commissioning and delivering service. It required local authorities to move from a position where service standards were set, delivered and monitored within the same organization, to a situation in which there was a division between those who defined the service and those who delivered it.

Besides reducing costs and improving efficiency, another byproduct of this approach government hoped to see was a change in the nature of industrial relations in the public sector, to more like that which is seen in the private sector. Trade unions, the governments believed, had pushed up costs through their wage demands and prevented improved services by their working practice restrictions. Again, without the discipline of the market, this might be possible, but competition would force moderation in pay and lead to more cost-effective work arrangements.

The idea of market rationality being used as the yardstick for organizational decision making was greeted with varying degrees of hostility within the public sector, though there were some government authorities that were more positive. In particular, local authority officers and members were simply not used to an imposed set of indicators by which the effectiveness of their operations could be judged. Moreover, it was felt that these initiatives paid little heed to the state of the external market or the ability of in-house staff to compete.

Nevertheless, managers had to meet their legal obligations. Many local authorities developed their own way of identifying what would form part of individual contract packages. This process was guided to a greater or lesser extent by the existence of corporate objectives, reflecting the management culture, or the nature of political control, which itself affects the predomi-

nant norms—most importantly, regarding the importance of financial management. Some authorities embraced CCT with enthusiasm. Others
rejected the underlying philosophy that cost effectiveness should be the
only measure of quality and complied with the law to the minimum extent
necessary.

There also existed a strong lobby in local government that argued for the
retention of an in-house team that, although subject to the monitoring rigor
demanded by CCT, could still enable the council to:

Mirror its own values and objectives by retaining direct control over
delivery;

Reduce the overhead costs on other services by assisting in spreading
the central service charge over a wider area;

Provide employment for local people;

Have the flexibility to respond to emergencies;

Protect itself from commercial cartels and price rigging; and

Provide a model of good employment practice.

For many authorities, initial hostility gave way to acceptance, and in
some cases they realized that the legislation might have its benefits. CCT
provided an opportunity to expose some services to the market where there
were:

A perception of poor in-house delivery, evidenced by the number of
complaints;

A lack of customer awareness in service provision;

High cost of provision;

Exposure to unacceptable risk of service failure;

An existing external market to provide the service; and

Difficulty in recruiting quality staff.

In many ways, these reasons mirror that which applies in the private sector. There seems to be a similar mixture of positive and negative imperatives, ideological and pragmatic reasoning. Outsourcing was regarded by
some as a means to pursue service excellence or, as in the case of IT, to improve service quality. There are examples where it has also been used to do
the dirty work for councils, for example, to exit from restrictive trade union
deals. Similarly, CCT has been used as a cost-cutting device, either in itself

or to ensure that the in-house service provider could compete with external providers. In some cases, CCT has been embraced as a lever for change, to effect a cultural transformation toward greater performance orientation and a more innovative approach to service delivery. The response to CCT became less of a defensive reaction and more of a vehicle for strategic change. More pragmatically, some local government members saw the opportunity to reduce the costs of services without cuts in service provision, particularly during a period of centrally imposed cash constraints.

BENEFITS OF OUTSOURCING TO LOCAL GOVERNMENT

There have been a number of studies on the cost savings arising from CCT as a result of the tendering process.[3] Cost effectiveness is, however, not merely a measure of the cost of the provision of a service but consists of two complementary themes. One is cost, the other is quality: the degree to which the service meets the needs and expectation of users. Often the two benefits are seen as intertwined by commentators.

Studies of quality outcomes have been limited. Bailey and Davidson pull together some of this research.[4] They conclude those findings of improved quality may be overgeneralized because of conflict over the definition of quality, because of a lack of expert knowledge of service characteristics, and because of the vested interests of those on the client side to demonstrate their own effective performance through improving quality standards. From their own research they conclude that a managerial/professional approach to quality is predominant. This places the emphasis on processes, standard setting, and external independent accreditation. There is very little evidence of any significant involvement of providers or users of services that may be disappointing if one of the catalysts for CCT was consumer involvement or influence. There has been considerable emphasis on the management of the process in the belief that this will bring quality, rather than management outcomes.

PROBLEMS WITH OUTSOURCING IN LOCAL GOVERNMENT

The problems articulated by a number of local authorities include:

The inability of contractors to espouse the unwritten public sector values in providing service;

The inability to monitor contractor performance properly, due to budget cuts in both the auditing function and in the client group;

The difficulty of establishing true measures of value for money, either because of the political sensitivity of the question or because there is no established market price (because of the absence of a developed market in some services);

The problem of the relationship between quality and price, particularly within the limitations imposed by the guidelines;

Poor contractor performance, particularly in planning service provision;

Financial instability of the contractor;

Potential conflicts of interest, where in an in-house service provision the service provider and the client have been the same;

Loss of expertise to the authorities that is unlikely to be recovered, thereby restricting future options; and

The staffing implications off CCT (redundancies, uncertainties, morale, lowering of wages, new work arrangements).

By late 1995, the Local Government Management Board (LGMB) in the United Kingdom was aware of only just over 200 cases in six years of CCT where problems had been sufficiently serious to warrant termination of the contract.[5] Approximately two-thirds of terminations involved external contractors. Nevertheless, in a LGMB survey in late 1995, 17 percent of respondents marked external contractor performance as unsatisfactory or very poor, only 5 percent of in-house service providers were similarly marked.

THE MANAGEMENT OF OUTSOURCING

Despite the force of legislation behind outsourcing there was still plenty of scope for different interpretations and approaches to CCT. Local government authorities still had to decide whether to submit an in-house bid. This consideration preceded a further set of decisions about which services, how much of the service, and in what style of package work the bid should be put out to tender.

There were fears expressed that authorities would package tenders in a way that would strongly favor in-house staff. In reality, there is little evidence of exotic packaging designed to frustrate a private sector bidder. Indeed, many governments have anticompetitive behavior laws that expressly forbid this and lay a duty on local authorities to foster a private sector market in order that bids might be obtained. Naturally, some authorities have been much more proactive than others in positively encouraging the market to bid for work. Some have sought the views of potential bidders while compiling specifications on their packaging and content. Others, while satisfying the government's requirements, have used a variety of strategies (management buyouts and partnering arrangements with existing private sector operators) to protect staff and safeguard some of the council's core values and objectives that were perceived to be threatened by the CCT regime.

In order to be clear as to what the process and rules would be in a context of an overall philosophy, one council established a central team to formulate an approach. The result is that managers of services are required to manage within a framework whose objectives are to:

Adopt mechanisms to safeguard the council's interests; develop strategies with the aim of increasing the quality of service;

Determine packaging for high quality, value for money services;

Introduce organizational arrangements to facilitate effective client roles;

Prepare specifications that reflect the budget and emphasize the council's public service ethos;

Introduce arrangements that would allow in-house teams to bid; and protect staff terms and conditions as far as possible.

There are considerations that need to be made for outsourcing in the public sector that are either wholly absent from the private sector or are not to the same degree important. Creating a mechanism to divide a department into client and contractor roles can be complicated if there is to be an in-house bid, particularly given any statutory rules that may apply. It is necessary to provide transparent trading practices if the internal bid is successful, otherwise "foul" will be called by the disappointed external contractors. There may be statutory minimum and maximum contract periods that prevent local authorities taking a view on what type of contractual relationship they seek.

As remarked earlier, there has been a growing acceptance by local authorities that outsourcing was an acceptable approach with some benefits to be realized through it, although there remained reservations about transferring work and staff to contractors that would not uphold the values espoused by councils. Some governments have been concerned to find less work being exposed to tender and won by the private sector than had been antici-pated. For example, in the United Kingdom, the government set up a review in 1996. The findings proposed an increase in the percentage of work to be tendered under each function (for example, for finance, this meant a rise from 35 to 65 percent) and a lowering of exemption levels.

Local authorities have expressed their concern about the effects of CCT on certain of these functions (legal, finance, personnel, road maintenance, garbage collection, and so forth) that they saw as strategically important. They were also worried about the market's capacity to respond with credi-ble alternatives. Many, no doubt, wanted to protect their own employees from being driven into contractor employment. Some local authorities be-lieve there is little evidence of anticompetitive behavior, or of the cheating and use of subterfuge to avoid CCT of which state or national governments often accuse them.

The continuing pressure to outsource a greater volume and type of work is driving some authorities to regard themselves, willingly or not, as client commissioners and procurers of services rather than as providers. This would mean a shift in their role to enabling and facilitating rather than do-ing. Yet, as in the private sector, there is still a need to define what core func-tions need to be retained for the task to be performed. Such activities as planning, audit, and standards are likely to be included in the list.

However, to a much greater extent than the private sector, the context in which these decisions will be made will be profoundly affected by those in power in central government. A change in the state or national governments may give local authorities more scope to be innovative in the way they ap-proach service delivery. This could mean greater variety in the balance be-tween internal and external provision, and potentially greater control over the manner of contractor performance. Whatever the mechanisms used or the level of scope to be innovative, the pressure to hold down costs and push up quality will remain.

NOTES

1. T. Colling (1993), "Contracting Public Services: The Management of Com-pulsory Competitive Tendering in Two County Councils," *HRM Journal* 3 (4): 1–15.

2. The changes that these governments imposed were, in their respective countries, commonly referred to as Thatchernomics (UK), Reaganomics (U.S.), and Rogernomics (New Zealand)—the word being a combination of the head of the government with *economic* since many of the changes were based on the ra-tional economic model.

3. Audit Commission (1984), *Further Improvements in Refuse Collection: A Review by the Audit Commission* (London: HMSO); Audit Commission (1987), *Competitiveness and Contracting Out of Local Authorities' Services* (London: HMSO); Audit Commission (1988), *Competitiveness Management of Parks and Green Spaces* (London: HMSO); B. Walker (1993); *Competing for Building Maintenance: Direct Labour Organizations and Compulsory Competitive Tendering* (London: HMSO); K. Walsh (1991), *Competitive Tendering for Local Authority Services: Initial Experiences* (London: HMSO).

4. S. J. Bailey and C. Davidson (1996), "Did Quality Really Increase for UK Local Government Services Subject to Compulsory Competitive Tendering?" Discussion Paper 33, Department of Economics, Glasgow Caledonian University, Glasgow.

5. Local Government Management Board (1995), *CCT Information Service Survey*, Report Number 12 (London: LGMB).

Appendix C

CASE STUDY: LATROBE REGIONAL HOSPITAL OUTSOURCING PROJECT

For most of this century at least, infrastructure provision in Australia has been the almost exclusive preserve of government, particularly of state governments. Traditionally, Australian governments have provided, for example, almost all of the nation's transport, electricity, gas and water infrastructure and services, and the great majority of education and health infrastructure and services. By the early 1990s, however, a change was occurring and state governments sought to promote privately financed projects.

Similarly, the Australian federal government, whose role in direct provision of infrastructure is largely limited to airports, defense, telecommunications, and some tertiary education, is now seeking to transfer to the private sector greater responsibility for ownership and operation of infrastructure. The reasons for the willingness of governments to change their approach are complex, but economic and financial necessity and a fundamental shift in political outlook are dominant influences.

The economic forces driving the change at the state level were:

On the one hand, a real limit to the extent that state governments could fund new or improved infrastructure, particularly in an environment of relatively static revenues and high accumulated debt, and on the other, a continuing growth in demand for economic and social infrastructure by both the business community and the public in general;

Constitutional limitations on the capacity of Australian states to raise additional taxation revenue;

Successive real reductions in the value of grants received from the federal government;

An increase in the proportion of total grants from the federal government that were tied to specific purposes and, therefore, not available for general purpose expenditure; and

Changes to funding arrangements by the Australian Loan Council that restricted state borrowing opportunities.

It was a policy of the Victorian state government that private enterprise be actively encouraged to invest in the state's future wherever benefits in terms of efficiency and cost effectiveness can be demonstrated.

The Infrastructure Investment Policy for Victoria ("the Policy"), released in August 1994, demonstrates the government's commitment to strengthening its partnership with the private sector.

POLICY OBJECTIVES

The Policy has the purpose of assisting Victorian government agencies and private proponents seeking investment in state infrastructure, facilities, and services. It sets out clear and concise guidelines, promoting greater certainty for business in making infrastructure investment decisions. The government is pursuing a number of objectives:

To procure assets, goods and services in the most efficient, cost-effective and timely manner;

To take advantage of new technologies and innovations, private sector management skills, and a wide range of financing techniques;

To promote the growth of new and existing Victorian businesses and employment; and

To strengthen the state's economy, producing sustainable social, cultural, and other quality of life benefits.

The Policy addresses a range of significant aspects of private enterprise involvement in the financing and provision of public infrastructure, including: setting out principles for assessing the merits of proposals for private sector investment; examples of appropriate forms of investment; the process to be adopted in developing infrastructure projects with the private sector; and provisions to apply to intellectual property and confidentiality.

It demonstrates an ongoing government commitment to reducing uncertainties faced by the private sector in pursuing project opportunities, while increasing efficiency of the bidding process and minimizing costs to the private sector. The Policy encourages competitive bidding and allocation of risk to those parties best positioned to assess and manage it, providing rewards for enterprise and risk taking through appropriate returns within a competitive environment while also securing benefits for the Victorian community.

APPROVAL PROCESS

A major concern for private sector parties, addressed by the Policy, is the incidence in Australia, as in other countries, of cancellation or radical change to projects on which considerable sums have been spent by bidders in research and preparation of bids.

The Policy has a three-stage approval process involving:

1. Approval by government to call for registrations of capability;
2. Approval by government to issue a detailed project brief; and finally
3. Approval by the responsible minister and the treasurer of proposed contracts as properly conforming with the previous project approvals, and a report to government confirming that the requirements of the project brief have been met by a bidder and hence that the project may proceed.

Government intends that once a project brief has been issued the project will proceed to implementation, subject only to achievement of the functional and other requirements specified in the project brief, including any cost to government.

APPLICATION TO HEALTH CARE

Health care forces have been slower to gain momentum due to the need to ensure adequate output measures of what public health care providers are spending on service delivery, and the complexities of describing the service needs to be met for the purposes of contractual obligations.

There is no reason why the delivery of public health care services should be any different from prisons or electricity or roads. In fact, the delivery of public hospital services by denominational health care providers such as the Sisters of Mercy and the Sisters of Charity are an example of how successful such arrangements can be.

Through the LaTrobe Regional Hospital Project, the Victorian government sought to demonstrate its commitment to improving access to high quality health care through greater private sector involvement in the provision of public health care services. This project was designed to provide the people of the LaTrobe Valley with a new, state-of-the-art hospital, and high quality health services at an efficient price, through private sector ownership and operation. It provides treatment and care on exactly the same basis as is currently available in publicly run hospitals. In partnership with Monash University, the operator of the new hospital is also expected to make a significant contribution to the education and training of health care professionals, with a unique emphasis on education and training for rural practice.

BACKGROUND

The LaTrobe Regional Hospital (LRH) previously operated two acute hospital campuses at Moe and Traralgon (ninety minutes drive from Melbourne by freeway) and a psychiatric facility at Hobson's Park near Traralgon. There is a 109-bed hospital at Sale, 64 km to the east and an 86-bed hospital at Warragul, 75 km to the west. The nearest major metropolitan hospital is at Dandenong, 110 km west of the LaTrobe Valley. For patients who choose private hospital treatment, the options are either a small 45-bed private hospital in Morwell or a private hospital in Melbourne.

The two acute hospital campuses had served the community well but were limited in service provision by duplication and aging facilities and had difficulty in attracting and retaining medical staff. The government considered that there were diseconomies in the then current structure of LaTrobe that resulted in suboptimal service delivery outcomes.

In 1995, following receipt and extensive research of independent reports that showed that the existing health care facilities in the LaTrobe Valley no longer met the needs of local and regional communities, the then Department of Health and Community Services in partnership with the Department of Treasury and Finance established a project team. The team was composed of department members and appropriate external advisers to develop a model under the infrastructure investment policy that would, when implemented, improve the efficiency of delivery of publicly funded health services in the LaTrobe Valley and Gippsland. External consultants specializing in probity, legal, finance, communications, design and construction, and industrial relations were appointed to the project. Communication and industrial relations strategies were developed and implemented.

In accordance with the Infrastructure Investment Policy for Victoria (IIPV), a registration of capability document was developed and released in July 1995 and a project brief and draft contract were subsequently issued to short-listed consortia in April 1996. Following extensive contract negotiations and the development of a transitional management arrangement, contracts for the building, owning, and operation of a new LaTrobe Regional Hospital and the management of the then existing three LaTrobe Regional Hospital campuses were executed by Australian Hospital Care, LaTrobe Regional Hospital Pty. Ltd., and the state on January 24, 1997.

Australian Hospital Care assumed management responsibilities of existing campuses on February 2, 1997. The builder, Multiplex Constructions, began site works in March 1997. The new 257-bed hospital was formally opened by the premier and the minister for health on July 24, 1998, and commissioned for operation on September 1, 1998, as required under the contract. To the best of our knowledge, it is the only hospital in Australia that has passed infection control tests on the first attempt. The hospital is operational and enjoying 100 percent occupancy rates.

Community acceptance is extraordinary. When the project first began, the community was hostile, sceptical of the private sector's ability to deliver first-class health services, and concerned about job losses and the potential for quality of care to diminish as the private sector operator pursued higher profit margins. Community action groups waged a strong antiprivatization campaign. Project team members were subjected to constant verbal barrages and the occasional flying chair.

However, by the time of the open day, July 19, 1998, community attitude had changed dramatically. Over 18,000 people turned out to tour the new facility. Since the commissioning date, an additional 230 parking spaces have been added to the previously required number of 402 to cope with demand.

The project's objectives were to:

Deliver a comprehensive health service to public hospital patients in the LaTrobe Valley that is also a referral service for the Greater Gippsland Region;

Ensure optimal and seamless integration of the new LRH services with the other health services provided to the people of Gippsland;

Ensure that high quality health services are delivered cost efficiently and effectively at or less than the projected cost of public sector service delivery from a single greenfields site;

Establish a model for an appropriate level of private sector participation in the delivery of health services;

Ensure that the project met government policy objectives and was implemented in accordance with the infrastructure investment policy for Victoria principles;

Transfer appropriate risks to the private sector, including the risks of owning any building and facilities associated with health service delivery;

Provide for all health services and facilities of the new LRH to be available for undergraduate education and professional training of medical students, doctors, nurses, and other health professionals as contemplated by the affiliation agreement with Monash University; and

Provide and encourage health education and training with a rural focus.

As previously mentioned, government seeks through the infrastructure investment policy process to allocate risk to those parties that government considers are best able to assess and manage that position. Accordingly, an appropriate risk allocation matrix and service delivery, along with community safeguard standards, needed to be developed by the project team. The risk matrix and service standards formed the backbone of the draft contract.

The risk matrix that applies in general to all hospital projects is divided into two stages. First was the development or construction phase and second was the operating phase. Consortia are required to acknowledge their acceptance of the risk allocation matrix in their registration of capability submission and again in responses to the project brief and draft contract. Consortia are expected to assume the following risks:

A.   Development Phase

Risk	Contracted Provider
	Approvals:
Planning approvals	*
Other government/public authority/local government approvals	*

Increases in local government charges	*
	Site and Site Conditions:
Site contamination/ environment/conditions	*
	Construction:
All risks	*
Cost to complete	*
Variations	*
Operational commissioning deadline	*
	Force Majeure during Development
Suspension and extension of obligations	*
Reinstatement	*
Sunset date	*
	Industrial Conditons:
Industrial disputes not aimed specifically at the project	*
	Completion and Commissioning:
Completion/certification	*
Commissioning plant/equipment	*
	Finance:
Procuring finance	*
Interest rate to date of signing, and interest rate change after date of signing	*
State and federal taxation change	*

B. Operating Phase

Risk **Contracted Provider**

	Licenses:
Accreditation	*
Public hospital patient demand	*

Revenue from public hospital patient services	*
Coast to operate to agreed standard	*
Other industrial disputes not aimed at the project	*
Operating performance/outcomes standards	*
Laws, policies and guidelines	*
Operating default	*
	Deviation from Standards:
Change in region's patient mix and demographic profile	*
Change in operating standards at state's request	*
Change in operating standards to maintain accreditation	*
Requirement for new facilities at state's request	*
	Financial:
Insurances	*
Interest rate risk	*
Debt repayment	*
Federal tax legislation	*
State tax legislation	*
Taxation risk generally	*
Changes in casemix and other state funding mechanisms applied to all Victorian publicly funded hospitals	*
	Facilities Suitability:
Building/plant durability	*
Design suitability for performance/ operability	*
Maintenance and replacement of any buildings/plant	*

	Changes in Law:
Federal legislation	*
State legislation and policy not aimed at the project	*
Teaching, training, and research	*
Change in control	*
	Force MajeureDuring Operating Phase.
Suspension and extension of obligations	*
Reinstatement	*
Sunset date	*

The asterisk under "Contracted Provider" signifies that it is government's intention to transfer those risks to the prvate sector and that the transfer will come into effect through the project contract. Bidders may choose not to accept some or all risks, but obviously the level of risk transfer away from government is part of the evaluation criteria.

In the case of LaTrobe, the successful bidder bears:

Service delivery and all operational risks: The service profile details the capacity required at the new LRH for each clinical specialty and provides for enhanced service provision in modern facilities complemented by advanced technology. The service plan specifies services and activity levels and key service capabilities that are required.

Casemix risk: Should the level of clinical service delivery for inpatient services fall below target, only those services that are delivered would be paid for. Should the level of clinical activity exceed targets as set from time to time within a particular year, the operator would need to rely on the same throughput pool arrangements for all Victorian public hospitals. Further, the successful bidder was required to accept the risk of future changes to, or substitution of, the casemix funding mechanism.

Demand risk: The new LRH must provide treatment to all patients regardless of whether a patient has health insurance, a patient's financial status, a patient's place of residence or whether a patient intends to elect or elects to be treated as a public or private patient.

Government does not underwrite a minimum service throughput: Terminal value risk (government is under no obligation to purchase the facility at the end of the contract period); operator to nominate the preferred site (all suitable government sites and some privately owned sites were made available to bidders); facilities and maintenance risk; maximum flexibility was provided to bidders through a concentration on outputs rather than process, with minimum concentration on bed numbers and facilities requirements; the successful bidder was required to accept the risks of physical design including determination of actual acute inpatient bed numbers required to meet specified outcomes, construction, fit-out, commissioning, and maintenance; and government was not prepared to make available either the Moe or Traralgon campuses to ensure that the region had a brand new purpose-built hospital and that there was no adverse impact on service delivery during the construction of the new LRH.

Service standards: Stringent minimum standards for the delivery of health services from the new LRH needed to be established as did mechanisms for addressing service delivery failures. These activities and measures of quality related to the management and delivery of health services at the new LRH are focused on issues of concern to patients.

Quality standards: Compliance with all legislation and Department of Human Services policies is required; Australian Council of Healthcare Standards (ACHS) standards were required to be met from commissioning of new LRH with formal accreditation achieved within eighteen months of commissioning; commonwealth outcome standards with respect to nursing home beds must be met. The commonwealth department of health and family services sent teams to the new LRH to monitor Commonwealth Outcome Standards; to ensure adequate standards of health care were provided immediately from when services were first delivered, the new LRH was required to establish clinical committees that address the requirements of patient care, medical appointments and credentialling, and human resources; government has the right to appoint an expert at any time to determine if the service standards are not being met even if none of the "service quality and quantity triggers" has been activated; new LRH must participate in data collection and surveys as required by department of health and family services, for example medical record coding audits, patient satisfaction surveys; community advisory board was established and reports directly to the minister for health; and the new LRH established a community advisory board that facilitates input from the community with respect to health care programs and service standards.

Community Safeguards: Government should be entitled to inspect the new LRH at any time; if patient health or safety is at risk, government must have the right (under contract and via legislation) to step in and operate the new LRH; failure to meet the quality standards or to provide the specified services results in default and a cure period then applies (length of cure period should be directly related to the severity and impact of the default); default should enable the state to withhold a percentage of the service payments and material default not rectified should give rise to termination of the contract (normal contractual remedies would apply); if the successful bidder defaulted, a regime should exit under which submissions could be called from preagreed operators to assume the new LRH contract; government should also be able to elect to assume the role of replacement operator or under certain circumstances build a replacement facility; and these issues, although not exhaustive of the LRH project brief's requirements, were provided to shortlisted consortia for their consideration and response.

SO WHAT WAS LEARNED AT THE LRH?

You can never do too much talking to stakeholders. Messages should be simple and repeated frequently. Staff must be kept informed of the project's progress through regular newsletters and open forums. Agreement should be reached at an early stage with affected trade unions and, therefore, staff. This can be achieved through the development of a memorandum of understanding that details the state's obligations up to the time of decommissioning the old facility, but does not bind the state to any obligation at the new privatized facility.

Transitional management arrangements need to be well thought out as problems arise. Services must continue to be delivered while staff recruitment takes place. Conflicts of interest or loyalty arise as decommissioning approaches. It is probable that providing access to staff for recruitment purposes is preferable to full transitional management arrangements.

The project team must be adequately resourced with both full-time employees and appropriate external consultants. Good consultants are hard to find. The state should appoint consultants before release of the registration of capability to ensure the best advisers are secured. Consultant costs need to be closely monitored.

Despite the occurrence of outsourcing the public still believes that the government is responsible for service provision. The private sector always has its hand out. Contracts need to be firm but not adversarial. Freedom of information requests are a frequent occurrence. Filing systems need to be well designed to cope with requests.

Experienced contract management staff are required to meet demands created by these complex contracts. Staff involved in the outsourcing should be groomed to take over contract management. A project manager, appointed by the winning consortium, is essential to ensuring that the owner and the operator who build, own, and operate projects are not at loggerheads during the construction period. This is because the builder is generally contracted to the financier (the owner) rather than the operator of the new facility. Make sure that a competent probity auditor is appointed to the project. Develop and publicize the probity plan. The probity plan should not be overly restrictive; common-sense principles should apply.

And finally, despite good planning and execution, it is only after three to five years of operation that the department will be able to say that projects of this nature are really a success or a failure.

Appendix D

KEY QUESTIONS FOR A LEAN ORGANIZATION

This book has discussed how to create a lean organization, that is, an organization that leverages value from its core competencies through strategic alliances and outsourcing. It is clear that there is no one route to the lean organization model; the concept of the lean organization is legitimately interpreted in different ways. However, the discussion in the preceding chapters suggests a range of policy measures that an organization moving toward the lean organization model ought to adopt.

In the final analysis, it is impossible to be pedantically prescriptive about the approach an organization should take in order to develop its core competencies, enter strategic alliances, shift toward a partnership culture or develop a network organization strategy. There are simply too may variables for the same answer to be right for every organization.

It is, however, possible to ask the same questions, to which there may well be different answers. Those organizations that are most successfully migrating toward the lean organization had already asked the questions that follow. They had found their own answers to them, and the challenge for those organizations that wish to emulate their success is to do likewise.

CORE COMPETENCIES

- Can the board of directors and/or senior managers define the organization's core competencies?

- If not, have core competencies been defined but not adequately communicated?
- If core competencies have not been defined, what action should be taken to do so?
- Who should play a part in defining core competencies: the board, strategic planners, SBU managers, line managers?
- Is everybody involved in defining core competencies clear about the three elements in a competence: technology, governance process, and collective learning?
- To what extent do the organization's core competencies underpin the organization's products and services?
- Have the competencies been benchmarked against other excellent competitors?
- If so, were the competencies found to be best in class?
- If not, what actions should be taken to improve the effectiveness of core competencies?
- If competencies have not been benchmarked, what needs to be done to gather performance data about them?
- Do products and services need to be more effectively aligned with core competencies?
- What proportion of investment is directed at building and developing core competencies?
- If this is low, do investment priorities need to be reexamined?
- Have managers looked at all the ways in which current core competencies might be exploited, for example, in related product areas?
- Are the core competencies strong enough to sustain the organization's success in the medium and long term?
- If not, can the competencies be strengthened with internal investment and development?
- If not, can the organization acquire additional relevant competencies through strategic partnerships or alliances?

EXISTING PARTNERSHIPS

- Does your organization currently work with any strategic partners?
- How do these partnerships contribute to the organization's overall business objectives?

- Is the contribution of these partnerships to business objectives regularly measured and monitored?
- Are there lessons from these successful partnerships that can be applied elsewhere in the organization?
- Has the organization entered any partnerships that failed to deliver their objectives?
- What lessons can be learned from those partnerships?

SEARCHING FOR NEW PARTNERS

- Has the board a clear view of how its business strategy is to be achieved, with or without partnerships?
- In which area of your organization's activities might the board need to search for new partners?
- Has the organization identified clear gaps in the fulfillment of its business strategy that could be filled with the aid of a partner or partners?
- What kind of partners might be needed in those areas, strategic or tactical, short or long term?
- In any given area, what contribution is your organization looking for from a prospective partner: assets, know-how, market position, intellectual property, cash, and so forth?
- In any given area, what can your organization contribute to a partnership: assets, know-how, market position, intellectual property, cash, and so forth?
- Has your organization established clear criteria for its prospective partner: cultural compatibility, financial strength, technical contribution, market contribution?
- Have prospective partners been fully evaluated against all relevant criteria?
- Can prospective partners on the short list realistically provide what the organization is looking for?
- Has your organization matched its core competencies against those of prospective partners?
- If so, is there complementarity or is there a risk of conflict?
- Do prospective partners on the short list have reasonable cultural compatibility with the organization?

- Is it likely that the prospective partners might be willing to enter an alliance with your organization?
- How can your organization frame its approach to the prospective partner(s) in an attractive and enticing way?
- At what level should the prospective partner be approached: board/director level, SBU level, departmental head?
- Who should lead the approach to the prospective partner?
- Has your organization considered what processes to use to consider any partnership offers that it receives?

NEGOTIATING A PARTNERSHIP DEAL

- In your organization, is there high-level sponsorship (usually from the board) for the proposed partnership?
- Before opening negotiations, have you defined what you want to achieve from the partnership?
- Have you identified those areas where concessions or compromise would be unwise?
- Have you defined those areas where it will be possible to be flexible in negotiations?
- Who will be involved in the negotiating team?
- Does the negotiating team contain a range of skills and knowledge together with negotiating and presentation skills?
- What are the limits of authority of the negotiating team?
- Are consultants needed during the negotiation?
- If so, has the role of the consultants been adequately defined?
- Has a timetable been set for the negotiations?
- What form of partnership will best meet the needs of the parties: collaboration, joint venture, merger?
- What is each party going to contribute to the partnership?
- Does what the other party is contributing to the partnership adequately match your own organization's expectations?
- Can the organization deliver what it says it will contribute?
- Can the partner deliver what it says it will contribute?

- Does the memorandum of understanding (or what you have called your legal documentation) encapsulate the full terms of the agreement?
- Does the memorandum of understanding define responsibilities for implementation and set a timetable?

IMPLEMENTING A PARTNERSHIP

- Does the final agreement include all relevant matters including contributions, management of the partnership, conflict resolution, apportionment of profits, and exit provisions?
- What level of autonomy is given to the partnership operation?
- What type and frequency of reporting is required from the partnership operation?
- Does the partnership have clear milestone events at which progress can be judged?
- Has the purpose of the partnership been widely communicated within your organization?
- Has there been wide buy-in to the partnership or are there still pockets of resistance that need to be addressed?
- Have any change management issues raised by the partnership been adequately addressed?
- Is there adequate machinery in place for communicating with the partner(s)?
- In what ways might information technology be used in order to communicate more effectively with the partner(s)?
- Is there a need to define the limits of information that may be exchanged with the partner(s)?
- Does staff working in the partnership need special training, for example, in languages or understanding a foreign culture?
- Is your organization organized in order to learn from the partnership?
- What structures underpin the organizational learning?
- How will organizational learning be captured and disseminated throughout your organization?
- In the short, medium, and long term, what criteria are you using to determine the success or failure of the partnership?

- How are you measuring those criteria?
- Are further opportunities for developing the partnership being adequately explored?

OUTSOURCING PARTNERSHIPS

- Does your organization already use outsourcing?
- If so, are those arrangements working satisfactorily and what lessons can be learned from them?
- If not, why are or were the arrangements unsatisfactory and what can be learned from them?
- Has the organization developed a comprehensive view of the role of outsourcing in its business strategy?
- It not, should such a review be undertaken?
- Does your organization have a clear view of its core competencies and, thus, its peripheral activities that might be candidates for outsourcing?
- Should outsourcing be limited to support functions, such as IT and accounting, or should it include manufacturing functions?
- If manufacturing is to be outsourced in whole or in part, what are the risks that your organization will lose core skills in technologies?
- Alternatively, is it necessary to outsource some aspects of manufacturing in order to acquire key skills either in technologies or manufacturing processes?
- What are the risks that your outsourcer might ultimately become a competitor in your core market?
- Are these risks acceptable and how can they be minimized?
- If manufacturing is outsourced, what steps can your organization take to erect a strategic block between the outsourcer and your market?
- Before choosing supplier, have you defined the criteria you will use in the selection?
- Have the outsourcing supplier's claims been carefully checked and have references been thoroughly investigated?
- Are you confident that the outsourcer can deliver what it says it will?

- What is the downside if it cannot and is there a contingency plan to deal with this situation?

- Has your organization made a realistic cost-benefit analysis of outsourcing, including the transaction costs that it entails?

- Do you feel there is a suitable cultural fit between your organization and the outsourcing supplier?

- Is the agreement sufficiently flexible to deal with your needs and meet changing requirements?

- Are the criteria by which the outsourcer will be judged defined with precision?

- What are the staffing implications of entering the outsourcing agreement and what are the costs of dealing with them?

- Are the circumstances and terms for ending the agreement clearly defined?

MANAGEMENT DISCIPLINES FOR PARTNERSHIPS AND OUTSOURCING

- Has your organization identified those managers who could be effective in working through partnerships and outsourcing?

- Is your organization's culture adept at working in partnerships, for example in searching for win-win situations?

- What cultural changes do managers need to assimilate in order to become more adept at managing through partnerships and outsourcing?

- How will your organization define the roles and responsibilities of managers who work with partnerships and outsourcing?

- What special training might managers need to work with partnerships and outsourcing?

- Does your organization have managers who would make good "brokers" in partnerships and alliances?

- Do managers have the necessary skills to use partnerships and alliances as learning opportunities and to develop that learning into organizational knowledge?

PARTNERSHIP CULTURE

- Is your organization's structure compatible with developing a partnership culture?
- Do the values that underpin your organization encourage people to work in partnership?
- How far has your organization developed internal partnership?
- Does your organization work with business teams that cross internal departmental or functional boundaries?
- What can be done to make those teams work more effectively?
- Can cross-functional teamworking be extended in the organization?
- How does your organization define roles and responsibilities for its staff?
- Does your organization truly empower employees and foster decision taking at the lowest possible levels?
- What steps does your organization take in order to manage conflict and personal stress, sometimes the unwelcome side effects of a networking culture?

TECHNOLOGY ENABLERS

- In which ways does the use of IT reinforce and develop core competencies?
- Do all employees have access to an appropriate level of IT support?
- Have they been trained to make the best possible use of that support?
- What can be done to enable IT to facilitate more effective business processes?
- In which ways can IT be used to promote more effective organizational learning?
- How can IT be used more effectively to promote communication within the organization and with external partners?

BIBLIOGRAPHY

Abrahamson, E., and Fombrun, C. (1994). Macrocultures: Determinants and Consequences. *Academy of Management Review* 19: 728–755.

Achordoguy, A. (1990). A Brief History of Japan's Keiretsu. *Harvard Business Review* 68 (4):58–59.

Alexander, M., and Young, D. (1996). Outsourcing: Where's the Value? *Long Range Planning* 29 (5):728–730.

Appelbaum, S. H., Leblanc, M., and Shapiro, B. T. (1998). The Aftermath of Downsizing. *Journal of Management Development* 17 (6):402–431.

Argyris, C. (1992). *On Oranizational Learning*. 2nd ed. Oxford: Blackwell Business.

Atkinson, J., and Meager, N. (1986). *New Forms of Work*. Report 121, IMS.

Audit Commission (1984). *Further Improvements in Refuse Collection: A Review by the Audit Commission*. London: HMSO.

Audit Commission (1987). *Competitiveness and Contracting Out of Local Authorities' Services*. London: HMSO.

Audit Commission (1988). *Competitiveness Management of Parks and Green Spaces*. London: HMSO.

Auditor-General of Victoria (1997). *Metropolitan Ambulance Service: Contractual and Outsourcing Practices*. Melbourne: Victorian Government Printer.

Badaracco, J. L. (1991). *The Knowledge Link: How Firms Compete Through Strategic Alliances*. Boston: Harvard Business School Press.

Bailey, S. J., and Davidson, C. (1996). Did Quality Really Increase for UK Local Government Services Subject to Compulsory Competitive Tendering?

Discussion Paper 33, Department of Economics, Glasgow Caledonian University, Glasgow.

Barley, S., Meyer, G., and Gash, D. (1988). Cultures of Culture: Academics, Practitioners and the Pragmatics of Normative Control. *Administrative Science Quarterly* 33: 24–60.

Bartlett, C. A., and Ghoshal, S. (1998). *Managing across Borders: The Transnational Solution*. 2nd ed. Boston: Harvard Business School Press.

Beamish, P. W. (1988). *Multinational Joint Ventures in Developing Countries*. London: Routledge.

Bertodo R. (1990). The Collaboration Vortex: Anatomy of a Euro-Japanese Alliance. *EIU Japanese Motor Business* (June): 29–43.

Bertodo, R. G. (1988). Evolution of an Engineering Organization. *International Journal of Technology Management* 3 (6):693–710.

Bettis, R. A., Bradley, S. P., and Hamel, G. (1992). Outsourcing and Industrial Decline. *Academy of Management Executive* 6 (1): 7–22.

Bleeke, J., and Ernst, D. (eds.) (1993). *Collaborating to Compete: Using Strategic Alliances and Acquisitions in the Global Marketplace*. New York: John Wiley and Sons.

Boisot, M. (1986). Markets and Hierarchies in a Cultural Perspective. *Organization Studies* 7: 135–158.

Borys, B., and Jemison, D. (1989). Hybrid Arrangements as Strategic Alliances: Theoretical Issues in Organizational Combinations. *Academy of Management Review* 14: 234–249.

Boyer, R., and Drache, D. (eds). (1997). *States against Markets: The Limits of Globalization*. London: Routledge.

Brandes, H., Lilliecreutz, J., and Brege, S. (1997). Outsourcing—Success or Failure? *European Journal of Purchasing and Supply Management* 3 (2):63–75.

Brannen, M. Y. and Salk, J. (1995). Putting Japanese and Germans Together: Negotiated Culture in a German-Japanese Joint Venture. Paper presented at Academy of Management Meeting, Vancouver.

Bryce, D. J., and Useem, M. (1998). The Impact of Corporate Outsourcing on Company Value. *European Management Journal* 16 (6):635–643.

Buono, A., and Bowditch, J. (1989). *The Human Side of Mergers and Acquisitions*. San Francisco: Jossey-Bass.

Business Europe (1993). Pros and Cons of Third-Party Distribution. *Business Europe* (December): 7.

Charan, R. (1991). How Networks Reshape Organizations—For Results. *Harvard Business Review* 69 (5):104–115.

Child, J., and Faulkner, D. O. (1998). *Strategies of Cooperation: Managing Alliances, Networks, and Joint Ventures*. Oxford: Oxford University Press.

Colling, T. (1993). Contracting Public Services: The Management of Compulsory Competitive Tendering in Two County Councils. *HRM Journal* 3 (4):1–16.

Collins, T. M., and Doorley, T. L. (1991). *Teaming Up for the 90s: A Guide to International Joint Ventures and Strategic Alliances*. Homewood: Business One Irwin.

Contractor, F. J., and Lorange, P. (eds.) (1988). *Cooperative Strategies in International Business: Joint Ventures and Technology Partnerships between Firms*. Lexington: Lexington Books.

Cooper, R. (1996). Lean Enterprises and the Confrontation Strategy. *Academy of Management Executive* 10 (3):28–39.

Corbett, M. F. (1994). Outsourcing and the New IT Executive. *Information Systems Management* 11 (4):19–22.

Crozier, M., and Friedberg, E. (1980). *Actors and Systems*. Chicago: University of Chicago Press.

Cummings, T. (1984). Transorganizational Development. In B. Staw, and T. Cummings (eds.), *Research in Organizational Behavior* 6: 367–422.

Daft, R. (1992). *Organizational Theory and Design*. 4th ed. St. Paul: West.

Department of Local Government (1997). *Competitive Tendering Guidelines*. Bankstown: Department of Local Government.

Department of Local Government (1997). *Pricing and Costing for Council Business: A Guide to Competitive Neutrality*. Bankstown: Department of Local Government.

DeSanctis, G., and Poole, M. (1994). Capturing the Complexity in Advanced Technology Use: Adaptive Structuration Theory. *Organization Science* 5 (2):121–147.

Dess, G., Rasheed, A., McLaughlin, K., and Priem, R. (1995). The New Corporate Architecture. *Academy of Management Executive* 9 (3):7–18.

Dicken, P. (1992). *Global Shift: The Internationalization of Economic Activity*. New York: Guilford Press.

Dicken, P. (1998). *Global Shift: Transforming the World Economy*. New York: Guildford Press.

Domberger, S. (1998). *The Contracting Organization: A Strategic Guide to Outsourcing*. Oxford: Oxford University Press.

Domberger, S., and Hall, C. (1995). *The Contracting Casebook: Competitive Tendering in Action*. Canberra: Australian Government Publishing Service.

Donaghu, M. T., and Barff, R. (1990). Nike Just Did It: International Subcontracting and Flexibility in Athletic Footwear Production. *Regional Studies* 24 (6):537–552.

Doz, Y. L., and Hamel, G. (1998). *Alliance Advantage: The Art of Creating Value Through Partnering*. Boston: Harvard Business School Press.

Durkheim, E. (1947). *The Division of Labor in Society*. Glencoe: Free Press.

Earl, M. J. (1996). The Risks of Outsourcing IT. *Sloan Management Review* 37 (3):26–32.

Farish, S. (1994). The Branson Factor, *PR Week* (9 September): 6–7.

Fichman, M., and Goodman, P. (1996). Customer-Supplier Ties in Inter-Organizational Relations. In B. Staw and T. Cummings (eds.), *Research in Organizational Behavior* 18: 285–329.

Fixler, D. J., and Siegel, D. (1997) Outsourcing and Productivity Growth in Services. *Structural Change and Economiuc Decisions* 10: 177–194.

Fombrun, C. (1988). Conflict and Cupertino in Interfirm Networks. Unpublished paper. Stern School of Business, New York University.

Forrest, J. E. (1992). Management Aspects of Strategic Partnering. *Journal of General Management* 17 (4):25–40.

Fox, A. (1974). *Beyond Contract: Work Power and Trust Relations*. London: Faber.

Frost, P., Moore, L., Louis, M., Lundberg, C., and Martin, J. (1991). *Reframing Organisational Culture*. Newbury Park: Sage.

Fukuyama, F. (1995). *Trust: The Social Virtues and the Creation of Prosperity*. Harmondsworth: Penguin Books.

Gasser, T. (1991). Managing without Boundaries: The Challenges to Business. *EFMM Quarterly Review*, Forum 91/3: 8–11.

Gertsen, M. C., Søderberg, A.M., and Torp, J. E. (1998). *Cultural Dimensions of International Mergers and Acquisitions*. Berlin: Walter de Gruyter.

Gerybadze, A. (1995). *Strategic Alliances and Process Redesign: Effective Management and Restructuring of Cooperative Projects and Networks* Berlin: Walter de Gruyter.

Glaister, K. W., and Buckley, P. J. (1994). UK International Joint Ventures: An Analysis of Patterns of Activity and Distribution. *British Journal of Management* 5: 33–51.

Glaister, K. W., Husan, R., and Buckley, P. J. (1998). UK International Joint Ventures with the Triad: Evidence for the 1990s. *British Journal of Management* 9 (3):169–180.

Golden, K. (1992). The Individual and Organizational Culture: Strategies for Action in Highly-Ordered Contexts. *Journal of Management Studies* 21: 1–20.

Gomes-Casseres, B. (1996). *The Alliance Revolution: The New Shape of Business Rivalry*. Cambridge: Harvard University Press.

Gore, W. L. (1985). The Lattice Organisation: A Philosophy of Enterprise. *Networking Journal* (Spring/Summer): 24–27.

Gray, B. (1989). *Collaborating*. San Francisco: Jossey-Bass.

Gray, P. (1994). Outsourcing and Other Strategies. *Information Systems Management* 11 (4): 72–75.

Greaver, M. F. (1999). *Strategic Outsourcing: A Structured Approach to Outsourcing Decisions and Initiatives*. New York: AMACOM.

Gulati, R. (1995). Does Familiarity Breed Trust? The Implications of Repeated Ties for Contractual Choice in Alliances. *Academy of Management Journal* 38: 85–112.

Hamel, G., Doz, Y. L., and Prahalad, C. K. (1989). Collaborate with Your Competitors—and Win. *Harvard Business Review* 67 (1):133–139.

Hammer, M. (1996). *Beyond Reengineering: How the Process-Centered Organization Is Changing Our Work Lives and Our Lives*. New York: HarperBusiness.

Hammer, M., and Champy, J. (1994). *Reengineering the Corporation: A Manifesto for Business Revolution*. St. Leonards: Allen and Unwin.

Hammer, M., and Stanton, S. A. (1995). *The Reengineering Revolution: A Handbook*. Sydney: HarperBusiness.

Handy, C. (1989). *The Age of Unreason*. London: Arrow Books.

Handy, C. (1992). Balancing Corporate Power: A New Federalist Paper. *Harvard Business Review* 70 (6):59–72.

Handy, C. (1994). *The Empty Raincoat: Making Sense of the Future*. London: Hutchinson.

Harrigan, K. R. (1986). *Managing for Joint Venture Success*. New York: Lexington Books.

Harris, A., Giunipero, L. C., and Hult, G. T. M. (1998). Impact of Organizational and Contract Flexibility on Outsourcing Contracts. *Industrial Marketing Management* 27: 373–384.

Harrison, B. (1994). *Lean and Mean: Why Large Corporations Will Continue to Dominate the Global Economy*. New York: Basic Books.

Hastings, C. (1991). Breaking Barriers by Networking. *EFMM Quarterly Review*, Forum 91/3: 12–13.

Hastings, C. (1996). *The New Organization: Growing the Culture of Organizational Networking*. Maidenhead: McGraw-Hill.

Hausner, B. (1998). Outsourcing: Evaluating Alternatives. *Pharmaceutical Science and Technology Today* 1 (4):148–152.

Heckman, R. (1999). Organizing and Managing Supplier Relationships in Information Technology Procurement. *International Journal of Information Management* 19: 141–155.

Henderson, J. C. (1990). Plugging into Strategic Partnerships: The Critical Connection. *Sloan Management Review* 31 (3):7–18.

Henderson, J. C., and Subramani, M. (1998). The Shifting Ground between Markets and Hierarchy: Managing a Portfolio of Relationships. Unpublished paper.

Henderson, J. C., and Venkatraman, N. (1993). Strategic Alignment: Leveraging Information Technology for Transforming Organizations. *IBM Systems Journal* 32 (1):4–16.

Hirst, P., and Thompson G. (1996). *Globalization in Question: The International Economy and the Possibilities of Governance*. Cambridge: Polity Press.

Hoogvelt, A. (1997). *Globalisation and the Postcolonial World: The New Political Economy of Development*. Basingstoke: Macmillan.

Hosmer, L. (1995). Trust: The Connecting Link between Organisational Theory and Philosophical Ethics. *Academy of Management Review* 20: 379–403.

Industrial Relations Services (1995a). Contracting-Out and Contracting-In Covered by TUPE. *IRS Employment Review* 515 (February): 8–13.

Industrial Relations Services (1995b). EOC Highlights the Gender Impact of Compulsory Competitive Tendering. *IRS Employment Review* 515 (June): 14–16.

Industrial Relations Services (1995c). Collective Redundancies and Transfer Undertakings. *IRS Employment Review* 515. (November): 14–15.

Industry Commission (1996). *Competitive Tendering and Contracting by Public Sector Agencies*. Report Number 48. Melbourne: Australian Government Publishing Service.

Institute of Municipal Management (1996). *Compulsory Competitive Tendering: Procedures Manual*. South Melbourne: Institute of Municipal Management.

Jacobs, R. A. (1994). The Invisible Workforce: How to Align Contract and Temporary Workers with Core Organisational Goals. *National Productivity Review* (Spring): 169–183.

James, H. S., and Weidenbaum, M. (1993). *When Businesses Cross International Borders: Strategic Alliances and Their Alternatives*. Westport: Praeger.

Jarillo, J. C. (1993). *Strategic Networks: Creating the Borderless Organization*. Oxford: Butterworth Heinemann.

Jennings, K., and Westfall, F. (1992). Benchmarking for Strategic Action. *Journal of Business Strategy* 13 (3):22–26.

Johansson, H. J., McHugh, P., Pendlebury, A. J., and Wheeler, W. A. (1993). *Business Process Reengineering: Breakpoint Strategies for Market Dominance*. Chichester: John Wiley and Sons.

Johnson, G. (1987). *Strategic Change and the Management Process*. Oxford: Blackwell Business.

Johnson, M. (1997). *Outsourcing . . . in Brief*. Oxford: Butterworth Heinemann.

Johnson, R., and Redmond, D. (1998). *The Art of Empowerment: The Profit and Pain of Employee Involvement*. London: Financial Times/Pitman Publishing.

Jones, C. (1994). Evaluating Software Outsourcing Options. *Information Systems Management* 11 (4):28–33.

Judenberg, J. (1994). Applications Maintenance Outsourcing. *Information Systems Management* 11 (4):34–38.

Kanter, R. (1989). *When Giants Learn to Dance*. New York: Touchstone Books.

Kelley, B. (1995). Outsourcing Marches On. *Journal of Business Strategy* 16 (4):38–42.

Kim, L. (1997). *Imitation to Innovation: The Dynamics of Korea's Technological Learning*. Boston: Harvard Business School Press.

King, W. R. (1994). Strategic Outsourcing Decisions. *Information Systems Management* 11 (4):58–61.

Kochan, N. (ed.). (1996). *The World's Greatest Brands*. Basingstoke: Macmillan Business.

Konsynski, B. R., and McFarlan, F. W. (1990). Information Partnerships—Shared Data, Shared Scale. *Harvard Business Review* 68 (5):114–120.

Kozin, M. D., and Young, K. C. (1994). Using Acquisitions to Buy and Hone Core Competencies. *Mergers and Acquisitions* 29 (2):21–26.

Kramer, R. M., and Tyler, T. R. (1996). *Trust in Organizations: Frontiers of Theory and Research*. Thousand Oaks: Sage Publications.

Lacity, M. C., and Hirschheim, R. (1993). The. Information Systems Outsourcing Bandwagon. *Sloan Management Review* 35 (1):73–86.

Lacity, M. C., Hirschheim, R., and Willcocks, L. (1994). Realizing Outsourcing Expectations. *Information Systems Management* 36 (1):7–18.

Lacity, M. C., and Willcocks, L. P. (1998). An Empirical Investigation of Information Technology Sourcing Practices: Lessons from Experience. *MIS Quarterly* 22 (3):363–408.

Lacity, M. C., Willcocks, L., and Feeny, D. F. (1996). The Value of Selective Outsourcing. *Sloan Management Review* 37 (3):13–25.

Lane, C., and Bachmann, R. (1996). The Social Constitution of Trust: Supplier Relations in Britain and Germany. *Organizational Studies* 17 (3):365–395.

Larson, A. (1992). Network Dyads in Entrepreneurial Settings: A Study of the Governance of Exchange Relationships. *Administrative Science Quarterly* 37: 76–104.

Laumann, E., Galaskiewicz, J., and Marsden, P. (1978). Community Structure as Interorganizational Linkages. *Annual Review of Sociology* 4: 455–484.

Leavy, B. (1996). Outsourcing Strategy and a Learning Dilemma. *Production and Inventory Management Journal* 37 (4):50–54.

Lei, D. (1993). Offensive and Defensive Uses of Alliances. *Long Range Planning* 26 (4):32–41.

Lei, D., and Slocum, J. W. (1992). Global Strategy, Competence Building and Strategic Alliances. *California Management Review* 35 (1):81–97.

Lendrum, T. (1995). *The Strategic Partnering Handbook: A Practical Guide for Managers*. Sydney: McGraw-Hill.

Lendrum, T. (1998). *The Strategic Partnering Handbook*. 2nd ed. Sydney: McGraw-Hill.

Lewis, J. D. (1990). *Partnerships for Profit: Structuring and Managing Strategic Alliances*. New York: Free Press.

Lewis, J. D. (1995). *The Connected Corporation: How Leading Companies Win through Customer-Supplier Alliances*. New York: Free Press.

Lewis, J. D., and Weigert, A. (1985). Trust as a Social Reality. *Social Forces* 63: 967–985.

Limerick, D., and Cunnington, B. (1993). *Managing the New Organization: A Blueprint for Networks and Strategic Alliances*. San Francisco: Jossey-Bass.

Lipnack, J., and Stamps, J. (1994). *The Age of the Network: Organizing Principles for the 21st Century*. New York: John Wiley and Sons.

Lipnack, J., and Stamps, J. (1995). *The Teamnet Factor: Bringing the Power of Boundary Crossing into the Heart of Your Business*. New York: John Wiley and Sons.

Lippit, J., and Van Til, J. (1981). Can We Achieve a Collaborative Community? Issues, Imperatives, Potentials. *Journal of Voluntary Action Research* 10 (3–4): 7–17.

Local Government Management Board (1995). *CCT Information Service Survey*. Report Number 12. London: LGMB.

Lorange, P., and Roos, J. (1991). Why Some Strategic Alliances Succeed and Others Fail. *The Journal of Business Strategy* (January-February): 25–30.

Lorenzoni, G., and Baden-Fuller, C. (1995). Creating a Strategic Center to Manage a Web of Partners. *California Management Review* 37 (3):146–163.

Luke, R., Begin, J., and Pointer, D. (1989). Quasi Firms: Strategic Inter-Organizational Forms in the Health Care Industry. *Academy of Management Review* 14: 9–19.

Lynch, R. P. (1990). *The Practical Guide to Joint Ventures and Corporate Alliances: How to Form, How to Organize, How to Operate*. New York: John Wiley and Sons.

Lynch, R. P. (1993). *Business Alliances Guide: The Hidden Competitive Weapon*. New York: John Wiley and Sons.

Lyons, M. (1991). Joint Ventures as Strategic Choice—A Literature Review. *Long Range Planning* 24 (4):130–144.

McCann, J., and Gilkey, R. (1988). *Joining Forces: Creating and Managing Successful Mergers and Acquisitions*. Englewood Cliffs: Prentice-Hall.

Martin, J. (1992). *Cultures in Organizations. New York:* Oxford University Press.

Martin, J., and Siehl, C. (1983). Organizational Culture and Counterculture: An Uneasy Symbiosis. *Organizational Dynamics* 12: 52–64.

Mattsson, L. G. (1988). Interaction Strategies: A Network Approach. Conference paper, American Marketing Association's Summer Marketing Educator's Conference, San Francisco.

Mayer, R., Davis, J., and Schoorman, F. D. (1995). An Integrative Model of Organizational Trust. *Academy of Management Review* 20: 709–734.

Meyer, N. D. (1994). A Sensible Approach to Outsourcing: The Economic Fundamentals. *Information Systems Management* 11 (4):23–27.

Micklethwait, J., and Wooldridge, A. (1996). *The Witch Doctors: What the Management Gurus Are Saying, Why it Matters and How to Make Sense of It*. London. Heinemann.

Milgate, M. (1999). Conditions for the Effective Formation, Management and Evolution of Cross-Border Alliances. Unpublished Master of Commerce (Honours) thesis, School of Management, University of Western Sydney–Nepean, Rydalmere.

More Than a Contractor. *Apparel Industry Magazine* 57 (12) (December 1996): 21–22.

Morgan, G. (1997). *Images of Organization*. 2nd ed. Thousand Oaks: Sage Publications.

Mueller, F. (1993). The Role of Know-How in Corporate Rejuvenation: The Case of Rover. *Business Strategy Review* 4 (3):15–24.

New Holland (1993). *The New Holland Case: Narrating a Company*. Milano: Baldini and Castoldi.

Ngwenyama, O. K., and Bryson, N. (1999). Making the Information Systems Outsourcing Decision: A Transaction Cost Approach to Analyzing Outsourcing Decision Problems. *European Journal of Operations Research* 115: 351–367.

Nohria, N., and Eccles, R. G. (1992). *Networks and Organizations: Structure, Form, and Action*. Boston: Harvard Business School Press.

Nohria, N., and Ghoshal, S. (1997). *The Differentiated Network: Organizing Multinational Corporations for Value Creation*. San Francisco: Jossey-Bass.

O'Shea, J., and Madigan, C. (1997). *Dangerous Company: The Consulting Powerhouses and the Businesses They Save and Ruin*. London: Nicholas Brealey.

Outsourcing and Contract Management Unit (1997). *Outsourcing and Contract Guidelines*. Melbourne: Department of Treasury and Finance.

Outsourcing and Contract Management Unit (1998). *Victorian Government Services Contracting Survey 1996–1997*. Melbourne: Department of Treasury and Finance.

PA Consulting (1994). *UK IT Sourcing Survey*. London: PA Consulting.

Peppard, J., and Ward. J. (1999). "Mind the Gap": Diagnosing the Relationship between the IT Organisation and the Rest of the World. *Journal of Strategic Information Systems* 8: 29–60.

Powell, W. (1990). Neither Market nor Hierarchy: Network Forms of Organization. In B. Staw, and T. Cummings (eds.), *Research in Organizational Behavior* 12: 295–336.

Prahalad, C. K. (1993). The Role of Core Competencies in the Corporation. *Research Technology Management* 36 (6):40–47.

Prahalad, C. K., and Hamel, G. (1990). The Core Competence of the Corporation. *Harvard Business Review* 68 (3):79–91.

Public Sector Management Office (1995). *Competitive Tendering and Contracting: Framework and Guidelines—User's Manual*. Perth: Public Sector Management Office.

Quinn, J. B. (1992). *Intelligent Enterprise: A Knowledge and Service Based Paradigm for Industry*. New York: Free Press.

Quinn, J. B., and Hilmer, F. G. (1994). Strategic Outsourcing, *Sloan Management Review* 35 (4):43–55.

Rackham, N., Friedman, L., and Ruff, R. (1996). *Getting Partnering Right: How Market Leaders Are Creating Long-Term Competitive Advantage*. New York: McGraw-Hill.

Reca, J. V., and Zieg, K. C. J. (1995). Privatization: An Analysis of Contracting
    Out of Government-Provided Services. *National Contract Management
    Journal* 26 (2):51–64.
Reich. R. B., and Mankin, E. D. (1986). Joint Ventures with Japan Give Away
    Our Future. *Harvard Business Review* 64 (2):78–86.
Riley, P. (1983). A Structurationist Account of Political Culture. *Administrative
    Science Quarterly* 28: 414–437.
Ring, P., and Van de Ven, A. (1994). Developmental Processes of Co-operative
    Inter-organizational Relationships. *Academy of Management Review* 19:
    90–118.
Robinson, S. (1996). Trust and Breach of the Psychological Contract. *Administra-
    tive Science Quarterly* 41: 574–599.
Rock, M. (1995). In, Out, Shake It All About. *Director* (August): 34–54.
Roodhooft, F., and Warlop, L. (1999). On the Role of Sunk Costs and Asset Spec-
    ificity in Outsourcing Decisions: A Research Note. *Accounting, Organi-
    zations and Society* 24: 363–369.
Rose, R. (1988). Organizations as Multiple Cultures: A Rules Theory Analysis.
    Human Relations 41: 139–170.
Rothery, B., and Robertson, I. (1995). *The Truth about Outsourcing*. Aldershot:
    Gower.
Sabel, C. (1993). Studied Trust: Building New Forms of Co-operation in a Vola-
    tile Economy. *Human Relations* 46: 1133–1170.
Sackman, S. (1991). *Cultural Knowledge in Organizations: Exploring the Collec-
    tive Mind*. Newbury Park: Sage.
Schein, E. (1985). *Organization Culture and Leadership*. San Francisco:
    Jossey-Bass.
Scott, A. (ed.) (1997). *The Limits of Globalization: Cases and Arguments*. Lon-
    don: Routledge.
Seabright, M., Levinthal, D., and Fichman, M. (1992). Role of Individual Attach-
    ments in the Dissolution of Inter-Organizational Relationships. *Acad-
    emy of Management Journal* 35: 122–160.
Selsky, J. (1991). Lessons in Community Development: An Activist Approach to
    Stimulating Inter-Organizational Collaboration. *Journal of Applied Be-
    havioral Science* 27: 91–115.
Senge, P. (1990). *The Fifth Discipline: The Art and Practice of the Learning Or-
    ganization*. Milsons Point: Random House Australia.
Senge, P., Kleiner, A., Roberts, C., Ross, R. B., and Smith B. J. (1994). *The Fifth
    Discipline Fieldbook*. London: Nicholas Brealy Publishing.
Service Competition Project Advisory Committee (1997). *Service Competition
    Guidelines*. Sydney: Council on the Cost of Government.
Shaw, J. (1990). A Cognitive Categorization Model for the Study of Intercultural
    Management. *Academy of Management Review* 15: 626–645.
Shepherd, A. (1999). Outsourcing IT in a Changing World. *European Manage-
    ment Journal* 17 (1):64–84.

Sheppard, B., and Tuchinsky, M. (1996). Interfirm Relationships: A Grammar of Pairs. In B. Staw and T. Cummings (eds.), *Research in Organizational Behavior* 18: 331–373.

Sisson, K. (1995). Organisational Structure. In S. Tyson (ed.), *Strategic Prospects for HRM*. London: Institute of Personnel and Developmnet.

Smith, S. (1996). Better Out Than In. *Computer Weekly* (May 23): 30–31.

Snow, C. C., Miles, R. E., and Coleman, H. J. (1992). Managing 21st Century Network Organizations. *Organizational Dynamics* 20 (3):5–20.

Snowdon, M. (1987). Austin Rover: The Joint Venture with Honda. *International Journal of Technology Management* 2 (1):67–73.

Snyder, A. M., and Ebeling, H. W. (1992). Targeting a Company's Real Core Competencies. *Journal of Business Strategy* 26: 26–32.

Sparke, A. (1993). *The Compulsory Competitive Tendering Guide*. London: Butterworths.

Staber, U. H., Schaefer, N. V., and Sharma B. (1996). *Business Networks: Prospects for Regional Development*. Berlin: Walter de Gruyter.

Stalk, G., Evans, P., and Shulman, L. E. (1992). Competing on Capabilities: The New Rules of Corporate Strategy. *Harvard Business Review* 70 (2):57–69.

Stevenson, W., and Bartunek, J. (1996). Power, Interaction, Position, and the Generation of Cultural Agreement in Organisations. *Human Relations* 49: 75–104.

Stokes, S. L. (1994). Life after Rightsizing. *Information Systems Management* 11 (4) (Fall): 69–71.

Suchman, M. (1995). Managing Legitimacy: Strategic and Institutional Approaches. *Academy of Management Review* 20: 571–610.

Szymankiewicz, J. (1993). Contracting-out or Selling-out? *Logistics Focus* (December): 2–5.

Taninecz, G. (1996). What Went Wrong? *Industry Week* 245 (23): 45–56.

Tapscott, D., and Caston, A. (1993). *Paradigm Shift: The New Promise of Information Technology*. New York: McGraw-Hill.

Taylor, E. (1991). Power Transformers—The Dynamics of Global Coordination. *Harvard Business Review* 69 (2):96–97.

Taylor, W. (1991). The Logic of Global Business: An Interview with ABB's Percy Barnevik. *Harvard Business Review* 69 (2): 91–105.

Thompson, G., Frances, J., Levačić, R., and Mitchell, J. (1991). *Markets, Hierarchies and Networks: The Coordination of Social Life*. London: Sage Publications.

Thompson, J. D. (1967). *Organizations in Action: Social Science Bases of Administrative Theory*. New York: McGraw-Hill.

Tichy, N. M., and Sherman, S. (1994). *Control Your Destiny or Someone Else Will: Lessons in Mastering Change from the Principles Jack Welch Is Using to Revolutionize GE*. New York: HarperBusiness.

Ungson, G. R., Steers, R. M., and Park S. H. (1997). *Korean Enterprise: The Quest for Globalization*. Boston: Harvard Business School Press.

Urban, S., and Vendemini, S. (1992). *European Strategic Alliances: Co-operative Corporate Structures in the New Europe*. Oxford: Blackwell Publishing.

Van de Ven, A. (1976). On the Nature, Formation and Maintenance of Relations among Organizations. *Academy of Management Review* 1: 24–36.

Van Kooij, E. (1990). Industrial Networks in Japan: Technology Transfer to SMEs. *Entrepreneurship and Regional Development* 2: 279–301.

Van Maanen, J., and Barley, S. R. (1984). Occupational Communities: Culture and Control in Organizations. In B. Staw and T. Cummings (eds.), *Research in Organizational Behavior* (6):287–365.

Volberda, H. W. (1998). *Building the Flexible Firm: How to Remain Competitive*. Oxford: Oxford University Press.

Von Krogh, G., and Roos, J. (1996). *Managing Knowledge: Perspectives on Co-operation and Competition*. London: Sage Publications.

Walker, B. (1993). *Competing for Building Maintenance: Direct Labour Organisations and Compulsory Competitive Tendering*. London: HMSO.

Walsh, K. (1991). *Competitive Tendering for Local Authority Services: Initial Experiences*. London: HMSO.

Weick, K. (1995). *Sensemaking in Organizations*. Thousand Oaks: Sage.

Welch, J. A., and Nayak, P. R. (1992). Strategic Sourcing: A Progressive Approach to the Make-or-Buy Decision, *Academy of Management Executive* 6 (1):23–31.

Whetten, D. (1982). Issues in Conducting Research. In D. Rogers and D. Whetten (eds.), *Inter-Organizational Co-ordination*. Ames: Iowa State University Press.

White, R., and James, B. (1996). *The Outsourcing Manual*. Aldershot: Gower Publishing.

Wilkins, A., and Dyer, W. (1988). Toward Culturally Sensitive Theories of Culture Change. *Academy of Management Review* 13: 522–533.

Willcocks, L., and Chong Ju Choi (1995). Co-operative Partnership and "Total" IT Outsourcing: From Contractual Obligation to Strategic Alliance? *European Management Journal* 13 (1):67–78.

Williamson, O. E. (1973). Markets and Hierarchies: Some Elementary Considerations. *American Economic Review* 63: 316–325.

Williamson, O. E. (1975). *Markets and Hierarchies: Analysis and Antitrust Implications*. New York: Free Press.

Wilson, L. (1994). *Stop Selling, Start Partnering: The New Thinking About Finding and Keeping Customers*. New York: John Wiley and Sons.

Winder, M. (1994). Transitional Outsourcing. *Information Systems Management* 11 (4):65–68.

Womack, J. P. (1992). The Lean Difference: Building a High Performance Enterprise. *Prism* (1st Quarter): 102–111.

Womack, J. P., and Jones, D. T. (1994). From Lean Production to the Lean Enterprise. *Harvard Business Review* 72 (2):93–103.

Womack, J. P., and Jones, D. T. (1996). *Lean Thinking: Banish Waste and Create Wealth in Your Corporation*. New York: Simon and Schuster.

Womack, J. P., Jones, D. T., and Roos, D. (1990). *The Machine That Changed the World*. New York: Simon and Schuster.

Yoshimura, N., and Anderson, P. (1997). *Inside the Kaisha: Demystifying Japanese Business Behavior*. Boston: Harvard Business School Press.

Yoshino, M. Y., and Rangan, U. S. (1995). *Strategic Alliances: An Entrepreneurial Approach to Globalization*. Boston: Harvard Business School Press.

INDEX

About the Author

MICHAEL MILGATE has worked with a number of national and international organizations as a consultant, in a variety of service and engineering-based industries, and focuses his research and lecturing on strategy, research methods, and marketing.